Beyond Equality and Difference

Beyond Equality and Difference

Citizenship, feminist politics and female subjectivity

Edited by

Gisela Bock and Susan James

London and New York

First published 1992
by Routledge
11 New Fetter Lane, London EC4P 4EE

Simultaneously published in the USA and Canada
by Routledge
a division of Routledge, Chapman and Hall, Inc.
29 West 35th Street, New York, NY 10001

Typeset in 10/12pt Times and printed by
Redwood Press, Melksham, Wiltshire

British Library Cataloguing in Publication Data
Beyond equality and difference: citizenship, feminist
   politics and female subjectivity.
   I. Bock, Gisela II. James, Susan
   305.42

Library of Congress Cataloging-in-Publication Data

Beyond equality and difference: citizenship, feminist politics, and
female subjectivity/edited by Gisela Bock and Susan James.
p.   cm.
Papers originally presented at a conference held at the European
University Institute Florence in Dec. 1988.
Includes bibliographical references.
1. Feminist theory – Congresses. 2. Equality – Congresses. 3. Sex
differences (Psychology) – Congresses. I. Bock, Gisela. II. James,
Susan.
HQ1190.B49 1992
305.42'01 – dc20 91–47137

ISBN 0–415–07988–8. – ISBN 0–415–07989–6

Contents

Contributors

Gisela Bock is Professor of History at the University of Bielefeld and External Professor at the European University Institute, Florence. Here she directed the European Culture Research Centre which sponsored the conference from which this book originated. Her publications include books on Campanella (1974) and Machiavelli (1990), *Die 'andere' Arbeiterbewegung in den USA* (1976), *Zwangssterilisation im Nationalsozialismus: Studien zur Rassenpolitik und Frauenpolitik* (1986), *Maternity and Gender Policies*, edited with Pat Thane (1991) and articles on women's and gender history in various languages.

Rosi Braidotti is Professor of Women's Studies at the University of Utrecht. She is the author of *Patterns of Dissonance* (1991) and many articles and translations.

Adriana Cavarero teaches philosophy at the University of Verona. She is the author of *Dialettica e politica in Platone* (1974), *Platone, il filosofo e il problema politico: l'epistolario e la lettera VII* (1976), *La teoria politica di John Locke* (1984), *L'interpretazione hegeliana di Parmenide* (1984) and many articles.

Jean Bethke Elshtain is the Centennial Professor of Political Science and Professor of Philosophy at Vanderbilt University. Her books include *Public Man, Private Woman: Women in Social and Political Thought* (1981), *Meditations on Modern Political Thought* (1986), *Women and War* (1987) and *Power Trips and Other Journeys* (1990). She is author of numerous essays in scholarly journals and journals of civic opinion. She has been a fellow at the Institute for Advanced Study, Princeton, and a scholar-in-residence at the Bellagio Conference and Study Centre, Bellagio, Italy.

Jane Flax teaches political theory at Howard University and is a psychotherapist in private practice. She has written articles on feminist, psychoanalytic and political theories and is the author of *Thinking Fragments: Psychoanalysis, Feminism and Postmodernism in the Contemporary West* (1990). She is currently working on a new book on subjectivity.

Susan James is a lecturer in the Faculty of Philosophy at the University of Cambridge and a fellow of Girton College, Cambridge. She is the author of *The Content of Social Explanation* (1984) and is currently working on a book about theories of the passions.

Karen Offen is a historian and independent scholar, affiliated with the Institute for Research on Women and Gender, Stanford University. She has co-edited two documentaries, *Victorian Women: A Documentary Account of Women's Lives in Nineteenth-Century England, France and the United States* (1981), and *Women, the Family and Freedom: The Debate in Documents, 1750–1950* (2 vols, 1983), and is at present completing a book on the women question in modern France. Her most recent publications focus on the comparative history of feminism and the historiography of women and the French Revolution.

Carole Pateman is Professor of Political Science at the University of California at Los Angeles, where she teaches political theory and women's studies. Her most recent books are *The Sexual Contract* (1988), *The Disorder of Women: Democracy, Feminism and Political Theory* (1989) and, edited with M. Shanley, *Feminist Interpretations and Political Theory* (1991). She is currently the President of the International Political Science Association.

Deborah L. Rhode is Professor of Law and former Director of the Institute for Research on Women and Gender at Stanford University. Among her most recent work is *Justice and Gender: Sex Discrimination and the Law* (1989). She is the editor of *Theoretical Perspectives on Sexual Difference* (1990).

Silvia Vegetti Finzi teaches in the Sezione di Teoria dell'Educazione e della Personalità at the University of Pavia. She has written many articles on feminist themes and is the author of *Il bambino della notte: divenire donna divenire madre* (1990) and *Storia della psicoanalisi: autori opere teorie 1989–1990* (1991).

Patrizia Violi is Assistant Professor in Semiotics at the University of Bologna. Her main fields of research are semantics and semantic theory. Among her books is one on language and sexual difference, *L'infinito singolare: Considerazioni sulla differenza sessuale nel linguaggio* (1986).

Acknowledgements

The origins of this book lie in a conference held at the European Culture Research Centre at the European University Institute in Florence, as part of a programme of interdisciplinary and international research. The conference took place in December of 1988, and we are grateful to the European University Institute for allowing us to hold it in the beautiful Renaissance setting of the Villa Schifanoia, to the staff of the villa who helped to make the occasion so pleasant, and to the translators who made it possible for us all to communicate with one another.

Several scholars who are not represented in this volume contributed their knowledge and insight to the original discussion. We are indebted to Heidemarie Bennent for her analysis of the place of women in Kant's philosophy (see her *Galanterie und Verachtung*: *Eine philosophiegeschichtliche Untersuchung zur Stellung der Frau in Gesellschaft und Kultur*, 1985); to Temma Kaplan, who pressed us to explore the various kinds and senses of equality; to Andrea Maihofer for her informative account of the recent German debate about equality and difference; and to Anna Rossi-Doria, who broadened our understanding of the historical dimensions of the idea of female difference. In addition, our thanks are owed to Valeria Russo, both for her useful comments and for her work in organizing the conference.

We would not have been able to include Karen Offen's essay without the permission of the University of Chicago Press, who allowed us to reprint it. We thank them for their generosity.

Finally, in the course of preparing this volume, we have been assisted by Iain Fraser and Allan Grieco, who provided initial English translations of the Italian essays, and by Philip Riley, who meticulously corrected some of the page proofs. We have received invaluable help and advice from our editors, Janice Price, Sue Roe and Moira Taylor and from Routledge's anonymous reader who made many astute comments on an earlier version of the manuscript. We are grateful to them all.

Gisela Bock
Susan James

Introduction: Contextualizing equality and difference

Since the 1980s, feminist discourse has been shaped by an intense and controversial debate surrounding the conceptual couple 'equality' and 'difference'. What are the meanings of these terms? What is to be gained from their juxtaposition? What can their analysis contribute to our grasp of gender relations in the past, present and future, to our understanding of what women were, are or will be? How does this opposition illuminate the relations between women and men? What does it reveal about relations among women themselves? Discussion of questions such as these has yielded a wealth of insights. It has opened up new levels of reflection among feminists about the character of feminism, and prompted a reconsideration of its significance for society at large.

This volume aspires to contribute to the exploration of this theme in several ways. Most importantly, however, it aims to counteract excessively abstract and sometimes confusing treatments of equality and difference by contextualizing each of these terms and the opposition between them. While it certainly does not aim to conclude the existing debate – quite the contrary – the book is built around an underlying assumption, expressed in the title *Beyond Equality and Difference*, that our understanding of this pair of concepts can be most fruitfully advanced by contextualizing their many dimensions. By looking at the shifting senses of the terms 'equality' and 'difference' as they are employed by different people in different situations, we are reminded that they are not static – no more static, indeed, than the experiences and forms of existence to which they refer.

EQUALITY AND EQUALITIES, DIFFERENCE AND DIFFERENCES

So far, a central theme of this debate has been the clarification of its constitutive terms. Despite the fact that they are deeply ingrained in western discourses on gender relations, as well as in a philosophical tradition where they are regarded as gender neutral, these have turned out to be richer and more ambiguous than they appeared. Unsurprisingly, perhaps, the attempt to arrive at a relatively stable and shared understanding of their meanings has itself been marked by differences – differences between academic disciplines on the one hand and between nationalities on the other. A major motive for assembling the contributors to this volume was thus to approach the issue from a variety of perspectives and pass such insights as had been gained across academic and national boundaries. Specialists in history, political science, philosophy, epistemology, law, linguistics, psychology and psychoanalysis all took part in this meeting; and while their various and even conflicting views did not always reflect the outlook merely of their own disciplines, many of their contributions were nevertheless shaped by the subject-matter and methods belonging to a particular area of academic study.[1] One reason for gathering their essays together in this volume is therefore to present a wide variety of approaches to a single issue.

In addition to this kind of difference, it has become almost commonplace to assume that contrasting positions in the controversy over equality and difference can be divided along national lines. According to a widely held view, both 'French feminism' and 'Italian feminism' extol female difference, while 'Anglo-American feminism' focuses exclusively on equality. Such stereotypes, which tend to creep in when people are talking about countries other than their own, are liable to be grossly over-simplified. In order to get away from them, and to indicate some of the subtleties that characterize feminist debate both within and between national cultures, this volume brings together the work of feminist scholars from various parts of the world – from Australia, Britain, Germany, Italy, the Netherlands, the United States – several of whom have spent much of their lives outside their countries of origin and have to some extent weakened their ties with the cultures in which they grew up.[2] It aims to indicate that, while prevailing assumptions about national types of feminist discourse are not altogether unfounded, there are also significant limits to their validity.

Three limits deserve to be particularly mentioned, the first of which concerns the connotations of the neologism 'biology'. Because national traditions are indeed part of the context within which feminist discourse has developed, by both inclusion and rejection, they have helped to shape the various 'national types' within the feminist movement. Thus, while Anglo-American and German feminists have criticized theories of sexual difference on the grounds that they run the risk of biologism, their French and Italian counterparts have remained comparatively unmoved by this objection. In order to understand their disagreement, we need to look at the contexts within which it arises. This criticism of difference has been most forcefully expressed in countries where biologism, whether socio-biology or eugenics, has been an important and dangerous social movement, often linked to racism. In twentieth-century Italy and France, however, biologism in its various forms has been much less influential in the articulation of theories and in political practice.

A knowledge of history can therefore help to remind us how difficult it is to generalize about the promises and dangers inherent in the various 'national types' of feminism; but it would of course be foolish to regard these as monoliths, set in stone. Almost three decades after the beginning of the second wave of feminism, the dominant feminist discourse of any western country is the outcome of a long period of controversy and even strife about key issues and key policies; it may represent a compromise or the view of a majority and is bound to be changing all the time. This is particularly true of the notions of equality and difference, concepts which continue to shift in response to fresh political and theoretical interests, and evolving strategic opportunities. In the United States, for example, these terms continue to be shaped by the influential writings of Carole Gilligan,[3] by the defeat of the Equal Rights Amendment, by deconstructionist views of difference and by a new interest in feminist theories emanating from Europe and Australia. In Germany a comparable debate is under way, partly as a response to theories developed in France, Italy and the United States, and partly as the result of fresh insights into the 'first wave' of the German women's movement, including its Jewish branch.[4] Were it not for continuing upheavals such as these, there would be no occasion for this book.

Finally, this volume aims to dispel the illusion that the advocates of equality and difference can be sharply divided by nationality, and to show that the feminist discourses of a single country rarely celebrate either unqualified difference or unqualified equality. Instead, they all aim, in a range of idioms, to deconstruct the traditional meanings of these terms, to reconstruct new, woman-centred senses of equality and difference and to devise new relationships between them.

Such forms of contextualization may suggest ways of reaching beyond the dichotomy equality/difference. But this is not to suggest that we have already moved beyond it, or that the controversy which continues to surround it is superfluous. In this volume, we aim to explore some aspects of the debate rather than to even out the various views defended or to resolve the disagreements between them. On the contrary, their very diversity is offered as an important facet of contemporary feminism, to be studied in its own right.

The factors which breed such diversity are of course manifold, but it nevertheless seems possible to trace four areas of disagreement which play a large role in sustaining the deep-seated tensions between equality and difference. First, a sense of mutual insecurity is fuelled by the fact that both these ideas can be, and have been, used against women; formal equality has all too often been defined in male terms, and appeals to female difference or otherness continue to be used to justify the inequality of the sexes. Advocates of each side of the debate therefore run certain recognized political risks. Second, the women's movement of the 1960s and 1970s helped women to arrive at liberating but utterly diverse insights into what it means to be a

woman and a feminist, insights which themselves express the tension between equality and difference. Suspicion of women's self-denial – 'How can
someone who doesn't like being a woman be a feminist?' – seems to collide
with the desire for a new freedom – 'Why would anyone who likes being a
woman need to be a feminist?'[5] The difficulty of breaking out of this
personal double-bind is often reflected at a more general level in the attempts of feminist theory to arrive at broader claims about womanhood: 'I
have no difficulty in stating that I am a woman. But if I am asked, "What is a
woman?", I waver.'[6]

Third, the tension between equality and difference bears not only on the
analysis of relations between women and men, but also on the sameness or
differences between women. As one Afro-American woman put it in 1968:
'In black women's liberation we don't want to be equal with men, just like in
black liberation we're not fighting to be equal with the white man. We're
fighting for the right to be different and not be punished for it.'[7] No wonder,
then, that the tension is most pronounced of all in the area of intersection
between feminist theory and feminist politics where the questions 'Equal to
whom?' and 'Different from what?' arise most vividly. Here the issue is not
just what women were and are, but what women want to be, and hence what
a society which puts an end to domination and androcentrism might look
like.

Throughout its history, women's liberation has been seen sometimes as
the right to be equal, sometimes as the right to be different. The debate
surrounding these two outlooks in today's feminist politics may be summarized in the following terms. On the one hand, the issue concerns whether or
not a feminist politics based on a goal of equality – of equal treatment, equal
rights, equal work and so on – aims to assimilate women to men, to erase
gender difference and construct a gender-neutral society. Some advocates of
equality favour the idea of such gender neutrality, while others dispute the
claim that this is what real equality would consist in.

On the other side lies the question of whether or not a feminist practice
based on the ideal of difference – a world in which women are not subject to
male-defined values and institutions which pretend to universal validity –
plays into the hands of a tradition that has used the notion of female
difference to justify inequality and aspires to a goal which is not, after all,
desirable. Some advocates of sexual difference favour the idea of a dual
world containing both masculine and feminine values and institutions.
Others reject the view that the expression of female difference either would
or should result in a cultural or political dualism of this sort.

On both sides, moreover, there are those who consider the conceptual
couple 'equality and difference' as dichotomous and its terms as mutually
exclusive, and those who aim to articulate other relationships between
them. Some feminists regard female difference as a starting point and
equality as a goal (to be achieved, for example, through affirmative action);

others (such as those who demand that men and women should have equal access to academic positions but plead for and practice a distinctive kind of female scholarship) treat equality as a means to the goal of female difference. Certain feminist positions can be and have been supported by an appeal either to equality or to difference.

In a field so full of reflections and ambivalence many meanings are obviously in play, and the opportunities for misinterpretation are legion. To minimize misunderstanding, the essays by Italian authors in.this volume require special comment, since they have not only been translated from one language to another, but at the same time been removed from their cultural background into a context where the special qualities of Italian feminism are not widely appreciated. Indeed, a further aspiration of this book is to bring this Italian perspective to the attention of Anglophone feminists.

THE ITALIAN CONNECTION

Since the 1970s, Italian feminist discourse has developed an original and distinctive conception of sexual difference, as a condition not of gender equality but of women's liberty.[8] This vision clearly sets Italian feminism apart from much of the Anglo-American tradition. But the Italian theories and practices of sexual difference (*pratica* and *pensiero della differenza sessuale*) also differ somewhat from the similar ideas developed in France, notably by Luce Irigaray. In particular, Italian *pensiero della differenza sessuale* is less deeply rooted in psychoanalytic theory than its French counterpart, tending to draw instead on the idioms of philosophy, political theory and politics.

The divergence between these trajectories owes something to differences of national culture. In Italy, psychoanalysis did not have as great an impact on intellectual life as in France, and there was no dominant school in relation to which feminists felt constrained to place themselves. Instead, there was a vigorous political establishment: not only a long-established Christian Democrat government, but also the largest, most powerful and most innovative Communist Party in the west, which adhered to a traditional socialist view of how the 'woman question' was to be solved. The abolition of social classes through class struggle would bring about equality, understood as the inclusion of women in everything that socialism held dear – in the party, in unions and in non-domestic labour. Meanwhile, other women's issues, such as those belonging to the domestic sphere, would somehow resolve themselves.

Radical Italian feminism developed in a highly volatile political context, alongside male-dominated leftist movements which had their own bones to pick with the Communist Party. It was thus forced to confront not only traditional conservatives and traditional communists, but at the same time a new type of male leftist, many of whom adopted, with respect to women, a highly traditional stance. In these circumstances Italian feminism grew up quickly. Through direct experience both within and outside the Communist Party, feminists acquired an exceptionally concrete understanding of what the most 'progressive' forces on the male political spectrum understood by women's equality. To combat the prevalent conception of equality as sameness, as an invitation to join men on men's terms which feminists came to call 'emancipationism', they developed a sophisticated range of theoretical insights and political practices centred on their distinctive notion of female difference.

Partly because of this background, *pensiero della differenza sessuale* is inclined to insist more vehemently than other strands of feminist thought on the view that all traditional discourses about women, most particularly those which hold out a promise of equality, contain a male bias. Nor does it regard it as sufficient to uncover the bias in dominant ideals of equality and then put the problem aside. Instead, Italian feminists assume that analysing and criticizing the notion of equality will remain a consistent part of their theory and politics for as long as the situation warrants; for as long, that is, as society is marked by male domination and female subordination, by female inferiority and male superiority.

This emphasis on sexual difference, which characterizes so much Italian feminist thought, is not, of course, completely unparalleled; but it would nevertheless be a mistake to assimilate it too quickly to superficially comparable strands of feminist debate, for example to Anglo-American discussions of the idea of a separate sphere. While American historical analyses of the separate sphere have presented it not just as an area in which women were and are oppressed but also as a domain of female power, Italian studies maintain that, in domestic life as in the public arena, women are ruled by men. This conclusion contributes to the view, so central to *pensiero della differenza sessuale*, that a primary, originary female difference has, in all areas of social life, been homologized or assimilated to a male perspective which hides behind a mask of gender neutrality in order to subordinate women. The remedy for this state of affairs cannot lie in the traditional conception of women's difference, a conception which functions on male terms and has been used to keep women in their inferior place. Rather, so the Italian feminist movement insists, it lies in a new exploration of an autonomous *differenza sessuale*, understood as a basis for women's liberty.

Inevitably, defenders of this view are often asked: 'But what, then, is sexual difference? Is it natural, biological, ontological, essential, social, cultural or historical?' Equally inevitably, the reply, 'It is all of these',[9] will fail to satisfy many interlocutors who are seeking an answer that *pensiero della differenza sessuale* is not prepared to give. Implicit in the question 'What is sexual difference?' is a demand to know what women 'really are' and a tacit accusation of essentialism. To try to answer it directly would be to accept that there is something that women really are, a view that most Italian feminists reject. Their answer – 'It is all of these' – demonstrates their reluctance to accept the over-neat distinction between biology and culture that underpins the Anglo-American division between sex and gender and incorporates a vision of women's bodies as separable from culture.[10] Equally, it signals their conviction that it is no less essentialist to assume that women are fundamentally the same as men than to assume that they are fundamentally different. Finally, it expresses their view that we do not know any essence of women which is independent of their past and present conditions; we know only that it differs from what it is subordinated to and from what it has been made into as long as it has been defined by others.

By refusing to engage with the question of what women are, this Italian tradition upholds an image of a condition of liberty in which women will be free to shape themselves in any field they choose. Adriana Cavarero, Silvia Vegetti Finzi and Patrizia Violi argue that this autonomy needs to be explored and created in precisely those areas which have been the *locus par excellence* of women's domestication: in relation to maternity, the female body, female language and female subjectivity. As long as these fields are not shaped by women themselves, they will remain 'homologized', adapted to male-centred needs and functions and unavailable as areas in which women can represent themselves and express their difference.

Does this tradition of feminist thought renounce the value of equality altogether? Evidently not, since the liberty for which it strives is conceived as an equal liberty to shape oneself in accordance with whatever differences one finds significant. Nevertheless, these novel interpretations of liberty and equality present feminism with a heady challenge, since it is far from clear what liberty, understood as the coexistence of two different genders, would look like. At the very least, such a goal would involve the legitimacy and acceptance of difference, 'a society in which sexual difference is transformed from a disguised and repressed conflict into an open one'.[11] The means, however, to articulate and mediate between two gendered and free perspectives are still in the early stages of creation.

WOMEN'S CITIZENSHIP, INDEPENDENCE AND MATERNITY

While Italian feminist theory possesses a number of important and distinctive features, an insistence on its peculiarities runs the risk of artificially segregating it from its neighbours. As our Italian contributors point out, *pensiero della differenza sessuale* has a great deal in common with other feminist movements. This state of affairs is reflected in these essays, in which a small number of particularly significant and unsettling themes continually recur across national and disciplinary boundaries. In some cases, attention is focused on problematic social roles, such as those of the citizen or mother; in others, it is concentrated on broadly philosophical issues, such as the character of the relation between equality and difference; in still others, the question of how we can overcome the limits set by the opposition of equality and difference rises to the surface. All of these represent points of particular difficulty and interest within the current debate and provide a rich source of insights into its strengths and vulnerabilities.

One resonant theme concerns the part played by the distinction between equality and difference in the constitution of two separate spheres of society – a public, political sphere of equal citizens, and a private, non-political realm in which difference, including gender difference, may be recognized and expressed. Some of the neglected complexities surrounding this distinction are discussed by Carole Pateman, who shows how the duties to live and die for the state, usually attributed only to men, are for women citizenly duties which are performed in the private sphere. Women's difference, she argues, has so far been used to incorporate women as subordinates into a male political order; but changing circumstances now offer the possibility of rethinking the cross-cutting divides between public and private, equality and difference, and creating a genuinely democratic kind of citizenship in which both sexes are full citizens and their citizenship is of equal worth to them as women and men.

For Pateman, what is at stake here is women's freedom, a goal she shares with Adriana Cavarero, who reveals how, in traditional liberal theory, the purportedly gender-neutral figure of the citizen is implicitly male, so that female difference is repressed and invisible in the public sphere. The nature of this repression can be uncovered, Susan James suggests, by looking at the forms of independence which are nominally granted to all citizens but which in fact commonly belong only to men. By scrutinizing the theoretical and practical roles of independence we can learn how women are deprived of the kind of citizenship enjoyed by men, and at the same time begin to reassess the several interconnected values which are expressed in an ideal of citizenship.

A further aspect of the public/private distinction is taken up by Jean Bethke Elshtain and, in a very different vein, by Jane Flax, both of whom explore its connections with power and powerlessness. It is important to remember, as Elshtain points out, that women are not altogether powerless in the domestic sphere, even when they lack overtly political power. This emphasis on the importance of different forms of power and powerlessness is clarified and developed by Flax, who argues that the central concern of a feminist politics should be not equality or difference, but justice – an end to the domination of women by men.

While men and women have recently come to be widely regarded as equal in the public realm of citizenship, the bearers of equal rights, women's difference, as Pateman has pointed out, is still often thought of as encapsulated in the domestic sphere, most especially in their roles as wives and mothers. Motherhood is of particular interest here, as many of the essays in the book testify, for it is understood both as excluding women from many aspects of political life and at the same time as giving them distinctive political duties. On the one hand, motherhood is natural and private, an archetypal case of all that political society is defined against; on the other hand, women have a political duty to bear children. Many of these essays analyse aspects of this complex relationship. Pateman shows how motherhood is incorporated into the patriarchal state which constructs for women distinctive citizenly duties; Cavarero examines its place in the natural law tradition. Silvia Vegetti Finzi discusses the discourses of early modern doctors, educators and moralists on maternity and female sexuality and contrasts them with nineteenth-century psychoanalytic discourses, in which maternity has all but vanished. Against the background of modern reproductive technology she argues that women need to develop their own views of motherhood, views capable of redefining the political sphere and challenging the legitimacy of science. A somewhat similar conclusion is drawn by Elshtain, who argues that an appreciation of gender difference can serve to make concealed forms of power visible and effective. Finally, Gisela Bock challenges the view that National Socialism celebrated sexual difference and gave motherhood a place of honour; she shows how, contrary to this myth, it celebrated not maternity but paternity. Equality and difference of gender were subordinated to racial difference and equality to produce an extreme devaluation of maternity. Not only did anti-natalism come to be the core of National Socialist population policy, but female difference was used to justify the massacre of Jewish women, and to subject male and female victims alike to a 'monstrous equality without fraternity or humanity' (Hannah Arendt).

Seen from a historical point of view, the problems encountered by contemporary feminists as they grapple with the dichotomy between equality and difference are by no means novel, any more than the attempt to come to terms with the relationship between motherhood and citizenship is entirely new. Since the late eighteenth century, women have grounded their claim to public, civic and political acknowledgement on their maternal and wifely contributions to society. In the American and French revolutions, for example, women espoused the notions of republican motherhood and gendered virtue. Thus, when Olympe de Gouges published her *Declaration of the Rights of Woman and the Female Citizen* in 1791, she insisted on female difference, and especially motherhood, as the basis of various important aspects of women's equality.[12]

In this volume, a number of authors explore some of the historical dimensions of this theme. Carole Pateman points to the example of the British feminist Eleanor Rathbone, who envisaged full citizenship for women as women and demanded that the state should give mothers a generous allowance in their own right (more substantial than anything actually provided by any European welfare state) in acknowledgement of their equal citizenship. Karen Offen shows that in France and other parts of Europe, as well as in the United States, many women's movements grounded their claims to equality on sexual difference. For example, Hubertine Auclert, apparently the first woman publicly to describe herself as a feminist, suggested in her periodical *La citoyenne* that the 'minotaur state' should be replaced by the 'motherly state' and demanded that motherhood should be subsidized. The formula 'motherhood is a social function', which originated in France but soon spread to other countries, expressed a rejection of the view that maternity is a merely private or physiological matter, and a wish to see it incorporated in a new concept of citizenship.[13]

The baffling character of an equality which both excludes and includes women was tellingly identified by Hannah Arendt:

> From the beginning the paradox involved in the declaration of inalienable human rights was that it reckoned with an 'abstract' human being who seemed to exist nowhere . . . This right seemed to contradict nature itself since we in fact know 'human beings' only in the shape of women and men; and the concept of human being, if conceived in a politically useful way, must necessarily include the plurality of human beings.[14]

Arendt here pinpoints a paradox which continues to trouble feminist theorists. As both Pateman and Flax remark, we can be equal (undifferentiated) or different, but not both. Such formulations of the problem imply that feminists face a stark choice between two utterly opposed values and strategies, a choice which both stems from and reinforces the view that equality and difference stand for mutually exclusive approaches to questions of gender. It may be, however, that the available options are not as limited as this analysis suggests. The contributors to this book explore various ways of overcoming a dichotomous understanding of the relationship between equality and difference, challenging both the historical and philosophical construction of its terms and the supposedly hierarchical relationship between them. Some argue that, at least in certain theoretical contexts, the notions of equality and difference turn out to be interdependent; James, for example, shows that once we consider the psychological pre-conditions which implicitly underlie the forms of independence definitive of the liberal citizen, we find that political equality rests upon the recognition of various forms of difference, and vice versa. Other contributors, such as Bock and Offen, identify the way that types of equality and difference are interwoven in particular historical contexts so that any adequate analysis must take account of the complex interplay between them. A third group of authors advocate a rethinking of the idea of difference, a move away from the traditional emphasis on maternity and the traditional understanding of this term. Vegetti Finzi's contribution to this line of argument is joined by Rosi Braidotti's claim that feminist theoreticians should take time to reconsider the very roots of female difference which she locates in the relation between thinking and the female body.

Finally, some of the essays in this book suggest that feminism needs to move beyond both equality and difference and find new ways of interpreting and improving the condition of women. Deborah Rhode argues that, in legal contexts, appeals to female difference are less useful than appeals to women's disadvantage; and Jane Flax sketches the outline of a feminist politics centred on justice, understood as the end of women's subordination.

GENDER JUSTICE AND FEMALE SUBJECTIVITY

The arguments developed in the first two parts of this volume mainly use the analysis and criticism of past theories and events to identify pitfalls and shortcomings which contemporary and future feminisms might hope to avoid. The essays in the third part, by contrast, tend to be more overtly forward-looking; they strive to articulate a better future for women and to identify new problems which feminism must address. Central to these explorations are the topics of female subjectivity and gender justice.

The need for women to create their own subjectivity, to arrive at ways of representing and symbolizing their experiences, is a recurring theme which comes to the surface in the essays by Rosi Braidotti and Patrizia Violi. Both these authors address the ways in which our ability to understand ourselves is mediated through a male-centred language which must be analysed and revised. Violi argues that in patriarchal societies women lack the positive, collective self-representations which for men are embodied in myths and stories. A central task of feminism must be to find a language in which to express and symbolize sexual difference, thereby allowing it to escape from 'the secret place of individual consciousness' into the symbolic order. Braidotti defends the importance of a complementary project – the re-evaluation of the bodily roots of female subjectivity. A feminist conception of the subject must, she suggests, emphasize its embodiment and sexual differentiation. But to understand the character and implications of such a view of the subject we need to work out its connections to some of our most fundamental ideas – to the related notions of desire and thinking.

What might be the outcome of an exploration of this kind? While the theorists of *pensiero della differenza sessuale* answer 'Liberty', other authors in this volume envisage a related condition of justice. Some problems standing in the way of the achievement of this goal are discussed by Deborah Rhode, who shows that those attempts to use the law on behalf of women which have appealed solely to their equality, or solely to their difference, have suffered from serious theoretical limitations and encountered grave practical obstacles. It would be more fruitful, she suggests, to develop a flexible notion of women's disadvantage, while at the same time resisting the temptation of theoretical purity in the name of a pragmatic approach to legal reform. Something of this pragmatism also characterizes Flax's suggestion that feminists should regard justice as an 'anticipatory concept', a shifting ideal situated in a field of differences. Drawing on the insights of post-modernism and on Winnicott's conception of the transitional space, she argues that, as we articulate and rearticulate conceptions of justice, we must delimit the conditions and contexts in which it can be achieved and the purposes it can and cannot serve.

These last essays, therefore, explore ways of moving beyond equality and difference, beyond a framework which has animated feminist discussion for over a hundred years and, as this book attests, continues to do so.

NOTES

1 For further disciplines and interdisciplinary approaches see e.g. M. Strathern (ed.), *Dealing with Inequality: Analysing Gender Relations in Melanesia and Beyond*, Cambridge, Cambridge University Press, 1987; D. Rhode (ed.), *Theoretical Perspectives on Sexual Difference*, New Haven, Conn., Yale University Press, 1990. For classical approaches which do not include a perspective on gender see e.g. I. Berlin, 'Equality', in I. Berlin, *Concepts and Categories: Philosophical Essays*, Oxford, Oxford University Press, 1980, pp. 81–103; D. Rae *et al.*, *Equalities*, Cambridge, Cambridge University Press, 1981.
2 For French scholarship on the issues of this volume see esp. the references in the Italian contributors' essays, and the special issues of *Signs*, 6(1), 1980, and 7(1), 1981; E. Grosz, 'Philosophy, subjectivity and the body: Kristeva and Irigaray', in C. Pateman and E. Grosz (eds), *Feminist Challenges: Social and Political Theory*, Sydney, Allen & Unwin, 1986, pp. 125–43.
3 C. Gilligan, *In a Different Voice: Psychological Theory and Women's Development*, Cambridge, Harvard University Press, 1982.
4 See esp. T. Wobbe, *Gleichheit und Differenz: Politische Strategien von Frauenrechtlerinnen um die Jahrhundertwende*, Frankfurt, Campus, 1989; U. Gerhard *et al.* (eds), *Differenz und Gleichheit: Menschenrechte haben (k)ein Geschlecht*, Frankfurt, Helmer, 1990; M. Kaplan, *The Jewish Feminist Movement in Germany: The Campaigns of the Jüdischer Frauenbund, 1904–1938*, Westport, Conn., Greenwood Press, 1979.
5 Quoted in A. Snitow, 'A gender diary', in M. Hirsch and E. Fox-Keller (eds), *Conflicts in Feminism*, London, Routledge, 1990, p. 33.
6 A. Cavarero, 'L'elaborazione filosofica della differenza sessuale', in M. C. Marcuzzo and A. Rossi-Doria (eds), *La ricerca delle donne: studi femministi in Italia*, Turin, Rosenberg & Sellier, 1987, p. 185.
7 M. Wright, 'I want the right to be black and me', in G. Lerner (ed.), *Black Women in White America*, New York, Random House, 1972, p. 608.
8 For an important analysis of Italian feminist thought see T. de Lauretis, 'The essence of the triangle, or taking the risk of essentialism seriously: feminist theory in Italy, the US, and Britain', *Differences*, 1–2, 1988, pp. 1–37.
9 A. Caverero, 'Die Perspektive der Geschlechterdifferenz', in Gerhard *et al.*, *Differenz*, p. 96.
10 For the problems of translating the 'sex/gender' terminology into Italian see de Lauretis, 'Essence', and G. Bock, 'Challenging dichotomies: perspectives on women's history', in K. Offen, R. Pierson and J. Rendall (eds), *Writing Women's History: International Perspectives*, London, Macmillan, and Bloomington, Ind., Indiana University Press, 1991, p. 9.
11 R. Rossanda, 'Differenz und Gleichheit', in Gerhard *et al.* (eds), *Differenz*, p. 28.

12 M. B. Norton, *Liberty's Daughters: The Revolutionary Experience of American Women, 1750–1800*, Boston, Mass., Little, Brown, 1980; L. Kerber, *Women of the Republic: Intellect and Ideology in Revolutionary America*, Chapel Hill, NC, University of North Carolina Press, 1980; R. H. Bloch, 'The gendered meanings of virtue in revolutionary America', *Signs*, 13(1), 1987, pp. 37–58; J. W. Scott, 'French feminists and the rights of "man": Olympe de Gouges's Declarations', *History Workshop*, 28, 1989, pp. 1–21.

13 For an international overview over such feminist voices see G. Bock and P. Thane (eds), *Maternity and Gender Policies: Women and the Rise of the European Welfare States, 1880s–1950s*, London, Routledge, 1991.

14 H. Arendt, *The Origins of Totalitarianism*, New York, Harcourt Brace Jovanovich, 1968, ch. 9; see also her *The Human Condition*, Chicago, Chicago University Press, 1958, pp. 7–8.

Part I

Women's citizenship, independence and sexual difference

Chapter 1

Equality, difference, subordination: the politics of motherhood and women's citizenship

Carole Pateman

The feminist movement and feminist scholarship are frequently seen as divided between the advocates of equality on the one side and the advocates of sexual difference on the other. Some feminists are presented as demanding equality in the sense of the identical treatment of women and men, and others as demanding that the distinctive characteristics and activities of women should be given special consideration, and it appears that women are forced to choose, and have always been forced to choose, between the two. As Joan Scott has commented:

> When equality and difference are paired dichotomously, they structure an impossible choice. If one opts for equality, one is forced to accept the notion that difference is antithetical to it. If one opts for difference, one admits that equality in unattainable.[1]

This perception of the relation between 'equality' and 'difference' is not unique to the United States; but an extremely individualist political culture combined for long periods with a conservative Supreme Court has meant that a choice between equality and difference is often posed more sharply than in, say, Britain or Australia. One of the most recent examples is the verdict in the *Sears* case, in which the claim of the Equal Employment Opportunity Commission that a preponderance of men employed in commission sales resulted from discrimination against women workers was rejected in favour of the argument of Sears, Roebuck that this was the consequence of differences in the interests and voluntary choices of women and men.[2]

A common interpretation of the history of women's struggle for citizenship, and especially for the suffrage, is that it was simply a campaign for equality, for the 'rights of men and citizens' to be extended to women. This view misunderstands the way in which our predecessors fought for citizenship. From at least 1792, when Mary Wollstonecraft's *A Vindication of the Rights of Woman* was published, women have demanded both equal civil and political rights, and that their difference from men should be acknowledged in their citizenship. Most suffragists, for example, argued that womanhood suffrage was required as a matter of justice and to make government by consent a reality, and also that the distinctive contribution that they could make to political life as women was a major reason why they should be enfranchised. A rift in the feminist movement opened up in the inter-war years in the United States and Great Britain over the question of protective legislation for women workers and welfare measures for mothers and children; supporters of the Equal Rights Amendment and 'equal rights' were arrayed on the one side and the advocates of social reform and the New Feminists on the other. The rift was very real and the controversy sometimes heated. Nevertheless, positions on both sides were not as clear cut as the simple opposition between 'equality' and 'difference' suggests. Indeed, it is often overlooked that since all those involved had supported women's suffrage, the argument was carried on against the background of unanimous support for one very important aspect of 'equality'.

Nor was there a clear division between working-class proponents of 'difference' and 'protection' and middle-class demands for 'equal rights'. Some women workers in Britain opposed protective legislation because it excluded women from various areas of employment, and some women trade unionists and women workers supported the National Women's Party (NWP) which led the fight for the ERA in the United States. Moreover, the NWP insisted that it was not against protective legislation if it applied to both sexes; and its leader, Alice Paul, stated, for example, that women were 'the peace-loving half of the world and the home-making half of the world'.[3] In Britain, 'equality' feminists in the Open Door Council also supported protective legislation that applied to men and women, and were in favour of maternity benefits for women workers.[4] From the other side, members of the Women's Bureau in the United States, who opposed the ERA, tried to secure equal-pay legislation, and the New Feminists in Britain saw family allowances as a means to reduce a wife's dependency on her husband, that is, as a means of increasing 'equality'. Blurring the opposition even further, the Six Point Group demanded, 'alongside equal pay, that "[T]he economic value of the work of women in the home must be recognized"'.[5]

These examples should be sufficient to indicate that even when 'equality' and 'difference' have been associated with two wings of the feminist movement, the politics of the feminist movement is a good deal more complex than is often suggested. I want to investigate, in an exploratory fashion, another aspect of this complexity: what I shall call the politics of motherhood. The fact that only women have the capacity to become pregnant, give birth and suckle their infants is the mark of 'difference' *par excellence*. Childbirth and motherhood have symbolized the natural capacities that set women apart from politics and citizenship; motherhood and citizenship, in this perspective, like difference and equality, are mutually exclusive. But if 'motherhood' represents all that excluded women from citizenship, motherhood has also been constructed as a political status. Motherhood, as feminists have understood for a very long time, exists as a central mechanism through which women have been incorporated into the modern political order. Women's service and duty to the state have largely been seen in terms of motherhood, and to begin to examine the politics of motherhood it is necessary to see how women's duty is connected to men's service to the state as workers and soldiers.

Women's inclusion into the political order needs special emphasis, since it is often assumed that the problem of women's citizenship is one of exclusion. A major reason for the complexity of women's political status is that it has never been a matter of mere exclusion. Women's political standing rests on a major paradox; they have been excluded and included on the basis of the very same capacities and attributes. Feminist theorists have shown how political constructions of what it means to be a man or a woman are central to conceptions of the well-ordered polity. In my own work I have examined how the classic contract theorists presented sexual difference as the political difference between freedom (men) and subordination (women). Women were held by nature to lack the characteristics required for participation in political life, and citizenship has been constructed in the male image.[6] Women, our bodies and distinctive capacities, represented all that citizenship and equality are not. 'Citizenship' has gained its meaning through the exclusion of women, that is to say (sexual) 'difference'.

But this is only part of the story of the development of modern patriarchy. The classic theorists did not completely exclude women from the political order, from 'civil society'. The creation of modern patriarchy embodied a new mode of inclusion for women that, eventually, could encompass their formal entry into citizenship. Women were incorporated differently from men, the 'individuals' and 'citizens' of political theory; women were included as subordinates, as the 'different' sex, as 'women'. They were incorporated as men's subordinates into their own private sphere, and so were excluded from 'civil society' in the sense of the public sphere of the economy and citizenship of the state. But this does not mean that women had no political contribution to make and no political duty to perform. Their political duty (like their exclusion from citizenship) derives from their difference from men, notably their capacity for motherhood.

The eighteenth-century doctrine of republican motherhood provides an illustration of the multiple layers of meaning of motherhood as a political status. The political theory of civic republicanism emphasized active political participation by citizens imbued with civic virtue, who were also capable of bearing arms. Republican citizens were thus men and soldiers – but what of women? They were to be the subordinate companions of citizens, but with their own political task; they were to be republican mothers. In America, a republican mother was excluded from citizenship, but she had a crucial political part to play in bearing and rearing sons who embodied republican virtues. She remained an auxiliary to the commonwealth but an auxiliary who made a fundamental political contribution.[7] During the French Revolution – when the 'rights of men and citizens' were first proclaimed – women's political rights and activities were suppressed and their place declared to be that of republican mothers.[8]

Why should the republican mother not be a citizen? There was, from a feminist perspective, no rational reason at all. Women would express their citizenship, in part at least, through motherhood. From the 1790s onwards, the demand was made that women's private duty should become part of citizenship. A century after the French Revolution, in the 1890s and early 1900s, as Karen Offen has shown, a 'familial feminism' was predominant in France.[9] Feminists argued that the state should support women in their duty as mothers and improve the material conditions of motherhood, and that those who performed this national task should be granted the standing and rights of citizens.

This argument had been made during the period of the French Revolution by Mary Wollstonecraft. As I noted above, Mary Wollstonecraft argued simultaneously for equality and the recognition of difference. She called for equal civil and political rights for women and their economic independence from their husbands – stating, 'Let woman share the rights and she will emulate the virtues of man' – and, at the same time, for women's citizenship to be expressed differently from men's. Women had a 'peculiar destination' as mothers, and their equal citizenship would be expressed through their motherhood. She wrote that, 'speaking of women at large, their first duty is to themselves as rational creatures, and the next, in point of importance, as citizens, is that, which includes so many, of a mother'. She hoped that the day would come when men would be despised if they were not active citizens; 'and while he was employed in any of the departments of civil life, his wife, also an active citizen, should be equally intent to manage her family, educate her children, and assist her neighbours'.[10]

The problem with this feminist strategy is that it remains impaled on the horns of what I have called Wollstonecraft's dilemma. The dilemma arises because, within the existing patriarchal conception of citizenship, the choice always has to be made between equality and difference, or between equality and womanhood. On the one hand, to demand 'equality' is to strive for equality with men (to call for the 'rights of men and citizens' to be extended to women), which means that women must become (like) men. On the other hand, to insist, like some contemporary feminists, that women's distinctive attributes, capacities and activities be revalued and treated as a contribution to citizenship is to demand the impossible; such 'difference' is precisely what patriarchal citizenship excludes.

Contemporary arguments about the re-evaluation of women's capacities, especially motherhood, also raise another question: namely, how is 'motherhood' to be understood? Does 'motherhood' refer only to the relation between mother and child; or does 'motherhood' also refer to women's standing in the political order? One feminist argument, especially influential in the United States, treats motherhood in the former sense and focuses on 'maternal thinking'.

Sara Ruddick argues that all thought is a response to social practice; in this case, the practice or discipline of motherhood. Maternal thinking grows out of a mother's concern for the child's preservation, growth and acceptability (will the child be an 'acceptable' member of society?) and is centred around 'attentive love'.[11] The notion of maternal thinking does not involve a simple return to an argument from (women's) nature. Ruddick insists that 'maternal' is a social category, so that men, if they care for others, can be maternal thinkers. She argues that the conditions of women's motherhood have largely been defined by men, thus maternal thinking is always open to determination by the dominant culture and, hence, to inauthenticity. Maternal thinking has to be transformed by feminist consciousness, and then, Ruddick argues, 'the self-conscious inclusion of maternal thought in the dominant culture will be of general intellectual and moral benefit'. Once maternal thinking is brought into 'the public realm' the care of children can become 'a work of public conscience and legislation'.[12] Similarly, Jean Elshtain claims that, 'were maternal thinking to be taken as the base for feminist consciousness, a wedge for examining an increasingly overcontrolled public world would open immediately'.[13] The task for feminists, Ruddick states, is to formulate a 'theory of justice shaped by and incorporating maternal thinking'.[14]

An argument based on the 'difference' symbolized by motherhood has inevitably provoked a response from an advocate of 'equality'. Mary Dietz argues that maternal thinking reinforces the split between private and public. Maternal thinking is not political; it arises from a relationship between unequals (the mother and child) that is 'intimate, exclusive, and particular', and is thus opposed to democratic citizenship which is 'collective, inclusive, and generalized'. The bond between mother and child is quite different from the bonds of citizenship. To argue that maternal consciousness can be a basis for feminism and citizenship is to look at political life from the wrong way round. Only when women act as citizens, not mothers, can the policies advocated by feminists be implemented. Dietz concludes that 'accordingly, the values [feminists] must defend are not as such maternal (the growth and preservation of children) but political (freedom, equality, community power)'. Feminists should not reduce women's identity to the single dimension of 'mother', but should endeavour to '[nurture] the reality of women as, in large part, citizens'.[15]

The debate therefore continues to oscillate between 'difference' (maternal thinking should be valued and brought into the political arena) and 'equality' (citizenship not motherhood is vital for feminists) and so remains caught in Wollstonecraft's dilemma. There are also other problems when 'motherhood' is seen only in terms of the mother–child relation. For instance, attention is deflected from the structure of sexual relations and the meaning of 'sex' in contemporary society; in other words, little consideration is given to the context in which women become pregnant.[16] Instead, attention becomes focused on 'motherhood' as part of 'the family', the private sphere, and motherhood appears as either non-political or outside politics, and two solutions to women's predicament present themselves. One popular proposal is for 'shared parenting' within the family; men must be encouraged to be 'mothers'. But as Lynne Segal has commented rather sharply: 'watching childbirth, pushing prams, putting children to bed, many men now relate sensitively to women and children in ways unthinkable to their fathers – yet, the edifice of male power remains'.[17] The other proposal is that 'motherhood' be inserted into politics and citizenship in the form of maternal thinking. But 'motherhood', in another sense, has been incorporated into politics for a very long time.

Motherhood as a political status, as a major vehicle of women's incorporation into the political order, has shaped women's duty to the state and women's citizenship. I want to approach women's political duty and service from two directions: the structure of the welfare state and the question of the political obligations of citizenship. (Within the confines of the present essay, I cannot discuss the way in which much of women's political activity also reflects motherhood as a political status; for example, as participants in bread riots, as 'women's auxiliaries' in strikes or, more recently, as participants in the anti-nuclear movement or, like the Mothers of the Plaza de Mayo, taking action on behalf of the 'disappeared'.)

The basis of the 'social insurance' model of the Anglo-American welfare state is that individuals make a 'contribution' that then entitles them to the benefits, or what T. H. Marshall called the social rights of citizenship, of the welfare state.[18] Paid employment becomes central to the welfare state because the 'contribution' is taken from the pay-packet of the worker.[19] Except in feminist discussions it is rarely noticed that it is men, as 'workers' and 'bread-winners' and recipients of the family wage, who have been regarded as those 'individuals' able to make the 'contribution' to the welfare state.

Women have not been (seen as) capable of making the same contribution as men and so have not had the same entitlements in the welfare state. This was made plain by William Beveridge in his report, which laid the foundations for the comprehensive British welfare reforms of the 1940s, when he wrote: 'the great majority of married women must be regarded as occupied on work which is vital though unpaid, without which their husbands could not do their paid work, and without which the nation could not continue'.[20] The tasks of a wife, and mother, were not the 'work' associated with equality and citizenship, and wives and husbands were treated differently under the National Insurance Act of 1946. That is not to say that women have been left out of the welfare state. Rather, they have not usually benefited as citizens. Over the past decade or more, feminist scholars have shown how women, now the major beneficiaries of the welfare state and the majority of the poor, still tend to receive their benefits not, like men, in their own right, but as dependents and subordinates of male citizens, the bread-winners.[21] Thus, the structure of the welfare state embodies (the patriarchal construction of) sexual difference.

But women also had a contribution to make that reflected their difference from men. The paradoxical contribution demanded from women was – welfare. This was not the public welfare of the 'welfare state', but the contribution of private, unpaid welfare in their homes. Women, as mothers, nurture the next generation of citizens, and, as wives and daughters, tend to the sick, the infirm and the aged. The welfare state has always depended upon women's contribution, but it remains unacknowledged and set apart from (political) citizenship. In the present period of 'privatization', women's private tasks assume an even greater importance.

The early development of the British welfare state also illustrates the importance of a different kind of contribution or service to the state that is vital for an understanding of the politics of motherhood. During the First World War, the British government paid 'separation allowances' to the wives of soldiers and sailors and it was at this point, Susan Pederson argues, that the '"logic" of social citizenship structured around maintaining the domestic rights of the male citizen became established'.[22] In effect, the welfare state replaced the husband as 'bread-winner' while he was absent making another kind of contribution. As one MP commented, the allowance was 'paid by the state as part of the wage of the soldier'; it was not the entitlement of his wife.[23] Benefits paid to men as entitlements due for service as citizens, whether as workers or soldiers, could not belong to wives. 'Women' and 'citizenship' are opposed, and women had their own 'different' contribution to render.

The primary form that wives' (women's) service has taken can be seen by looking at the respective contributions of women and men from another direction; by considering arguments about the political obligation and duty of the citizen. The ultimate test of the allegiance of the citizen and the ultimate duty of citizenship are to die for the state. As one political theorist wrote recently: 'the duty to give life, should it be necessary to do so, in order to sustain or generate a political order is one of the central duties of citizenship'.[24] Michael Walzer also discusses another duty of citizens, 'the obligation to live for the state', or the duty not to renounce citizenship through suicide, that requires citizens to endure the vicissitudes of everyday living. Walzer notes that, for eighteenth-century writers, the capacity to commit suicide was part of the right to life; 'the best proof of [men's] standing as free and rational creatures'.[25]

I do not want to discuss the question of suicide but to ask a question that remains unasked in the discussions of political obligation with which I am familiar; namely, is the duty of men and women to die and live for the state interpreted and performed in the same way? In standard arguments about the two duties, theorists of citizenship do not ask whether either of them applies to women. Both the duty to die for the state and the duty to live for the state are typically discussed with reference only to men. The duty to die for the state is taken for granted to mean the duty of the citizen to take up arms at the behest of the state and, as Hobbes put it, 'protect his Protection', even if he must forfeit his life in so doing.[26] It is easy enough to see that bearing arms and dying on the battlefield for the state have been held to be beyond the reach of women. The 'jewel' in the arguments of the anti-suffragists was the insistence that women were unable and/or unwilling to use physical force and that their citizenship would, therefore, place the state in peril.[27] The argument still continues in the contemporary controversy over women and combat.

Few political theorists explicitly discuss the duty to live for the state, or the service owed to the state every day in the course of a lifetime, but discussions of citizenship in the welfare state make it plain that the major duty is to engage in paid employment – again, a duty of men. T. H. Marshall, for instance, argued that individuals have a general duty of service as citizens to promote the general welfare; he wrote: 'of paramount importance is the duty to work', and not merely to have a job, but 'to put one's heart into [it] and work hard'.[28] In Marshall's argument, the unpaid work of women which Beveridge mentioned, 'without which the nation could not continue', disappears without a trace. This is not the work of citizens, part of their political duty, but the work that women owe to the state because of their sex, which thus falls outside citizenship. None the less, women, like men, have a political duty to live for the state, not least because women can be called upon to die for the state during the course of their mundane, unrecognized duty. That women, too, have a duty to die for the state is not noticed by political theorists because the duty is fulfilled in the private realm, not in the public arena of the battlefield. Women's duty is suited to their ambiguous position in the state, exemplifying nature and (sexual) 'difference', not the conventional life of the public world of equal citizenship. Women's ultimate political duty is motherhood, to give birth for the state, and, if nature so decrees, to give their lives in creating new life, new citizens.

Michel Foucault has argued that in the modern era there has been a shift from sovereignty symbolized by the sword and the right of the sovereign to put his subjects to death, to a new form of rule and discipline concerned with the quantity and quality of life of the population.[29] Foucault fails to ask the question, 'where does that population comes from?' He thus ignores the fact that the patriarchal meaning of sexual difference and the manner of women's incorporation into the political order are an integral part of the interest of modern state in the number and condition of the population.

Many states, today and in the past, have been greatly exercised whether or not they have sufficient population to be 'great' and powerful, or to stand against other populations that are seen as a threat because of their size or ethnic composition. Whether or not women were performing their political duty has thus been a major concern of the state, and a wide array of measures have been deployed to ensure that their duty was fulfilled. An enthusiastic performance of their political duty could receive official reward in a manner similar to exemplary soldiers. In 1920, in France, where the size of the population has long been a source of anxiety to the state, particularly fecund women were acknowledged by a medal, with ribbons.[30]

Earlier in the twentieth century, in both Australia and the United States, a decline in the white birth rate led to fears of 'race suicide'. The position of women and the political duty of motherhood were, therefore, at the centre of national policy concerns. Inquiries were held into the problem, and in Australia in 1904 the childless woman was condemned as 'selfish' and portrayed by the most shrill pro-natalists as 'a menace to social purity and national stability'.[31] More recently, the Ceausescu regime in Romania enforced women's duty in the harshest fashion to try to attain a population of 30 million at the end of the twentieth century, banning contraception and abortion and policing women workers to ensure that all pregnancies were detected and brought to term. (The resulting large-scale abandonment of babies into squalid institutions by poor, overburdened mothers has, since the overthrow of the regime, received much publicity, unlike the policy itself.)

The state has been interested in the 'quality' and not merely the quantity of the population. If women have had the duty to give birth for the state, not all women have been seen as fit to be mothers. Middle-class white women, above all, as 'superior' genetic stock, have been seen as undermining the nation by limiting the extent of their service, or avoiding service altogether, by 'unnatural' means. Other women have been subject to measures to prevent them from fulfilling their duty; women from indigenous, migrant or black minority populations in western countries have been sterilized without their consent, and arguments surface regularly about the deleterious effects of differential birth rates of women classified according to IQ or class. As I was writing this essay, the *Philadelphia Inquirer* published a controversial editorial advocating incentives to encourage poor black women to use a new birth control implant, which could keep them from becoming pregnant for up to five years, and a judge in Visalia, California, ordered another black woman, who had been convicted of badly beating her children, to use the same device as condition of her probation.[32]

The most horrific and graphic example of this aspect of the politics of motherhood was the policy in Nazi Germany. The Nazi regime is often seen as pro-natalist and as placing a high value on motherhood, and pictures of rosy, flaxen-haired mothers and children are familiar enough. But, as Gisela

Bock's very important research has shown, Nazi 'racial hygiene' doctrine did not even regard all German women as fit mothers. From 1933 onwards, a public policy of forced sterilization and compulsory abortion was practised. The mentally and physically handicapped, in addition to the 'inferior' groups, the Gypsies, Jews, Slavs and so on, were the targets, and it was the extreme anti-natalism, not pro-natalism, which sets the Nazi regime apart from other western countries of the period.[33]

The service and sacrifice demanded of women as child-bearers and the service and sacrifice demanded of men as soldiers are often compared (even if they have never been brought together by political theorists). For example, President Theodore Roosevelt compared the 'cowardly' or 'self-ish' woman who shirked her duty to become a mother with the man who 'fears to do his duty in battle when the country calls him', and declared them both to be equally contemptible.[34] From the feminist side, August Bebel stated that 'a woman who brings children into the world does the community at least as great a service as a man who defends his country'. He noted that the casualty rate among child-bearers was probably greater than among soldiers on the battlefield and commented that 'this is reason enough to entitle women to complete equality with men'.[35] Again, the English feminist Maude Royden declared during the First World War:

> The state wants children, and to give them is a service both dangerous and honourable. Like the soldier, the mother takes a risk and gives a devotion for which no money can pay; but, like the soldier, she should not, therefore, be made 'economically dependent'.[36]

No one, she insisted, held that a man 'must depend on his wife for mainten-ance because he is a soldier ... You cannot, indeed, pay for all that motherhood means, but neither can you pay for a man to die. Yet soldiers are "endowed" by the State.'[37]

Royden's reference to 'economic dependence' brings motherhood together with both dimensions of men's service to the state. British feminists saw the separation allowances being paid during the war in a very different light from the prevailing view that they were part of the soldier-worker's pay. Feminists argued that the wives' allowances should be seen as an entitlement, as a right of a citizen in return for her service to the state that she gave in the home; as Eleanor Rathbone stated, the payment should be treated as 'a statutory payment to a woman in respect of her [citizenship] functions as a wife and a mother'.[38] Eleanor Rathbone was at the forefront of the wide movement in western countries that began in the early part of the twentieth century for state endowment for mothers. At her most radical she saw the endowment as a means of remedying the subordination of wives by helping to eliminate their economic dependence on the family wage of husbands. Rathbone contended that payment to mothers would 'once and for all, cut away the maintenance of children and the reproduction of the race from the question of wages'.[39] The way would then be open for women workers to be paid the same wages as their male counterparts.

Feminist comparisons of the risks run by mothers and soldiers, and arguments that an endowment for mothers should be payment for their service as citizens, ran up against Wollstonecraft's dilemma. Women's duty to give birth to the state is not a duty of citizens, and the casualties of motherhood are not included among those who have fallen in the service of their country. From this perspective, death in childbirth cannot be a sacrifice like that of a soldier, but must stand as a casualty of nature, as the antithesis of the human heroism of death under fire.[40]

Similarly, when family allowances (as the endowment for mothers came to be called) were finally instituted in Britain after the Second World War, the payment was made directly to mothers and so could be seen as a mark of recognition for their contribution – but as private persons, not as citizens. Moreover, family allowances were also widely viewed as a means of alleviating poverty among children and as a supplement to the family wage.

A feminist strategy that calls for the integration into citizenship of women's distinctive contribution, or compares women's service to that of men as workers or soldiers, rests on the assumption that 'women' and 'difference' need to be brought into the political order. The pertinent question is assumed to be whether sexual difference is politically relevant, or how 'difference' could be relevant. Thus, the vital question is overlooked of how to subvert and change the manner in which women have already been incorporated, and so to transform the relation between 'equality' and 'difference'. The task of political reconstruction remains daunting, but, at the end of the twentieth century, some significant changes – a few too recent to assess readily – have taken place in the context in which the politics of motherhood is played out.

Not only men but, at least in the United States, mothers are now soldiers. The American troops who recently waged war against Iraq included mothers among the women (about 6 per cent of the total force) who were deployed in non-combat positions. The comparison of the casualty rates of mothers and soldiers has also lost much of its strength now that the dangers of childbirth have been so greatly reduced for most women in western countries. For the very first time, the means are available for women to choose whether and when to perform their political duty, although a powerful movement now exists to enforce motherhood as an involuntary duty for women – rather in the way that men can be conscripted as soldiers – by banning contraception and abortion. In 1989, the US Supreme Court judged that it was constitutional for the States to prohibit the use of public facilities and employees for abortions; poor women were thus deprived of part of their social rights of citizenship. At the same time, there are indications that motherhood is beginning to be seen as a right and not only as a duty. Much of the publicity and rhetoric surrounding the new reproductive technology and so-called surrogate motherhood suggests that women have a right to be fertile or to expropriate the fertility of other (usually poor) women.[41] The welfare state, notwithstanding its patriarchal structure, has also changed the position of mothers. Welfare benefits enable a mother to choose to live, if not well in the Anglo-American system, at least independently of a man's economic patronage. (And artificial insemination – an old technique put to new uses – allows women to become mothers without engaging in sexual relations with men.)

Perhaps most obviously, more mothers than ever before are now workers, but women generally are still paid less than men so that their economic dependence remains, albeit less severe than in the past. Nor has the sexual division of labour in private life been greatly affected by women's participation in the public workplace, as the instructive example of Sweden reveals. National labour market policy and 'equality policy' since the 1960s have enabled and encouraged women to be worker-mothers, especially through the provision of generous income replacement payments for parents who care for very young children and public child-care facilities. Despite the numbers of young men to be seen pushing prams, very few fathers take parental leave, and the sexual segregation of the occupational structure is the greatest among the OECD countries. Even in a society with a remarkable degree of equality in many respects, the connection between male employment and citizenship (or, indeed, men bearing arms and citizenship) has not yet been broken.[42]

The meaning of 'equality' in Swedish 'equality policy' brings me back to my starting point: 'equality' and 'difference' are opposed, or, at best, some compensation is allowed for 'difference' (so women, for instance, have flexible working hours and maternity leave; child care is provided and shops are open in the evening). The large measure of formal equality now won by women still excludes 'difference' while leaving intact much of women's inclusion through 'difference'. Another major problem, however, is precisely that the terms of the argument have been framed as 'equality' and 'difference'. There are good reasons for this, as my historical examples have been designed to show. The examples should also illustrate that the heart of the matter is not sexual difference but women's subordination. 'Equality', like other central political categories, is a contested term; but whereas 'equality' in some of its possible meanings can encompass 'difference', no sense of 'equality' compatible with a genuinely democratic citizenship can accommodate subordination. By a 'genuinely democratic citizenship', I mean that both sexes are full citizens and that their citizenship is of equal worth to them as women and men. For that to be the case, the meaning of sexual difference has to cease to be the difference between freedom and subordination. The issue in the problem of 'difference' is women's freedom.

Some of the more fervent advocates of difference seem to imply that equality is not important. Yet one fundamental dimension of women's freedom is the freedom inherent in equal citizenship. It bears repeating that the rift in the 1920s over 'equality' and 'difference' was between women who had all fought for the equal citizenship of the suffrage. The equal political standing of citizenship is necessary for democracy and for women's autonomy. If the political meaning of sexual difference is to change, and women's citizenship is to be worth the same as men's, patriarchal social and sexual relations have to be transformed into free relations. This does not mean that all citizens must become (like) men or that all women must be treated in the same way. On the contrary, for citizenship to be of equal worth, the substance of equality must differ according to the diverse circumstances and capacities of citizens, men and women. Motherhood no longer fills women's lives, or takes women's lives, as it once did, nor is women's citizenship only a matter of motherhood, but motherhood and citizenship remain intimately linked. Only women can give physical life to new citizens, who, in their turn, give life to a democratic political order.

NOTES

I am extremely grateful for the assistance of Keith D. Watenpaugh in revising this essay.

1 J. W. Scott, *Gender and the Politics of History*, New York, Columbia University Press, 1988, p. 172.
2 US District Court for the Northern District of Illinois, Eastern Division, *EEOC v. Sears, Roebuck & Co.*, 1986, Civil Action no. 79–C–4373. (An appeal in 1988 confirmed the judgement; the case covered the period 1973–80. The verdict, and the expert testimony of historians on opposite sides, has led to a prolonged and often acrimonious debate.)
3 Cited in C. L. Bacchi, *Same Difference: Feminism and Sexual Difference*, Sydney, Allen & Unwin, 1990, p. 45.
4 H. Smith, 'British feminism in the 1920s', in H. Smith (ed.), *British Feminism in the Twentieth Century*, London, Edward Elgar, 1990, pp. 59–60.
5 Cited in Bachi, *Same Difference*, p. 66.
6 See C. Pateman, *The Sexual Contract*, Cambridge, Polity Press, and Stanford, Calif., Stanford University Press, 1988. Unlike the other contract theorists, Hobbes holds that men and women are free by nature. On Hobbes see C. Pateman, '"God hath ordained to man a helper": Hobbes, patriarchy and conjugal right', in *The Disorder of Women: Democracy, Feminism, and Political Theory*, Cambridge, Polity Press, and Stanford, Calif., Stanford University Press, 1989.
7 See L. K. Kerber, *Women of the Republic: Intellect and Ideology in Revolutionary America*, New York, Norton, 1980.
8 See J. B. Landes, *Women and the Public Sphere in the Age of the French Revolution*, Ithaca, NY, Cornell University Press, 1988, especially ch. 4.
9 K. Offen, 'Depopulation, nationalism and feminism in *fin-de-siècle* France', *American Historical Review*, 89 (3), 1984, pp. 665–6.
10 M. Wollstonecraft, *A Vindication of the Rights of Woman*, New York, Norton, 1975, pp. 145–6, 189, 194.

11 S. Ruddick, 'Maternal thinking', in J. Trebilcot (ed.), *Mothering: Essays in Feminist Theory*, Totowa, Rowman & Allanheld, 1983, p. 227.
12 ibid., p. 226.
13 Cited in M. Dietz, 'Citizenship with a feminist face: the problem with maternal thinking', *Political Theory* 13 (1), 1985, p. 23.
14 Ruddick, 'Maternal thinking', p. 226.
15 Dietz, 'Citizenship', p. 20.
16 I have discussed these matters in *The Sexual Contract*.
17 L. Segal, *Is the Future Female?*, London, Virago Press, 1987, p. 211.
18 T. H. Marshall, 'Citizenship and social class', in *Sociology at the Crossroads and Other Essays*, London, Heinemann, 1963.
19 The importance of paid employment for men in the development of the welfare state is discussed in C. Pateman, 'The patriarchal welfare state', in *The Disorder of Women*.
20 Cited in J. Dale and P. Foster, *Women and the Welfare State*, London, Routledge & Kegan Paul, 1986, p. 17.
21 For some empirical evidence see Pateman, 'The patriarchal welfare state', pp. 241–2.
22 S. Pederson, 'Gender, welfare, and citizenship in Britain during the Great War', *American Historical Review*, 95 (4), 1990, p. 985.
23 ibid., p. 997.
24 J. Dunn, *Political Obligation in its Historical Context*, Cambridge, Cambridge University Press, 1980, p. 251.
25 M. Walzer, *Obligations: Essays on Disobedience, War and Citizenship*, New York, Simon & Schuster, 1971, p. 176.
26 T. Hobbes, *Leviathan*, ed. C. B. MacPherson, Harmondsworth, Penguin, 1968, p. 375.
27 The phrase is from B. Harrison, *Separate Spheres: The Opposition to Women's Suffrage*, London, Croom Helm, 1978, p. 73.
28 Marshall, 'Citizenship', pp. 123, 124.
29 See M. Foucault, *Discipline and Punish*, trans. A. Sheridan, New York, Vintage, 1979, and *The History of Sexuality*, vol. 1, trans. R. Hurley, New York, Vintage, 1980.
30 Offen, 'Depopulation', pp. 669–70.
31 Cited in R. Pringle, 'Octavius Beale and the ideology of the birth-rate: the Royal Commissions of 1904 and 1905', *Refractory Girl*, 3, 1973, p. 20.
32 Reported by T. B. Rosentiel, *LA Times*, Thursday 20 December 1990, p. A32.
33 See G. Bock, Chapter 5 in this volume.
34 Cited in B. Erenreich and D. English, *For Her Own Good*, New York, Anchor Press, 1978, p. 171.
35 A. Bebel, *Woman in the Past, Present and Future*, London, Reeves, 1886, p. 149.
36 Cited in S. Pederson, 'The failure of feminism in the making of the British welfare state', *Radical History Review*, 43, 1989, p. 91.
37 A. M. Royden, 'The future of the woman's movement', in V. Gollancz (ed.), *The Making of Women: Oxford Essays in Feminism*, London, Allen & Unwin, 1917, p. 140.
38 Cited in Pederson, 'Gender', p. 1003.
39 Cited in B. Cass, 'Redistribution to children and to mothers: a history of child endowment and family allowances', in C. Baldock and B. Cass (eds), *Women, Social Welfare, and the State*, Sydney, Allen & Unwin, 1983, p. 57.
40 The difficulty of reinterpreting the meaning of motherhood so that it appears to

be public service and sacrifice like that of soldiers is nowhere better illustrated than in Simone de Beauvoir's famous feminist study, *The Second Sex*, ed. and trans. H. M. Parshley, Harmondsworth, Penguin, 1975. She argues that, in risking their lives as hunters or warriors, men transcend a merely natural, animal existence. Women, cursed by being 'excluded from these warlike forays' (p. 95), merely repeat or reproduce life rather than placing their lives in jeopardy for 'reasons that are more important than the life itself' (p. 96). This is why young people laugh at a pregnant woman, 'who has become life's passive instrument' (p. 513).

41 New international dimensions of the politics of motherhood have also developed that are far removed from the international co-operation between members of the women's movement in the past. Current problems have to be seen in a neo-colonialist context, in which oral contraceptives ('the pill') were tested on Third World women and a trade exists in the – sometimes kidnapped – babies of poor Third World women to the affluent west.

42 See e.g. H. M. Hernes, 'The welfare state citizenship of Scandinavian women', in *The Welfare State and Woman Power: Essays in State Feminism*, Oxford University Press, 1987, ch. 7.

Chapter 2

Equality and sexual difference: amnesia in political thought

Adriana Cavarero

This chapter aims to show that modern political thought is characterized by a fundamental repression of sexual difference, that the very theoretical structure of the modern system of power ignores female sexual difference by absorbing it into an abstract paradigm of the individual, which is understood as male and universal.[1] This amnesia arises at various levels, and in this essay I shall be concerned with a *model* of the modern power system. The first and decisive formulation of this model is found in seventeenth-century theories of natural law, which divide state from society: and since it suits the purposes of my enquiry, I shall make use of this schematic distinction.

'BEFORE' THE MODERN

Since modernity conceives of itself as the outcome of a break, as a radical contrast with what preceded it, it is interesting to ask what was 'before' modernity. In relation to what does modernity posit itself as an entirely novel and different political order?

The political birth of modernity can be precisely located in the seventeenth-century natural-law theories of Hobbes and Locke, to their attempt to oppose (and declare illegitimate) a political model which may in turn be traced back, as far as its theoretical structure is concerned, to Aristotle's *Politics*. Needless to say, this structure had been changed and reworked, sometimes substantially, between Aristotle and the *ancien régime*. Nevertheless, the Aristotelian approach remained a source of authority and inspiration which fixed the fundamental categories of the pre-modern political model until the beginning of the seventeenth century. Two of its central elements are of particular interest in the present context: (a) the allegation that there are natural and historical *differences* between individuals, which can be translated into a pyramidal hierarchy or political order, and (b) the distinction in the *polis* between the sphere of politics and the sphere of the household.

(a) Aristotle's political theory is a consistent part of his anthropology[2] which takes the free adult male (roughly equivalent to the Athenian citizen) as the paradigm of human nature. Thus, to the question 'What is man?' (where the term 'man', *anthropos*, claims to stand for humankind), Aristotle replies by focusing on the free adult male and stating that 'man is a rational animal' and, *ipso facto*, 'a political animal'.[3] Once man, the full essence of human being, is held to correspond to the free adult male, other human beings who differ from him will be defined in terms of their various differences, which are regarded as marks of deficiency or inferiority.[4] Thus we have women, who are sexually different by virtue of not being male and hence inferior, the slaves, who are different by virtue of being unfree and consequently inferior, and adolescent males, who are different by virtue of being non-adult and as a result remain inferior until they reach the age of majority.

These differences are natural and structural, and each type of inferiority is marked by a lack of rationality. They serve to reserve the political sphere for men only, that is for free adult males. Men, however, are not conceived as abstractly equal, but are held to differ among themselves in their wealth, nobility, birth, etc. Thus, even when Aristotle speaks of equality, he always means equality in one respect which is at the same time compatible with inequality in another respect; for instance, all free males are equal in so far as they are equally free but unequal as regards wealth, virtue or nobility.

This political model consequently has many possible forms. Depending on which of the differences ascribed to free adult males is given priority, it can accommodate government by all free adult males (democracy), government by the nobility or the wealthy (oligarchy) or government by the most virtuous (aristocracy). Each of these makes use of a hierarchical model which locates the various differences among males in a particular place and provides for different functions, powers and rights relating to them. This model of hierarchically arranged differences remained essentially unchanged in its logical structure, despite variations in detail, up to the threshold of modernity. In fact, in the pre-modern epoch, we find a complex system of power, in which differences in birth, class and property are reflected in differences of powers and rights. In the England of Hobbes and Locke, for instance, a peer of the realm, a yeoman and a merchant were by no means equal individuals, neither possessing the same rights nor subject to the same laws and courts. People were born marked by differences and hence socially located in certain fixed places.

(b) This hierarchical structure characterizes the strictly political sphere which is accessible to males alone. The sexual difference between men and women (like the difference between free men and slaves, or adults and minors) does not mark a difference which can be translated into political terms, but a prior distinction of spheres of existence. The woman belongs to the sphere of the household and never oversteps the domestic realm to which she is confined by nature, by her natural gendered being, whereas man, if free and adult, realizes his special rational nature in the sphere of politics.[5]

This Aristotelian distinction between the sphere of the *polis*, *politika*, and the sphere of the household, *oikonomika* (from *oikos*, i.e. house),[6] presupposes a concept of the political as the maximum realization of the male essence and a corresponding concept of the *oikonomika* as being functional for and dependent on the political. Since the male has to be born and raised, and since he has bodily needs which must be met, the sphere of the household satisfies these vital requirements in such a way that the male, free from need, may devote himself to his highest end, namely political life. In Aristotle's terminology, this is equated with the good and happy life. There accordingly emerges a clear distinction between a public sphere where the rational fullness of those who are fully human can be realized, and a private sphere, concerned with survival and marked from the outset by a negativity which is evident in the very term 'private', i.e. de-prived, lacking (full humanness); it corresponds to the Greek *idiota*, which has, significantly, acquired a pejorative meaning in modern vocabulary.[7]

Thus, within the theoretical framework of Aristotelianism, female sexual difference marks a role of dependence on the adult male which corresponds to the confinement of women to their natural place, the private sphere of the household. Moreover, the rational nature of the adult male gives him a capacity to command and impose order; thus, as well as occupying the political sphere he also, as master, dominates woman in the domestic sphere. Master of the house and citizen of the *polis*, he posits himself as a human being *par excellence*. Woman, by comparison, is a human being of an inferior kind, incomplete, deficient, worthy and capable only of obeying orders. Also inferior, by comparison with the paradigm of the free adult male, are degraded males, the slaves, and still immature males, adolescents; like women, they are confined to the home and dependent on the master. So, although it is true that differences among adult males play a role in the political sphere where they define various forms of political constitution, it is the essential difference between free adult males on the one hand and women, slaves and adolescents on the other that preserves the sphere of politics for free adult males with all their innumerable differences.

The distinction between *politika* and *oikonomika*, or rather between public and private, remains essentially unchanged until the pre-modern epoch. It also survives beyond this era. It is one of the most obvious symptoms of the repression, the amnesia, of sexual difference, a fact to which I shall return later in this essay. For the moment, however, let me simply point out that, since the abolition of slavery, it is above all women who remain confined in the domestic sphere of service and procreation. (The adolescent, whose membership of this sphere is due to his immaturity, was always destined for politics.) It may seem that queens were an exception to the rule, but this is not altogether the case. For them, female sexual difference is the mark of an inferiority which places them at the end of the line of inheritance to the throne; and in addition they are denied the right of primogeniture which is the decisive factor in the monarchical system. In any case, the existence of a few queens in no way undercuts the internal and functional separation, in the antique model, between the sphere of politics and the sphere of the home, built around the sexual difference between male and female. This difference remains prior to the differences that differentiate the hierarchical organization of the political structure, whatever its historical form.

THE STATE

The theoretical and logical structure that marks the modern state was born specifically as a decisive rejection of Aristotelian political doctrine; and since it was on that doctrine that the historical system of rule preceding the modern state was *de facto* based, it was born also as a decisive rejection of that historical situation. It is essential to note that I am here referring to the political sphere in the strict sense, since, as we shall see, the Aristotelian distinction between the sphere of politics and the sphere of the home may be called into question in exceptional situations, but remains essentially untouched.

One of the ways in which modern political thought rejects its predecessors – in theory and in history – is evident in its reliance on the logical fiction of a state of nature, assumed as a starting hypothesis. The new political theory of the state claims that all individuals are equal by nature and have the same powers and rights. Here, then, we are dealing with a concept of absolute equality: because everyone is equal to everyone else by virtue of showing an original essence of human nature, no one has any entitlement to rule anyone else. This fiction – or logical hypothesis – of the state of nature is extremely important, since it allows the radical elimination of the hierarchical conception of society based on the differences among men. The object and outcome of the assumption of the original natural equality of all individuals are precisely the neutralization of the differences/inequalities which maintained the previous system of power. It is important to emphasize that we are dealing here with a logical category, a powerful fiction that delegitimizes and wipes out history. In other words, we are here in the presence of a radical erasure which makes a *tabula rasa* of whatever existed historically (and of the doctrine that sustained it) and starts from the general concept of humankind in its natural condition.

Although it may seem obvious, it is nevertheless helpful to remember that humankind is necessarily made up of men and women. Insisting on this fact is neither otiose nor superfluous but reminds us that natural individuals are sexually differentiated. If the object of the logical assumption of a state of nature is to wipe out all the differences among natural individuals, one might expect that sexual difference, too, would be wiped out in the sense that, even though natural individuals are necessarily either men or women, nevertheless their different sexualization will not be translated into differences of powers and rights. While this might be what we would logically expect, it is, amazingly, not what happens. In fact, the minds of modern political thinkers are marked by a powerful repression of female sexual difference. We are dealing here with an innate repression which I would define as a syndrome of 'universalization of masculinity' which manifests itself on at least two levels: an elementary one and a complex one.

The elementary level of repression is expressed in the way that modern political theoreticians simply *fail to see* women. Their mind's eye sees in the state of nature (and hence in the social contract and the political society that results from it) only men, while women are a sort of 'background', an appendix of mothers and wives, vaguely perceived in the distance and not further explored. What operates in these thinkers, in various ways,[8] is a (very ancient) coincidence between the human order and patriarchalism, so that in one way or another the observation of humankind in its natural state makes them 'spontaneously' see only individuals of the male sex. Viewed in this perspective, then, the modern state is a community of males marching in tight order and reconstructing its logical genesis by appeal to the state of nature. The state of nature is, moreover, no more than a logical hypothesis, a starting point from which, through the mechanism of the social contract between equal individuals, the legitimate political order, the state, can be constructed. Women, excluded because they are invisible to a theoretical viewpoint marked by the repression of sexual difference, come along in the van as an illogical encumbrance.

On this elementary level, the amnesia is so 'naïve' that the need for a logical justification is not felt. In fact, whereas the Aristotelian doctrine clearly perceived female sexual difference and thereupon excluded it from politics as embodying an inferior degree of rationality, the elementary level of modern repression seeks no reasons for the exclusion of women: they are not there simply because they are not 'visible'. The actual history of the modern state clearly reveals this elementary repression. When women at a certain point claimed full citizenship and equal rights, the state found itself, as it were, suddenly facing them, and from a political viewpoint saw them for the first time; no doubt with indignant fear and angry surprise.

There is, however, another aspect of history, concerned with the internal evolution of modern law, where we encounter a more complex level of repression of female sexual difference. While it is indeed true that modern theories of the state simply do not 'see' women, it is equally true that in another way the male subject of these theories claims for himself a universal valency which enables him to overcome the finitude and particularity of his sex and transforms him into a paradigm of humankind as such. This generalization of the male into a neutral or universal being[9] is a very ancient matter; yet the rationalizing, abstractive capacity of modern theory brings it to its maximum fulfilment.

The sphere of politics is of course only one of the spheres where the complex repression of female sexual difference finds fertile ground, since no modern discipline is immune from it. It permeates ordinary language itself. One ordinarily says, for instance: 'men are children of God' or 'men are destroying nature', meaning by 'men' not only males of the human species but females too. 'Men' applies to men and women, whereas 'women' applies to women only. It is helpful here to recall once more the Greek background to this issue. In Aristotle (as in Plato and others) we find a correspondence between 'man', understood as the human species in general, and 'male', which was to pass into most western languages as the universalization of the male and which was never thought about as a problem.

This twofold valency of the male, on the one hand male and on the other neutral or universal, had an unprecedented impact on modern political thought. In this context, the repression of female sexual difference does not take the form of an exclusion, as it does in the elementary level of repression, but of a homologizing, assimilating inclusion. The male subject, though male in essence and in name, counts potentially for women too. In this perspective, women are not *another* subject (with an equally genuine origin and therefore equal dignity and empowerment) but are a sort of empirical specification of the sole male subject. They are, let us say, the female-sexed part of men. In political doctrine this means that men, first as natural individuals and then as citizens, precisely because of their neutral/universal valency virtually include women too. Thus when women decide to claim rights and citizenship, the dominating political doctrine proceeds to apply this inclusive/homologizing power already possessed by the male subject. Modern law has in fact included women as equal to men, as if women, despite female sexual difference, were men. Modern law is therefore (as both theory and history show) completely modelled on the male subject and can take in women only by homologizing them with the male subject which operates as a basic paradigm. Thus, in modern legislation concerning maternity leave, pregnancy is treated as an illness which prevents female workers from working.[10] This is because the male subject, for whom the law is designed, does not experience pregnancies, but only disabling physiological changes or illnesses. The phenomenon of pregnancy comes to be 'adapted' to the language and the categories which sustain the law. Moreover, the protection of maternity, which might seem to be specific to the female subject, is usually oriented towards a concept of protecting the rights of the unborn or the new-born.

At this second and complex level, the repression of female sexual difference is less 'naïve' and more incisive because homologization precludes the possibility of women being subjects, capable of projecting themselves and deciding about themselves on the basis of rights that would take account not of the view that women are like men although they are women, but of the ineffaceable fact that they are women. Indeed, feminist thought, in some of its recent manifestations,[11] emphasizes that female freedom cannot be inscribed in politics unless there is a fundamental recognition of the fact that humankind is undeniably and ineradicably marked by sexual difference, that it is made up of men and women, and can in no way be reduced either to a sexless universal paradigm that would be valid for both sexes, or to a male paradigm that claims validity for the female sex too.

It is necessary to distinguish here between a sexless universal paradigm (what is normally called the human person) and a male paradigm. In reality these are not two distinct paradigms but two interrelated sides of one single paradigm. Nevertheless, it is not uncommon to find in feminist thought a type of analysis which allows itself to be bewitched by the sexless universal paradigm and tends to regard it as separable from and not compromised by the male paradigm. These feminists are consequently inclined to overlook the fact that the concept of the human person is in itself irremediably compromised by the male valency that has become logically precipitated into it. To show that this bewitching is neither legitimate nor useful, I shall offer a historical example and a theoretical argument.

The historical example is an instance of what I have tried to illustrate hitherto: the positing of the so-called 'human person'. The neutral, universal, sexless subject has never existed either in fact or in theory, except as a universalistic cover-up of the repression of female sexual difference brought about by the male subject. The male subject, working out representations of the world oriented to himself, is so shamelessly capable of regarding himself as universal that it has been possible to describe a situation in which men alone can vote as one of 'universal suffrage'.

Against this background, it is necessary to reflect upon the fact that every culture, every language and every representation of the world is a translation in figurative terms of the sexed subject that dominates it and has developed it. (This subject is obviously historical, since the Athenian citizen is neither the same as the slave nor the *citoyen*.) A truly universal and sexless paradigm could thus be developed only by a human being without sex or at most by a hermaphrodite. Given the impossibility of easily locating such creatures, it seems useful to distrust neutral universal paradigms, especially to the extent that they reveal their origin in the claim of the male subject to identify himself with humankind as such, as has in fact happened in various ways since the days of Aristotle.

The theoretical argument against the legitimacy of the neutral universal paradigm is a sort of appeal to concreteness, or to what Hannah Arendt calls the factuality of the real.[12] It is undeniable that human beings are of two sexes. If we are concerned for truth, truth must give an account of, and meaning to, the fact that there exist men and women rather than bisexed or unsexed individuals. It must give an account of this fact as of something that belongs to human existence as such: for ever, at present and every time somebody comes into the world.

Aristotle did explicitly take account of it without beating about the bush, but in his own way; he transformed sexual differences between men and women into the power of men over women. Modern theory renews this power but with a less clear and thus more dangerous logic, a homologizing logic founded on the repression of female sexual difference. The real problem which now runs through various theoretical approaches and political practices of feminism is not that of denying sexual difference but of denying that it ought to be transformed into the power of one sex over the other. This means also rejecting homologization of the female sex to the allegedly universal paradigms of the male sex. It must be rejected because homologization does not mean generosity but an extremely potent form of power.

BETWEEN EXCLUSION AND HOMOLOGIZATION

The two levels of repression of sexual difference at work in modern natural-law theories of the state thus place women in a contradictory position where they face either exclusion or homologization. Modern history engages in continuous oscillation between these two poles. Women are either excluded from knowledge, rights and politics, or else admitted and homologized. Movements for women's emancipation have run this very course, by fighting exclusion and demanding homologizing admission. Such a course was rendered possible (though certainly not handed over on a plate) by the neutral universal valency of the male subject which, right from the outset, marked the egalitarian logic of the modern state; but it cannot be regarded as completed even today. Not only does formal equality by no means correspond to substantive equality; in addition, even formal equality itself has not altogether been accepted by the prevailing order.

The model of women's emancipation usually works by claiming homologization with the male subject. In doing so, it risks working towards the erasure rather than the affirmation of sexual difference. This criticism of the emancipationist[13] model may appear too severe, but it is intended more as a bold analysis rather than an arrogant condemnation. No woman who works as an intellectual can fail to bless female emancipation, since the very possibility of her present occupation is one of its consequences, and a gain in comparison with the fairly recent epoch in which women were totally excluded from knowledge. Nevertheless, this blessed state of affairs should not prevent us from emphasizing how the knowledge to which women have been admitted is, in content and form, completely modelled on its protagonist, the male subject. For instance, the philosophy and history in which women of my generation were trained, from elementary school to university, are the philosophy and history of men.[14] They are a knowledge which, in the wake of the simple as well as the complex repression of female sexual difference, claims that the philosophy and history of men are universal philosophy and history, with a homologizing power *vis-à-vis* women.

But the fact that there are now situations (very diverse ones and not only inside the academic world) in which some women speak about women and among women shows that the homologizing effect of knowledge is not definitive or unbreakable. It may be simply a stage with a useful function, a sort of transition from exclusion to freedom with respect to intellectual explorations on and by women that may pass via homologization. This does not necessarily mean that it is an obligatory passage in absolute terms; but historically this has been the transition through which many women have passed. The conception and practice of sexual difference now shared by many women have made it possible to see the risks of homologization which resulted from the demand that women should be admitted to the sphere of abstract equality modelled on the male paradigm. Viewed from a perspective of sexual difference, homologization can be regarded no longer as a goal, but at most as an instrument to be used in the struggle for female freedom. As the philosopher Luce Irigaray has said, it is not enough to free oneself from the master in order to be free. Freedom should be founded on the capacity of the female subject to speak herself, think herself and protect herself. She must give herself an autonomous meaning which takes account of the fact that women are women and not men. As long as women see their freedom in wanting to be like men – via homologization – the male political model that sustains it will triumph over female freedom. The male One and All will continue in its repression of female sexual difference.

SOCIETY

So far I have concentrated on the political model in the strict sense, on a model of the state the fulcrum of which is the paradigm of the equal, abstract, serial individual, unmarked by any difference and yet male. The same model includes, however, another and functionally related level of modern political theory which concerns society. In this sphere, differences shoot up like mushrooms, and are captured in 'social stratification' which usually refers to differences in economic and cultural resources. The protagonist of the modern political model is thus a two-faced individual, or one with a twofold essence: in relation to the state and its laws, it is equal to everyone else; in relation to society, it is marked by the most varied differences. For instance, a Milanese industrialist and an Apulian labourer are absolutely equal before the law and the state but differ markedly with respect to their social situation. Society in fact lives on the differences/inequalities that distribute different roles, functions and destinies among persons. It would therefore seem that modern society, as a sphere distinct from the state, reflects the pre-modern system of power. But this is not the case. In fact the modern political model has itself worked out the concept of society in accordance with its own special logic, making it, too, emerge from the presupposition of the state of nature.

To demonstrate this point I shall briefly go back to Locke (it is no accident that he is a constant theoretical reference point for the western democracies). Locke's natural individual is twofold: made up of reason, and in this respect equal to everyone else, but also of passions. This twofold substance has two logical consequences. On the one hand, the state and its principle of equality are based on reason; on the other hand, the passions, above all the passion to possess, give rise to private property which maps out a society of rich and poor, owners and wage-earners. My concern here[15] is only to emphasize how, starting from the twofold nature of the natural individual, the polity divides into distinct spheres, characterized respectively by abstract equality (the state) and concrete differences (society). By contrast with the hierarchical pre-modern model, society – the sphere of differences – is not reflected in differences of rights or political powers, but is presented, somewhat ideologically, as a free field of resources for which in theory subjects can compete.

But since the initial paradigm, even with these two faces, is the male subject with his claims to neutral/universal valency, we find here a situation resembling the one we have already encountered. The repression of female sexual difference, at both the elementary and a complex level, is reproduced point by point in the logic of society. The elementary level of repression consists once again in the simple exclusion of women. The 'market', a fundamental aspect of society, in its initial historical phase excludes women. Owners and wage-earners are seen only as men, are, let us say, naturally and obviously male. A market of men alone is stratified according to differences among males and is woven of their competitive conflicts.

But not for long. When it becomes advantageous for the market, women are admitted to it, at opportune moments, at fixed times and in specific sectors. They are admitted, homologized to the male paradigm and subjected to the established conditions of productivity at all costs, merciless competition and will to power. This homologizing paradigm constrains women to become uniform with the male subject by erasing female sexual difference to such an extent that female sexual difference, even at its biological level, comes to be regarded as an obstacle to homologization. Pregnancy is a stumbling block to be avoided, a career obstacle, a vertical drop in productivity.

The homologizing effect of the complex repression of female sexual difference thus not only absorbs women into the paradigm of the productive man, but is manifested, sometimes with ridiculous effects, in the technical vocabulary and conceptual logic of society. For instance, the categories of those working in the market are always described in the masculine plural. Thus, in Italian – one of the languages that marks gender in the plural by endings – we have *operai* (workers), *impiegati* (employees), *commercianti* (businessmen), *statali* (civil servants), etc. Not only this, but we have *tessili* (textile workers) and *insegnanti* (teachers) despite the fact that these two categories are overwhelmingly made up of women. One painful oddity is that textile workers, precisely because they are mainly women, have exceedingly unfavourable work contracts compared to, for instance, metalworkers, who are mainly men. Nevertheless, textile workers continue to be talked about in the masculine gender.

This undue universalization of the male can also be easily detected in modern languages that do not mark gender in the plural, for instance in the language of sociology. Here we often find classifications of the following kind: the old, the young, the handicapped, the unemployed *and* women. In this classification, women obviously belong to each of the social groups indicated, but are then also added as a separate social group. This occurs because female sexual difference is an inferiorizing factor and, although it is already understood to belong in each of the 'disadvantaged' social groups just mentioned, has to be listed separately as a condition that may occur on its own. In fact, men and women are not a mere bipolar couple in the vocabulary of sociology, as may be clear from this list: the old, the young, the handicapped, the unemployed *and* men. The effect is ridiculous because maleness is not a state of humankind, but humankind as such and universally.

My criticism here resembles my objection to the 'emancipationist' model. I do not hope that women will leave the market and society, but I do hope that they will remain in it as free subjects, capable of realizing themselves in a social model of their own, and not as an inferior version of the male subject. To put the point another way, female sexual difference is not just *one* of the differences that the male/universal subject enumerates among those differences which, modelled upon himself, make up a composite object called 'society'. Female sexual difference, if it is not the victim of powerful repression, implies that in society there should be – above all and before any other difference whatsoever – two different subjects: *two* and different, not *one* and homologous.

THE DOMESTIC SPHERE

I claimed earlier that modern political theory represents a definitive break with the logical and historical approach of the previous system of power which, though highly complex and at times innovative, has its conceptual roots in Aristotle's *Politics* – an approach characterized above all by the distinction between the political and the domestic sphere. It might be expected, then, that modern political theory, in striking a blow at the very foundations of the ancient order, would also strike a blow at the domestic sphere. Yet this did not happen. For modern theory, politics concerns both the state and society. The separate domestic sphere, however, remains untouched and unstudied or, rather, essentially accepted, repeated and recycled. Despite its desire to reject and radically reform the Aristotelian approach, modern political theory *forgets* to take the domestic sphere into account, so that it is incorporated in the modern outlook as a sort of enormous repression.

All this concerns the very disciplinary redefinition of political science itself, a complex problem that cannot be dealt with here. I wish to point merely to the persistence of an ancient conception of the domestic sphere, parallel to the new conception of the state and of society. It persists without becoming an object of the new science, but along the lines of a dichotomized, schizophrenic logic – as a manifest incongruity within the system, though one which is very useful, and indeed indispensable to its continued functioning. The schizophrenia of the system is revealed on the macroscopic scale by the fact that the state/society model lives side by side with a domestic model characterized by values which are entirely different and opposed, and which can be summed up as follows.

First, within the state, the principle of abstract equality posits equal, serial individuals who are placed in a horizontal dimension of equivalent single units. The domestic sphere, by contrast, is made up of connected individuals who differ in essence (mother, father, children) and who perform distinctive functions within a network of interdependent relations centred around the figure of the mother. Second, society is conceived as being governed by an individualistic-competitive paradigm; it follows the dictates of 'productive' labour which can be translated into money terms and which aim at money and profit. In the home, instead, we have an altruistic paradigm of care and dedication; it follows the dictates of 'reproductive' work which is unpaid, cannot be translated into money terms and is unilaterally performed by the mother and wife for the other members of the domestic unit.

According to the ancient Aristotelian model, the house does indeed remain the place of social reproduction, which is understood to be the work of women. Obviously the new complexity of the state/society sphere is reflected in the domestic sphere, reducing and compartmentalizing it on the one hand, but on the other hand loading it with new needs, new functions and new burdens, such as the utilization of public services and a sort of modernization of maternity which adds the difficulty of dealing with bureaucracies to the tasks of nursing and cooking, thereby presupposing that women have infinite time at their disposal.

Here, then, as is already the case in Aristotle, female sexual difference becomes visible and is characterized by a 'natural' role. Here the complexity of functions demanded of women's work compels women to invent survival strategies based not only on psycho-physical training to combat the strains of overwork, but also on a real and deep understanding of the complexity of their tasks and on their ability continually to restructure them. Since these are well known, I shall not dwell on them. I wish to emphasize, however, that the male figure of the master is not yet quite eliminated even at the level of family law, and still persists in various ways as the *patria potestà* or 'head of household'. Whatever the intentions that lie behind the recent reforms of family law, including its apparently egalitarian formulations, it definitely lacks the strength to break down the cultural model of the home.

It is important to ask what might happen to modern political theory if the domestic model were actually to be broken down, changed, rethought. What would happen to the system as a whole if the function of social reproduction assigned to the home and to female labour were to remain unfulfilled? These questions help us to see that the repression of the domestic sphere in modern political theory is not an error of omission but a profoundly functional, essentially immovable choice. Hitherto, no party of any tendency whatever has shown any serious desire to confront the issue of the domestic sphere in its political programme. At most, this problem is fleetingly touched on, and even when questions such as the recognition of housework or the improvement of social services are raised, the underlying set-up is not discussed. Perhaps there is a growing awareness that the cultural model of the home is untouchable in the sense of being necessary and vital to the system as a whole, even if, ironically, it continues to be spoken of as marginal and without value.

Thus, however much the repression of the domestic sphere and the consequent schizophrenia of the overall system are indices of its obvious logical inconsistency, they also indicate the equilibrium of a system which requires the exploitation of female domestic labour. To eliminate this exploitation would be to bring the whole system into crisis.[16] Moreover, it is above all women who bear the weight of this contradiction. For women, the logical schizophrenia between the state/society sphere and the domestic sphere is reflected in the schizophrenic experience of two models inside their own skin. *Homologized* to the neutral/male model in their extra-domestic work and bound by its norms of individualism, competitiveness, conflict, etc., they are at the same time *differentiated* in accordance with the wife/mother model in their domestic work and committed to altruism, care, service. This is not merely to play a dual role but to experience downright schizophrenia between the emancipationist and domestic models. In these models female sexual difference either disappears or swings into the foreground as the depository of a 'natural' function of mothering – a female sexual difference loaded with schizophrenia, that can never constitute the horizon for our autonomous project of liberty.

CONCLUSION

Forgotten, and constrained by the folds of multiple repression, female sexual difference experiences the principle of equality as an effect of exclusion and homologization, camouflages itself in social stratification as an inferiorizing condition of human existence, and is caught by centuries of tradition in the domestic sphere where it appears in a role of obligatory unpaid service. In this disquieting picture of modern political theory, being a woman is thus everything and nothing, or better, it is a nothing that has to adapt to being everything. For those who are not subjects, who do not consist in mind and body of their sexed gender (*genere sessuato*), who do not possess the symbolic representation that inscribes them in the world, are nothing by themselves, but at most a function in the world of the other.

Thinking in terms of sexual difference (*il pensiero della differenza sessuale*) is thus not simply a philosophical exercise, but the inaugural act in a political project that assumes women to be subjects capable of freedom and of self-signification. Like any political project which turns around a material subject (since body, history, destiny and desire are what give material to the female subject), thinking in terms of sexual difference is also a hermeneutic key that allows the modern concept of equality to be perceived as a principle which is false in its logical foundation and homologizing in its concrete effects. Equality between two different beings cannot be the dissolution of one of them in the other. The modern concept of equality predicates the undifferentiated and serialized character of those who are considered equal, and in the arbitrariness of this predication has already wiped from the earth races, cultures and ethnic groups. But women are not a race, nor a culture, nor an ethnic group. They are a primary difference inscribed in human existence, they are and have always been one of the two sexes. It is so and not otherwise. A principle of equality that reflects the truth of this *twoness* will thus necessarily be a principle that denies the legitimacy of the rule, in whatever shape and whatever logical guise, of one over the other.

It is possible to be both different and equal, if each of the two different beings is free and if the kind of equality at stake radically abandons any foundation in the logic of abstract, serializing universalization of the male One. It is possible to be both different and equal if not only a new logical foundation of the concept of equality can be developed, but a new model of society and of politics. The dimension of sexual difference cannot be accommodated by adjusting and integrating it into the existing model of society and politics, but demands a radical rethinking of the basic logic of the model. It demands a novel view of ways of coexisting and of liberty in a humanity made up of men and women.

But the repression of sexual difference is, in the present state of power relations, still silent and deep.

NOTES

1 The view that the modern state is founded on a political and legal universalism which is modelled on the male paradigm has become widely accepted in women's theoretical reflection. I shall confine myself here, as in most of the following, to some of the voices in the Italian debate: A. Cavarero, 'L'ordine dell'uno non è l'ordine del due', in A. Cavarero, *Il genere della rappresentanza: materiali e atti di 'Democrazia e diritto'*, Rome, Editori Riuniti, 1988, pp. 67–80; M. L. Boccia, 'La

ricerca della differenza', ibid., pp. 7–25; A. Rossi-Doria, 'Il voto alle donne; una storia di contraddizioni', ibid., pp. 29–41; A. Cavarero, 'L'emancipazione diffidente: considerazioni teoriche sulle pari opportunità', *Reti*, 2, 1988, pp. 42–52; M. Campari and L. Cigarini, 'Fonte e principi di un nuovo diritto', *Sottosopra*, January 1989, pp. 6–7.

2 See G. Sartori, *Elementi di politica*, Bologna, Il Mulino, 1987, pp. 245–6.

3 Aristotle, *Politics*, 1253a, 2 ff.

4 See e.g. A. Cavarero, 'Il bene nella filosofia politica di Platone e di Aristotele', *Filosofia politica*, II(2), 1988, pp. 309–21; L. Lange, 'Woman is not a rational animal: on Aristotle's biology of reproduction', in S. Harding and M. B. Hintikka (eds), *Discovering Reality*, Dordrecht, Reidel, 1983, pp. 1–15; E. V. Spelman, 'Aristotle and the politicization of the soul', ibid., pp. 17–30.

5 See H. Arendt, *The Human Condition*, Chicago, University of Chicago Press, 1958, pp. 28–37.

6 For this distinction, which was crucial and lasting for the history of the west, setting the roles and spheres defined as male and the female, see esp. J. B. Elshtain, *Public Man, Private Woman*; *Women in Social and Political Thought*, Princeton, NJ, Princeton University Press, 1981.

7 See Arendt, *Vita activa*, p. 43.

8 On differences between authors who deal with this issue see G. Conti Odorisio, 'Matriarcato e patriarcalismo nel pensiero politico di Hobbes e Locke', in I. Magli (ed.), *Matriarcato e potere delle donne*, Milan, Feltrinelli, 1978, pp. 37–56; J. Flax, 'Political philosophy and the patriarchal unconscious: a psychoanalytic perspective on epistemology and metaphysics', in Harding and Hintikka, *Discovering Reality*, pp. 261–81; C. Pateman, *The Sexual Contract*, Cambridge, Polity Press, 1988, and Chapter 1 in this volume.

9 On this crucial issue see my article 'Per una teoria della differenza sessuale', in A. Cavarero *et al.*, *Diotima: il pensiero della differenza sessuale*, Milan, La Tartaruga, 1987, pp. 41–79.

10 See E. Wolgast, 'Wrong rights', *Hypatia*, II(1), 1987, p. 33; and D. L. Rhode, Chapter 8 in this volume.

11 Within the Italian context, I refer here to the trend of thought related to Diotima, the philosophical community of Verona, and the Libreria delle Donne (Women's Bookstore) in Milan, who recognize a debt to Luce Irigaray; see esp. her *Sexes et parentés*, Paris, Editions de Minuit, 1987. Obviously, the definition of 'feminism' is neither easy nor uncontroversial. For some explorations that relate to various national contexts see esp. A. R. Calabrò and L. Grasso (eds), *Dal movimento femminista al femminismo diffuso*, Milan, Angeli, 1985; *Memoria: rivista di storia delle donne*, esp. 19–20, 1987 (on the feminist movement of the 1970s); Libreria delle Donne di Milano, *Non credere di avere dei diritti*, Turin, Rosenberg & Sellier, 1987; R. Braidotti, 'Donne e filosofia in Francia', *Memoria*, 15, 1985, pp. 39–51; T. Winant, 'The feminist standpoint: a matter of language', *Hypatia*, II(1), 1987, pp. 123–47; K. Offen, 'Defining feminism: a comparative historical approach', *Signs*, 14, 1988, pp. 119–57, included as Chapter 4 in this volume.

12 H. Arendt, *La vita della mente*, Bologna, Il Mulino, 1987, p. 85; English original *The Life of the Mind*, New York and London, Harcourt Brace Jovanovich, 1978.

13 Editors' note: In Italy, the term 'emancipationism' (*emancipazionismo, emancipazionista*), coined earlier but widely current among feminists since the 1970s, refers to forms of feminism based on the claims which are analysed here as homologization; in the Anglo-American debate they correspond, though not entirely, to feminism based on 'equality' as focal concept. For reasons of clarity and brevity, the term 'emancipationism' has been retained in the translation.

14 For the complex problem of the 'gendering' (*sessuazione*) of the two disciplines

see among recent studies A. Cavarero, 'L'elaborazione filosofica della differenza sessuale', in C. Marcuzzo and A. Rossi Doria (eds), *La Ricerca delle donne*, Turin, Rosenberg & Sellier, 1987, pp. 173–87; R. Braidotti, comments, ibid., pp. 188–202; P. di Cori, 'Prospettive e soggetti nella storia delle donne', ibid., pp. 96–111; G. Pomata, comments, ibid., pp. 112–22; G. Bock, *Storia, storia delle donne, storia di genere*, Florence, Estro Editrice, 1988; *Les cahiers du Grif*, 37–8, 1988, special issue on 'Le genre de l'histoire'.

15 For a further exploration see my 'La teoria contrattualistica nei "Trattati sul Governo" di Locke', in G. Duso (ed.), *Il contratto sociale nella filosofia politica moderna*, Bologna, Il Mulino, 1987, pp. 149–90.

16 How far this system is capable of translating the schizophrenia between public and private into an internally functional model that renders the 'inconsistency' of the two spheres 'consistent' can be seen from an analysis of the logical model of the welfare state; see N. Fraser, 'Women, welfare and the politics of need interpretation', *Hypatia*, II(1), 1987, pp. 103–21.

Chapter 3

The good-enough citizen: female citizenship and independence

Susan James

The theory and practice of democratic liberalism are much criticized at present on the grounds that they exclude women from full citizenship.[1] They do this in two ways: by denying women the full complement of rights and privileges accorded to men, and, more insidiously, by taking for granted a conception of citizenship which excludes all that is traditionally female. The cluster of activities, values, ways of thinking and ways of doing things which have long been associated with women are all conceived as outside the political world of citizenship and largely irrelevant to it.

This revolutionary but by now familiar argument draws strength from a particular interpretation of liberal theory as built around a set of complementary dichotomies. Dominating these is the opposition between public and private. This is variously interpreted, but at least encompasses the divide between the overtly political institutions of society and the domestic sphere of the home and family. It is supported by a series of polarities between equality and difference, reason and emotion, man and woman, disinterest and interest, impartiality and partiality, independence and dependence. The first terms of these pairs characterize the public sphere, while the second serve to limit it by showing what it excludes; both invest it with authority, and contribute to a conception of what is and what is not of value in political life. Moreover, in so far as public political life is seen as male, and is defined in opposition to the private, domestic sphere of women, women lack full membership of the political world and are not full citizens.

One of the greatest achievements of recent feminist philosophy has been to show that this analysis answers not only to the condition of our forebears but also to that of contemporary women living in the liberal western democracies. Despite the giant emancipatory strides of the past hundred years, women are still denied full citizenship. And despite its egalitarian aspirations, democratic liberal theory still nurtures a conception of politics which implicitly marginalizes and disadvantages women. Struck by the force of this argument, many feminists have turned their backs on liberalism, convinced that its patriarchal assumptions are so deeply embedded as to be beyond reform.[2] It has, in their view, nothing to offer feminists, who must look elsewhere for a novel and emancipatory conception of citizenship.

This outright rejection of liberalism often draws support from the analysis already sketched – the tendency to view the theory as a precarious structure, built of oppositions which must stand or fall together. If one dichotomy collapses (the private/public distinction, for instance) the rest will come tumbling down. In this essay I shall argue that it is a mistake to see the oppositions around which liberal theory is organized as lined up like two rows of dominoes, each male term facing its inferior female counterpart with implacable hostility. The relations within and between pairs are, as I shall seek to show, much more diverse. Focusing on the opposition between independence and dependence, I shall argue that a more cautious investigation of the place of this polarity in the liberal conception of citizenship reveals not only that the distinction between its terms is not as clear cut as some feminist stereotypes would suggest, but also that there is more continuity between liberal and feminist conceptions of citizenship than is generally appreciated.

This argument bears on two problems within feminist theory. Most obviously, it will, I hope, be of use in current debates about female citizenship. In addition, however, it may contribute to the task of creating a conception of politics which takes account of sexual difference. If the liberal notion of the political realm is implicitly male, it has to be modified or replaced – we need a new conception of the political. The task of forming one is, however, constrained by the concepts we possess; not just anything can count as political, after all, and we are bound to appeal to existing criteria in arguing, for example, that problems previously regarded as 'personal' have a political dimension. In this context, continuities between the old and new thinking are a valuable resource, to be used rather than despised. The extent to which current feminist theorizing trades on a liberal conception of the independent citizen is not discreditable, a sign of lack of progress or false consciousness. Instead, it is part of a process of transformation which both unmasks an instability within liberal thought and points the way towards a different image of the citizen.

My exploration of this theme begins by considering three areas – physical, economic and emotional – in which liberal theory holds that citizens must be guaranteed a degree of independence. I then analyse some of the ways in which women are (still) deprived of such a guarantee. The third section of the essay turns to the issue of emotional independence, and criticizes one common response to the liberal status quo – the development of a theory in which emotional independence has no place and is held to be of no political value. In the final section I then offer a different interpretation of this fundamental idea; I suggest that a richer conception of emotional independence enables us to see that it is not simply opposed to dependence, and enables us to reassimilate it into the framework of a feminist politics.

CITIZENLY INDEPENDENCE

The opposition between independence and dependence is commonly included in the list of dichotomies that articulate the liberal distinction between the public and the private. Whereas the domestic realm is characterized by dependent relations between, for example, men and women or parents and children, the political sphere contains individual agents whose equal status as citizens presupposes a degree of mutual independence.[3] In order to vote, express their opinions or stand for office, citizens must be free from what are counted as coercive constraints, and must be guaranteed the kinds of independence that this condition requires.

The justification for this sort of citizenly independence does not derive simply from the idea that the aim of the state is to maximize individual freedom. Instead, it derives from the more specific view that it is the job of a democratic polity to provide conditions in which each citizen can contribute to at least some political decisions in his or her own voice.[4] Coercive conditions are consequently those in which the voices of individuals are distorted, and it is in the name of undistorted political self-expression, rather than any wider-ranging personal freedom, that coercion is to be avoided.

Within the liberal tradition, certain kinds of dependence have long been recognized as hindrances to political participation. First, in order to speak in their own voices, citizens must be physically independent, free from bodily violation or the threat of it. Second, citizens are not in a position to express their political views if by doing so they run the risk of losing the means to provide for themselves and their dependants, the risk of either destitution or slavery. These freedoms are traditionally secured by individual rights to life, liberty and property, rights which are in turn interpreted in the light of the demand that the citizen should have the security or independence to contribute to the polity in his or her own voice.[5]

The ability to speak in one's own voice is central to democratic liberalism. But it is cross-pressured by a further demand that citizens should be capable of displaying a third kind of independence, this time an emotional one. Full citizens, it is held, must be capable of a degree of impartiality. To speak impartially, in the sense that concerns us here, is not to speak in one's *own* voice, informed by one's own particular interests and affections, but to speak from a more distant standpoint, as one person among others. There are various ways in which liberal theories presuppose the impartiality of individual citizens. Sometimes it is assumed that only people who are capable of making impartial judgements are able to recognize just and legitimate political institutions. More commonly, it is argued that if all citizens are eligible to hold office, anyone may in principle become a legislator and may be expected to adopt an impartial outlook.[6]

Impartiality, in this comparatively weak sense, requires a kind of emotional independence. On the one hand, one must be able to withstand emotional blackmail by others. And on the other, one must be able to withstand the force of one's own personal feelings, whether they are directed towards others or oneself. For example, the impartial legislator not only places affection for family or friends in a broader context of 'the affections people feel for their family or friends'. He or she also has to gain some distance on self-regarding feelings, such as a desire to be seen as the person who negotiated the successful resolution of a conflict. These emotions, as much as externally directed ones, can interfere with impartiality by putting the self too prominently at the centre of the picture.

The independence of full citizens is therefore a complex affair, the physical, economic and emotional aspects of which reflect the need for individuals to speak as private persons and as legislators; to be capable, if you like, of speaking in two voices which may or may not agree. The forms of independence that this presupposes are, I have suggested, central to the conception of citizenship with which we are concerned. Nevertheless, it is important not to exaggerate their extent. There is a danger that we may slip into thinking of the full citizen as the commited, participating activist or legislator. In fact, what I shall call, in homage to Winnicott, the good-enough citizen of liberalism[7] requires only a modest degree of independence and is by no means obliged to participate in political life; his or her independence is held to be sufficiently protected by a familiar bundle of rights and civil liberties, which, as we know all too well, provide only minimal security against dependence and exploitation.

Whatever their limitations, however, the existence of these protective measures testifies to an underlying liberal belief that independent citizens are not found but made, forged out of a collection of elaborate social arrangements designed to provide certain kinds of security. Furthermore, the interpretation of these measures reflects the changing views of society as to how the independence of citizens is to be understood. The introduction of the secret ballot, for example, created circumstances in which male citizens could vote with their own voices, without the threat of physical or economic reprisal. It is an unusually simple example of the attempt to guarantee the same minimal level of independence to all full citizens, thereby ensuring a measure of equality and giving each the same opportunity to fulfil their role as participators.

The quest for citizenly equality undertaken by those who campaigned for the introduction of the ballot box has recently been dismissed as both illusory and pernicious. The construction of citizens as political equals, it is argued, can only be achieved either by ignoring the many differences between individuals or by denying that the differences are relevant to politics. Thus, liberal theory has dismissed differences of gender, race, ethnicity, class or temperament as of merely private significance, and has created a relatively featureless political realm in which the selected properties of citizens are those of men – a realm which blanks out the identities of individuals by neglecting their differences.[8]

This argument correctly emphasizes a marked tendency within liberalism;

but it also over-simplifies the attitude of liberal theorists to equality. Liberalism does of course aim to construct citizens who are political equals. But in doing so it is not oblivious to the differences between them. In order to give all citizens the same minimal level of physical and economic independence, for example, it is necessary to treat some differently from others. Despite the centrality of universal rights within its tradition, liberal theory is sensitive to this fact and recognizes the political significance of differences in so far as these are obstacles to citizenship. For example, an impeccably liberal argument claims that mothers should be awarded a family allowance to compensate them for the loss of their economic independence while they bear and bring up children. To put the point another way, exponents of this liberal view recognize that the difference between mothers and others jeopardizes the economic independence of mothers, and holds that the state should intervene to guarantee that their independence is preserved.[9]

In this case, mothers are singled out for special treatment – the effects of their difference can only be alleviated by treating them differently. There is thus a sense in which liberal theory takes account of difference, not as something that is politically valuable in itself, but as something that is politically relevant because it threatens the equal independence of citizens. In this and similar contexts, equality and difference are not seen as mutually defining opposites, but are held to stand in a relationship of means to ends.

FEMALE CITIZENS

Discussion of the theoretical resources of liberalism serves in part to emphasize the enormous gap that exists between these very resources and the way they have been brought to bear on political practice. For although liberal theory contains, as we have just seen, some means to take account of the differences between individuals, it has signally failed to pay attention to differences of gender in its construction of a norm of citizenship. The conception of citizenly independence outlined in the last section has consequently been the subject of a series of powerful feminist criticisms which have pointed out how women, while formally accorded citizenship, are prevented by their gender from participating fully in political life.

One of the most forceful strands of this attack focuses on the types of independence analysed in the last section and shows how women are deprived of them. As we saw, democratic liberal theory requires that citizens should be able to exercise their civil rights without threat of physical violation. But this independence has not been extended to women in practice, and in theory is cross-cut by the tenets of partriarchy.[10] It is true, of course, that women, like men, may vote, address meetings, hold office and so on, secure in the knowledge that the law will protect them against attack. But because violence has not in general been understood to include sexual violence against women, they have remained vulnerable in a way that affects their ability to participate in political life.

Since the threat of sexual violence is so pervasive, ranging from minor harassment to battery and rape inside or outside marriage, it is not immediately clear that it is an obstacle to *political* participation, nor that it limits the minimal kind of physical independence that liberalism guarantees the citizen. Fear of sexual violence may, for example, prevent women from going out at night, and a liberal may agree that this is a bad thing. But he or she may protest that it does not impinge on the minimal independence that is necessary for citizenship – it does not directly prevent women from engaging in the public world of politics. Here we come up against a familiar problem of specifying what in social and political life prevents what. Fear of going out at night or the threat of a beating at home can of course prevent women from doing many things, including exercising their civil rights; it may, for example, deter them from attending political meetings. Sexual violence against women, whether in public or at home, is not specifically and exclusively directed against women as citizens; but in so far as it can and does limit their participation in politics, women lack the physical independence of their male counterparts.

Again, it may be objected that this point applies quite generally to a number of disadvantaged groups in society whose physical security is not assured. Men of colour, as much as women, may for example be threatened with violence if they run for office. This of course is true. But the objection misses the particular ways in which the physical independence of women, as women, is not guaranteed. Women are, to a vastly greater extent than men, vulnerable to various forms of sexual violence which society has been slow to recognize as illegitimate and in many cases still condones.

What, now, about economic independence – the ability to exercise one's civil rights, secure against the threat of destitution or slavery? It is important to bear in mind what a very minimal guarantee this is, for men or women; but once again, the ways in which women are deprived of it are special to them, and reveal another sense in which they are excluded from full citizenship. Recent feminist scholarship has drawn attention to the many factors that contribute to the economic dependence of women,[11] of which the most obvious is perhaps the traditional reliance of married women on their husbands. A married woman who has no income of her own depends on her husband for economic support, and her participation in political life may be subject to his good will. He may, for example, threaten to cut her allowance if she joins a certain party, goes to a particular rally or whatever. The precariousness of her position is brought out by the fact that, whereas it would be illegal for an employer to cut a woman's wages on account of her political preferences, the husband is within his rights, and thus exercises considerable power over his wife.

Within traditional marriages, then, women lack the economic security of citizens. But it may be objected that it is usually possible for women to work and that, armed with an independent income, they are protected against the kind of threat I have just outlined. Even where this is true, however, the objection underestimates the impact upon women of a variety of social arrangements which disadvantage them economically, sometimes to the point of destitution. Consider the facts that women's work is less well paid than that of men, that women's benefits are often calculated on the assumption that they are not self-supporting, and that many women with young children cannot afford to work. These arrangements, and others like them, conspire to create conditions in which some women, by virtue of their gender, are faced with a choice between destitution and economic dependence. For the destitute, political participation is not usually a practical possibility. For the dependent, it is under the control of the paymaster.

If this analysis is correct, women are not guaranteed even the level of independence that enables citizens to participate freely in political life. We must next ask, however, whether they are guaranteed the emotional independence required in particular of legislators. Because liberal theorists do not expect citizens to display emotional independence (do not expect them to think and act impartially) in everyday life, they do not devote as much attention to the construction of impartiality as to the construction of physical and economic independence. Theories which appeal to the impartial standpoint to justify particular conceptions of justice or obligation tend simply to assume that willing individuals can adopt it. And theorists who recognize that impartiality resembles physical and economic independence in being the fruit of elaborate social arrangements, tend to assume that it is simply the outcome of carefully adjusted political institutions. The institutions within which policies are decided on and laws are made must be so designed as to encourange and reinforce the emotional splitting required of legislators.

It remains to ask, then, whether the implicit condition that legislators must be capable of impartiality serves to exclude women from this aspect of citizenship. A number of the ways in which women's characteristic roles and experiences provide, by comparison with the experiences of men, an un-training for the impartial standpoint have recently been explored by feminist writers. In addition, the still-gendered division of labour has been shown to impose strains on women which make it harder for them than for men to exercise the skills required of legislators.[12]

Central to both these strands of argument is the perception and self-perception of women as carers, reflected both in a traditional understanding of what it is to be womanly or feminine, and in the character of women's work. Women's work, both past and present, is overwhelmingly concerned with looking after others – with bringing up children, making practical arrangements, cooking, cleaning, nursing and so on. In this work, further-more, women give priority to those for whom they are caring; whether they concern themselves with their physical needs, respond to the quirks of their characters or engage with their emotions, they treat those they are looking after as special individuals for whose well-being they have a particular responsibility.

The activities typically undertaken by women can be described, without strain, as partial, personal or particular, since the affections and concern that go into them are usually directed to particular people and set within specific relationships such as those of mother to child, nurse to patient, secretary to boss, wife to husband. At the same time, these qualities contribute to a deeply rooted interpretation of femininity, so that to be a woman is, in part, to display them. The womanly woman is caring or partial, that is to say, she thinks and behaves in ways that are antithetical to the norm of impartiality valued in legislators. So while women can, of course, judge impartially, they do so at a price – the price of compromising their femininity, as this is widely understood. This imposes a kind of psychic strain which is felt and reinforced in a host of ways.

I have been analysing some of the ways in which democratic liberal societies fail to live up to the ideal, itself an explicit feature of liberal political theory, that all citizens should be guaranteed the independence or security to participate in the polity. Women, I have suggested, are systematically denied this independence, so that the practice of liberalism offers little encouragement to feminists. I shall now go on to consider some feminist responses to this state of affairs.

INDEPENDENCE AND FEMINISM

If patriarchal liberal practice fails to provide for women the guarantees of citizenship enshrined in democratic liberal theory, it is natural to ask whether the theory is of any use. Does it have anything to offer to feminism? Current feminist thinking contains a variety of responses to this question and the divergences between them are particularly evident in the range of criticisms brought against the norm of citizenly independence. The discussion of independence therefore provides an appropriate place to consider, and reconsider, both the relationship of liberalism and feminism and the place of citizenly independence in a feminist politics.

Analyses of the ways in which women are not guaranteed either physical or economic independence, such as those summarized in the preceding section, can be used for various theoretical ends. They can be harnessed to the conclusion that the very idea of citizenly independence is a mistake and a delusion. But many feminist writers take the opposite tack, and point to the dependence of women as an aspect of their oppression, a scandal that lies neglected within supposedly, democratic polities. They draw attention to women's dependence in order to criticize it; to show how women are being deprived of something valuable, which is also their due.[13] These writers share with liberal theorists the belief that independence is a central and advantageous condition of citizenship. Their complaint is that the conditions of independence have been interpreted so as to exclude women.

This acceptance of at least one liberal value is perhaps clearest in discussions of physical independence. In general, feminists and liberals agree that freedom from the threat of physical violation is a fundamental condition of a democratic polity. In pointing out that physical violation includes sexual violence, feminists are not usually challenging the value of physical independence but are rather demanding that it be reinterpreted in a way that will give women physical independence in both public and private realms. The benefits of such a change would of course extend far beyond the sphere of political participation. But it, too, would become more accessible to women, who would be constructed as fuller, if not full, citizens.

The case of economic independence is a little more equivocal, though here too there is an underlying sympathy between liberals and many feminists. Feminists who analyse the disparities in the economic status and opportunities of men and women do not generally rejoice at their own findings. As a rule, they see the inferior economic position and consequent dependence of women as an injustice, a travesty of the theory to which liberals are committed that cries out for remedy. In so far as these feminists agree that the economic dependence of women limits their political participation, and that this state of affairs is undesirable, they share the liberal view that minimal economic independence is a condition of citizenship.

If an air of ambivalence surrounds this conclusion, it arises not from any attachment to economic dependence, but from two rather separate doubts. First, it is not clear that the liberal guarantee of economic independence amounts to much, for men or women; in some versions of liberal theory this commitment is pressed so hard by a conflicting commitment to personal freedom that only the skimpiest of financial safety-nets appears justifiable. Second, the lack of consensus about how to interpret the condition of economic independence means that it is not altogether clear what is being demanded for women. Nothing less than what is allowed to men, certainly. But that may not be enough to make women full citizens.

Nevertheless, analyses of the actual condition of women in liberal democratic societies tend to uphold the liberal conception of physical and economic independence as conditions of citizenship. The same cannot be said, however, of feminist treatments of emotional independence, many of which are fiercely critical of the view that impartiality is a central political value. The attempt to view oneself as one person among others reflects, according to these accounts, a misguided aspiration to adopt an independent, universal, objective and rational standpoint, by single-mindedly ignoring the differences between people. It epitomizes a male approach to politics centred on the ideal of equality, and excludes the values and ways of thinking characteristic of women. These values and ways of thinking are in turn charaterized by exclusion, as partial, situated, dependent, subjective, non-rational and respectful of difference.[14]

Emotional independence is, then, an issue over which liberal and feminist theorists decisively disagree. Whereas liberals interpret this independence as impartiality, and regard it as a valued quality of legislators, many feminists see it as an attempt to stifle and exclude difference by appealing to a spuriously objective standpoint. Moreover, this is one major reason for their rejection of liberal political theory in general. How should we view this conflict? In the remaining part of this essay I shall explore further the view defended by cultural feminists, who argue both that the ideal of impartiality is a miasma which functions as an ideological cover for a patriarchal standpoint, and that the correlative female values of dependence, partiality and so forth should be regarded as the normative core of a truly feminist politics.

Writers engaged in working out this strand of feminist argument tend to portray the emotionally independent liberal citizen as a stern and isolated person, lacking emotional warmth and personal attachments. To be impartial, he understands, is steadfastly to judge all cases by the same criteria, criteria which are in turn enshrined in a set of rules. In order to be applicable to all cases, these rules must focus on the properties that citizens hold in common, such as their needs and rights. For if a great many disparate and particular properties are allowed as grounds for legitimate claims (gender, race, educational background, psychiatric history, personal loves and hates, aesthetic preferences and so on) the rules will not provide a basis for comparing the diverse cases of different citizens. The rules thus have to be comparatively narrow, and must be rigorously applied. Furthermore, the rules reflect an understanding of our true humanity; they isolate the properties that people do in fact share, which form the basis of our social life together.

From this account, it is easy to get the impression that the liberal legislator is something of a moral bigot – rigid, insensitive, unimaginative and convinced that he has a monopoly of the truth. This idea is reinforced when his values are contrasted with the nominally female dispositions towards flexible negotiation, emotional attachment and the appreciation of difference. Who would not rather belong to a feminist polity? To a certain extent, however, this egregious portrait is founded on a misrepresentation of the liberal value of emotional independence. First, liberal theory need not suppose that, in order to display the emotional independence required of legislators, one must be without strong emotional attachments. Legislators may, for example, feel a fierce and protective love for their children. To display emotional independence is just to be able to distance oneself from these attachments when making political decisions. More important, emotionally independent legislators need not treat emotional attachments as irrelevant to political decisions. Sticking to the same example, an independent stance does not prevent a legislator from appreciating that, precisely because parents often love their children profoundly, the well-being of those children is enormously important to them. Finally, an independent legislator does not distance himself from all feelings and desires, but gives some of them priority over others. To lose sight of this point is to fall prey to the view – itself a mainstay of the public/private distinction – that the objects of emotions and desires are necessarily personal, rather than drawn from the political realm.

There is thus a tendency among cultural feminists to underestimate the liberal ideal of emotional independence by parodying the impartial outlook of the legislator. But they would, I think, reject even a more moderate conception of independence, on the grounds that a feminist politics should celebrate emotional dependence. The model for this kind of relationship is drawn from the family, and especially from the relations between mothers and children. Here, the ties of love are held to make emotional independence irrelevant; conflicts can be worked out as they arise by the mutual adjustment of desires and goals, and there is no place for rules, or for criteria as to what may or may not count as a benefit or disadvantage. A concern for one another's well-being is enough to ensure that differences are resolved and that feelings of resentment, frustration or anger are contained.[15]

There are many difficulties with this view, not least its romanticization of family life. The one that concerns us here, however, is the manner in which cultural feminism proposes simply to replace one political value – emotional independence – with its opposite. This strategy has two connected disadvantages: first, it leaves the opposition between independence and dependence intact, thus running the risk of excluding from political life whatever crops up on the independent side of the divide; second, by retaining an aspect of the traditional division between public and private it makes it difficult to elucidate any sense in which dependence is a *political* value. Emotional dependence is, after all, primarily presented as a private virtue, firmly rooted in the domestic, female, apolitical institutions of society, where it is reflected in all sorts of practices and habits of thought. Cultural feminism suggests that analogues of these attitudes and practices could be extended beyond the bounds of what is currently regarded as the private sphere and incorporated into a new kind of politics – situated, sensitive to difference and caring.

Such a vision is undoubtedly enormously attractive. But any attempt to work it out must confront the fact that it defines emotional dependence in terms of emotional attachment; the practices associated with emotional dependence are fuelled by affections such as those between mothers and their children, those between lovers or those between friends. To extend these practices (or something like them) beyond the private sphere would be to extend them into a territory where people are not bound by emotional ties and may perceive themselves as having little more in common than the fact that they happen to be living under the same political jurisdiction. A satisfactory political system must provide a basis for distributing resources and resolving conflicts among these people, as well as among the members of groups equipped with a conception of their common good. But these people lack the very quality that cultural feminism puts at the centre of politics, namely emotional dependence. It is therefore not obvious that a theory based on this value can apply to them. To put the point more generally, it is not obvious that emotional dependence can function as the central value of a theory which overlaps sufficiently with our existing conceptions of politics to be regarded as persuasive. This is not to deny that the family is a political institution. It is just to deny that all the problems a political theory must face arise in the context of the family and its analogues.

INDEPENDENCE AND SELF-ESTEEM

The presupposition that citizens should have a degree of emotional independence is, as we have seen, interpreted in liberal theory as the requirement that citizens should be at least potentially impartial, in the sense of being able to distance themselves from their personal affections and interests when making political decisions. Impartiality requires a degree of independence because it involves splitting oneself off from certain desires and emotions, whether one's own or those of others. Moreover, liberal theorists tend to take it more or less for granted that people can adopt an impartial standpoint, and pay comparatively little attention to the question of what conditions have to be met in order for them to do so. They are strikingly uninterested in the construction of emotional independence.

This lack of concern is, however, even more marked than our account so far suggests. For as well as assuming that legislators have the ability to be impartial, there is a further, altogether neglected sense in which democratic liberal theory tacitly supposes that citizens are emotionally independent. It is a central tenet of this theory, as we found earlier on, that each citizen should participate in the polity in their own voice. Each vote, for example, is the vote of a separate individual and should reflect his or her judgement. Liberal theorists have persistently investigated the physical and economic conditions of such independent membership. But when we enquire about the psychological conditions in which individuals are able to speak in their own voices, we find that these same theorists fall strangely silent. Having a voice of your own is, it seems, almost a defining characteristic of being an individual, and the possibility that a person might lack one does not arise.

Once we look more carefully, however, it is evident that the condition of speaking in one's own voice embodies a number of complexities. If I am to speak in my own voice, I must at least see myself as *having* an individual voice. But this capacity rests on two further requirements. In the first place, I must see myself as separate from others, for it is otherwise difficult to see how I can grasp the idea of a voice being mine. In the second place, I must see myself as possessing a *voice* that is mine. For there may be ways of perceiving myself as a separate individual, yet as lacking the ability to speak for myself. This latter condition, a vital part of the presuppositions that build up the conception of the individual citizen, is hard to pin down. To possess a voice it seems that one must conceive of oneself as having the ability to assess situations and speak one's mind about them, not as an expert, but (to beg the question) as one voice among others, worthy to be heard. A person who is without this self-understanding will not meet the primary requirement of citizens – having a voice of their own.

From a liberal perspective, this set of presuppositions may appear so basic as not to be worth mentioning. Yet it can be undercut in a number of ways. Suppose, for example, that I secure my own identity by speaking to please others, rely on others for the vindication of my views, depend heavily on the approval of others for my continued sense of self. My voice will not then be my own in the sense that liberalism assumes. To speak in one's own voice one must possess the psychological traits just sketched which might be summed up as self-esteem – a stable sense of one's own separate identity and a confidence that one is worthy to participate in political life. Self-esteem is thus a second kind of emotional independence that lies, albeit silently, at the heart of liberal political theory.[16]

It is perhaps not surprising that the presupposition of self-esteem has been overlooked by liberal theorists, for it is at once less tangible than the other kinds of independence associated with citizenship, and psychologically more profound. If people are assumed to possess it, it can be ignored. But once it is acknowledged as a characteristic of citizens which has to be created and protected, its interpretation immediately becomes problematic. Intuitively, it seems that self-esteem can be fostered and damaged by so many diverse practices that the process of sorting out those that bear on citizenship will threaten, among other things, the liberal conception of the political sphere. Liberals may therefore be tempted to leave it alone.

Nevertheless, the recognition of self-esteem as a crucial kind of emotional independence provides a way of reconsidering the opposition between independence and dependence. First, an explicit understanding that self-esteem is an aspect of the independence associated with citizenship may deepen our analysis of the ways in which this norm excludes women. There is already a good deal of evidence to suggest that women in patriarchal societies are liable to lack self-esteem. A range of studies have suggested that there are many ways in which it is more difficult for women than for men to gain a firm and comfortable sense of separate identity, and consequently more difficult for them to act autonomously and take responsibility for their decisions.[17] Moreover, these studies have tended to see women's lack of self-esteem as a disadvantage, an obstacle which limits the kinds of relationships they can form and sustain. Self-esteem is thus regarded as valuable, and in so far as women (or for that matter men) lack it they are held to be vulnerable in many aspects of their lives. Attempts to tackle this issue can consequently be seen as dealing directly with a tacit presupposition of liberalism, while sharing with liberal theory the conviction that self-esteem is a desirable individual trait. Among the many social roles in which it may stand individuals in good stead is that of the citizen, and an appreciation of the political significance of self-esteem may enable us to bring the insights contained in these studies to bear on the question of female citizenship.

The insistence that self-esteem, like other forms of citizenly independence, is not found but made may thus provide feminists with another critical tool for assessing the tenets of liberalism. In addition, the claim that self-esteem is an aspect of emotional independence may encourage cultural feminists to reconsider their view that emotional independence is without political value. As we have seen, cultural feminism has followed liberalism in equating emotional independence with a thoroughgoing impartiality, and has then rejected impartiality as antithetical to a politics centred on dependence. They have opposed dependence, understood as emotionally engaged caring, to independence, understood as impartiality. What, though, if emotional independence is interpreted not as impartiality but as the self-esteem presupposed by the liberal conception of the individual? Is it then so clear that emotional independence is incompatible with, or opposed to, a caring concern for others in all their difference? The recovery of self-esteem as a value common to feminism and liberalism reveals that the relation between emotional dependence and emotional independence is complementary rather than antagonistic. By focusing its attention on the emotional dependence of mothers and children at one extreme and the impartiality of Kantian legislators at the other, feminist theory, and particularly cultural feminist theory, has overlooked this fact. Instead, it has constructed a dichotomy which, while intended to unmask the inadequacy of liberalism, has also contributed to the growth of an unduly narrow conception of feminist politics.

This mistake can, however, be remedied. Once we recognize that self-esteem acts as an intermediary between the poles of emotional dependence and the emotional independence required of citizens, a more fruitful discourse emerges: the emphasis of liberal theory on impartiality no longer appears utterly worthless; but, by the same token, the scope of feminist political theory comes to be greatly enlarged.

It is helpful here to look in more detail at some of the connections between self-esteem and the emotional independence that full citizens need. First, a person who lacks self-esteem cannot, it seems, be expected to display this kind of independence. Such a person will be unable to exercise their own judgement without looking over their shoulder for the approval or agreement of the people on whom they are emotionally reliant; and in addition, they will not be able to treat these latter agents as some among others. In short, a citizen who lacks self-esteem will not be able to gain the requisite distance on the emotions and desires of either self or others.

The understanding that this is at least one way in which agents can fail to be impartial seems to be implicit within liberal theory and is reflected in its assumptions about the emotional independence of citizens. Part of the justification for the belief that all citizens should be seen as potential legislators is the presumption (unjustified as it may be) that all citizens have self-esteem. Moreover, this connection is what gives the idea of emotional independence as a whole its explicitly political value. Self-esteem may be a desirable quality of agents for all sorts of reasons. But its contribution to the ability to see oneself as one among others, and hence to assess the competing claims of people who may have almost no common interests, is at least an important part of what makes it politically significant.

Let us now turn to a second connection between emotional dependence and self-esteem. Psychoanalytic theories of development increasingly suggest that self-esteem is the outcome of secure, loving relations between a young child and his or her parent figures – the outcome of just the kind of relations that cultural feminists associate with the family and classify as dependent.[18] So while a particular pattern of early experiences is doubtless not the only way to acquire self-esteem, good-enough relations between mother-figure and child nevertheless exemplify the qualities that give rise to it. Equally, however, the capacity to love and care successfully for others *as* others presupposes self-esteem on the part of the carers. A mother, for example, who lacks self-esteem and depends for her own identity on her children's need for her may hinder them from developing into separate (self-esteeming) individuals. If these two links are taken together, a two-way connection between emotional dependence and self-esteem is revealed: on the one hand, the relations regarded as paradigmatically dependent presuppose the existence of agents who possess self-esteem; on the other, these very relations are seen as a condition of the acquisition of self-esteem.

When this set of interconnections is joined to the relation between self-esteem and impartiality, an aspect of the political significance of the family becomes clear, and the traditional view of the family as archetypically apolitical, in turn enshrined in the distinction between public and private, is undermined from a new direction. For we are now in a position to see that the family can be instrumentally important to the political sphere, by virtue of being an institution or set of practices in which a vital quality of democratic citizens – self-esteem – develops. The burying of this connection is just one of many ways in which liberal theory has obscured the political significance of work traditionally done by women. Nevertheless, it is a connection of the greatest importance. For anyone who takes seriously the idea that self-esteem is indeed a condition of full citizenship will surely wish to consider what sorts of family relations are productive of self-esteem, and whether the current positions of women within the family are such as to promote it. In this, they will treat the domestic and political spheres not as opposed, the loci of two distinct and incompatible types of relationship, but as complementary and potentially mutually supporting.

I have argued that, by treating the relationship between emotional dependence and independence as one of mutual exclusion, much current feminist political theory has hampered its understanding of liberalism and drawn a constrictingly narrow boundary around its own interpretation of citizenship. The alternative analysis of independence I have offered is not opposed to dependence, but rather points the way towards a conception of the citizen which is sensitive both to the emotionally dependent relations traditionally associated with women, and to the male norm of impartiality so important to liberalism. It thus proposes a way to reconcile independence and dependence.

At the same time, it implicitly questions the idea that there is a sharp or insurmountable divide between equality and difference. I have already argued that difference is not so alien to liberal theory as some feminists claim. In addition, however, my interpretation of independence presents the appreciation of difference as an aspect of self-esteem, and thus as a condition of the equal independence of citizens to which liberalism aspires. To be able to voice one's own opinions in the polity one must esteem one*self*, as one is, rather than believing that some of one's characteristics – one's gender, colour or class, for example – disqualify one from participation. One must esteem oneself as a woman, black, white, Bengali, worker, mother, Hindu, old-age pensioner, republican or whatever. This suggests that true self-esteem can only be created and maintained in practices that are sensitive to and respectful of difference. But it also suggests that the appreciation of difference is not an *alternative* to impartiality in politics. Instead, one grows out of the other.

NOTES

I am particularly grateful to Gisela Bock, Teresa Brennan, Cynthia Farrar and Quentin Skinner for their helpful comments on an earlier draft of this essay.

1 T. Brennan and C. Pateman, 'Mere auxiliaries to the commonwealth: women and the origins of liberalism, *Political Studies*, XXVIII, 1979; M. Thornton, 'Sex equality is not enough for feminism', in C. Pateman and E. Gross (eds), *Feminist Challenges*, Sydney, Allen & Unwin, 1986; C. Pateman, 'Women and consent' in *The Disorder of Women: Democracy, Feminism and Political Theory*, Cambridge, Polity Press, 1989; I. M. Young, *Justice and the Politics of Difference*, Princeton NJ, Princeton University Press, 1990; J. Landes, *Women and the Public Sphere in the Age of the French Revolution*, Ithaca, NY, Cornell University Press, 1988.
2 N. Fraser, *Unruly Practices*, Cambridge, Polity Press, 1989; Young, *Justice*; J. B. Elshtain, *Private Man, Public Woman: Women in Social and Political Thought*, Princeton, NJ, Princeton University Press, 1981; A. Jagger, *Feminist Politics and Human Nature*, Brighton, Harvester, 1983.

3 See e.g. Cavarero, Chapter 2 in this volume, and C. Pateman, 'The patriachal welfare state', in *The Disorder of Women*.
4 This view is deeply embedded in the liberal democratic tradition, e.g.: 'There is no difficulty in showing that the ideally best form of government is that in which the sovereignty, or supreme controlling power in the last resort, is rested in the entire aggregate of the community; every citizen not only having a voice in the exercise of that ultimate sovereignty, but being, at least occasionally, called on to take an actual part in the government, by the personal discharge of some public function, local or general.' J. S. Mill, *Representative Government*, ed. H. B. Acton, London, Dent, 1972, ch. 3, p. 207.
5 For a recent affirmation of this view of citizenship see J. N. Shklar, *American Citizenship: The Quest for Inclusion*, Cambridge, Mass., Harvard University Press, 1991.
6 The view that anyone may become a legislator is held e.g. by J. S. Mill (see note 4) but is also shared by exponents of a Rousseauvean strand in liberal democratic theory. According to this view, citizens learn to be concerned about a wider range of issues than their own private interests. See C. Pateman, *Participation and Democratic Theory*, Cambridge, Cambridge University Press, 1970, ch. 2; J. Cohen, 'Deliberation and democratic legitimacy', in A. Hamblin and P. Pettit (eds), *The Good Polity: Normative Analysis of the State*, Oxford, Blackwell, 1989.
7 See D. Winnicott, 'Communication between infant and mother, mother and infant, compared and contrasted', in Institute of Psychoanalysis, *What Is Psychoanalysis?*, London, Ballière Tindall and Cassell, 1968.
8 See Cavarero, Chapter 2 in this volume; I. M. Young, 'Polity and group difference: a critique of the ideal of universal citizenship', in Cass R. Sunstein (ed.), *Feminism and Political Theory*, Chicago, Chicago University Press, 1990; E. V. Spellman, *Inessential Woman*, London, Women's Press, 1988.
9 For the complexities surrounding this recognition of difference see C. Pateman, Chapter 1 in this volume.
10 C. A. MacKinnon, *Sexual Harassment of Working Women*, New Haven, Conn., Yale University Press, 1989; E. Wilson, *What Is to Be Done about Violence against Women?*, Harmondsworth, Penguin, 1983; for further bibliography on this topic see the appendix to C. A. MacKinnon, 'Sexuality, pornography and method', in Sunstein, *Feminism*.
11 M. Wollstonecraft, *Vindication of the Rights of Women*, Harmondsworth, Penguin, 1982, pp. 252–9; N. Fraser, 'Women, welfare and politics', in Fraser, *Unruly Practices*; H. Hartmann, 'Capitalism, patriarchy and job segregation by sex', in Z. Eisenstein (ed.), *Capitalist Patriarchy and the Case for Socialist Feminism*, New York, Monthly Review Press, 1979.
12 H. Marshall and M. Wetherell, 'Talking about career and gender identities: a discourse analytic perspective', and L. St Clair, 'When is gender a handicap? Towards conceptualizing the socially constructed disadvantages experienced by women', both in S. Skevington and D. Baker (eds), *The Social Identity of Women*, Calif., Newbury Park, Sage Publications, 1989.
13 See e.g. Wollstonecraft, *Vindication*; Pateman, 'Patriachal welfare state'.
14 See e.g. Cavarero, Chapter 2 in this volume. Also S. Benhabib, 'The generalized and the concrete other'; and I. M. Young, 'Impartiality and the civic republic', both in S. Benhabib and D. Cornell (eds), *Feminism as Critique*, Cambridge, Polity Press, 1987.
15 Some separatist versions of this view celebrate the mutual dependence of women and women, and women and children, as the source of a new feminist politics. See e.g. A. Rich, *Of Woman Born: Motherhood as Experience and Institution*, New

York, Norton, 1976; M. Daly, *Gyn/Ecology: The Metaethics of Radical Feminism*, Boston, Mass., Beacon Press, 1978. Other versions include the mutual emotional dependence of women and men. See e.g. S. Ruddick, 'Maternal Thinking', in J. Trebilcot (ed.), *Mothering: Essays in Feminist Theory*, Towota, NJ, Rowman & Allanheld, 1983, p. 226, and *Maternal Thinking*, London, Women's Press, 1990, pt 3; J. Bethke Elshtain, *Public Man, Private Woman: Women in Social and Political Thought*, Princeton, NJ, Princeton University Press, 1981, pp. 333 ff.

16 J. Rawls lists self-respect among what he calls primary goods. But for him self-respect is a quality which helps one to pursue one's conception of the good life, whatever that may be, rather than a prerequisite of citizenship. See his *A Theory of Justice*, Cambridge, Mass., Harvard University Press, 1971, pp. 440–96. For an interesting commentary on Rawls's theory from a feminist standpoint see S. Moller Okin, *Justice, Gender and the Family*, New York, Basic Books, 1989, ch. 5.

17 N. Chodorow, *The Reproduction of Mothering: Psychoanalysis and the Sociology of Gender*, Berkeley, Calif., and Los Angeles, University of California Press, 1987; J. Flax, 'Mother–Daughter relationships: Psychodynamics, politics and philosphy', in H. Eisenstein (ed.), *The Future of Difference*, Boston, Mass., G. K. Hall, 1980.

18 Chodorow, *Reproduction*; J. Flax, 'Political philosophy and the patriarchal unconscious', in S. Harding and M. Hintikka (eds), *Discovering Reality: Feminist Perspectives on Epistemology, Metaphysics, Methodology and the Philosophy of Science*, Dordrecht, Reidel, 1983.

Part II

Maternity, equality and difference in historical contexts

Chapter 4

Defining feminism: a comparative historical approach

Karen Offen

What is feminism? Who is a feminist? How do we understand feminism across national boundaries? Across cultures? Across centuries? These questions are raised every day, by activists in the contemporary women's movement, by scholars, in the press and in informal conversation. Everyone seems to have different answers, and every answer is infused with a political and emotional charge. The word 'feminism' continues to inspire controversy – indeed, even to evoke fear among a sizeable portion of the general public. If words and the concepts they convey can be said to be dangerous, then 'feminism' and 'feminist' must be dangerous words, representing dangerous concepts. Despite Virginia Woolf's attempt some fifty years ago to 'kill' the word 'feminism', it continues to be used. The concepts it stands for clearly retain 'a force of tremendous power'.[1]

Scholars who do claim the label of feminism owe it to the public and to one another to respond to these questions and to address the fear that induces would-be supporters to disclaim this label even when they support what we would consider feminist goals. To allow so many to get away with saying, 'I'm not a feminist, but . . .' seems highly problematic in the light of current political necessities. To speak effectively, we must arrive at some understanding of the term 'feminism' that we can agree on. However, to be truly useful such an understanding cannot be derived exclusively from contemporary Anglo-American culture;[2] it should reflect the cumulative knowledge we have acquired about the historical development of feminism in other comparable cultures.

What I am proposing here is a re-examination and reconceptualization of the public understanding of this word 'feminism', based on the history of the word and its cognates and on evidence of its use from comparative history. A historical understanding and definition of the term 'feminism' seem to me to be essential conditions for becoming more politically effective today and in the future.

EUROPEAN HISTORY AND THE HISTORY OF FEMINISM

The study of continental European women's history can contribute important insights to the exercise of defining feminism. It allows us not only to recover and dissect the prevailing and dissenting views on the organization of societies, embedded historically in the western debate on 'the woman question' (as this controversy came to be known in the nineteenth century), but also to explore the political dynamics of their interaction.

In the early 1970s, when my generation of historians, trained in the United States, began to investigate the history of European women and European women's movements, we understood feminism in a rather simplistic and straightforward way, according to a composite English-language definition then found in most American dictionaries. A feminist was, of course, defined as a person who espoused feminism. But what was feminism? The dictionary definition (in composite) read approximately as follows: a theory and/or movement concerned with advancing the position of women through such means as achievement of *political, legal or economic rights equal to those granted men*. This 'equal rights' perspective was also conveyed by the best-known histories of the American women's movement published prior to 1970, in which feminism effectively began in 1848 at Seneca Falls and the focus was on votes for women. The key notion here is the means to the end of 'advancement': 'rights equal to those granted men'.

Notice the extent to which this legalistic definition of 'equal rights' proposes the standard of male adulthood as the norm. It is a definition expressed in a vocabulary of 'rights' common to the western tradition but developed most explicitly in the political theory and practice of Great Britain and the United States, which have so long elaborated the rights and privileges of male individuals on grounds of principle. For women, the vote, the attainment of legal control over property and person, and entry into male-dominated professions and institutional hierarchies became the representative issues.

Those of us working in European history soon discovered that this English-language dictionary definition of feminism did not serve us well; we found its explanatory power inadequate in face of the accumulating evidence about the goals and activities of women's advocates and women's movements on the European continent during the nineteenth century and before. Although issues of access to male privilege and power were undeniably important for women and men in the European past, they sought other goals as well. Moreover, the ways in which Europeans expressed their claims seemed to differ considerably from those of the Anglo-Americans: Europeans focused as much or more on elaborations of womanliness; they celebrated sexual difference within a framework of male/female complementarity; and, instead of seeking unqualified admission to male-dominated society, they mounted a wide-ranging critique of the society and its institutions. Amy Hackett, a pioneering American historian of German feminism, proposed excluding the concepts of equality and rights from any broad definition of feminism, because claims for individual 'equality' and 'rights' were not categories germane to the discourse of leaders of the early twentieth-century German women's movement.[3] Yet, some of these women clearly considered themselves to be feminists and were so considered by their contemporaries.

Cheryl Register, a historian of Swedish feminism, similarly puzzled over the definition of feminism as she attempted to evaluate the contribution of the Swedish writer Ellen Key, for whom motherhood, not women's activity in the public sphere, was the central analytical point. How, she queried, should one evaluate 'a woman who stays independent of organizations and doctrines, extols private virtues, and sees love, an unlegislatable emotion, as the crux of liberation'? Such a woman, she added, 'looks suspiciously anti-feminist, unless we broaden our view of what feminism encompasses'.[4] Yet Ellen Key, who also demanded state subsidies for all mothers, including the unmarried, had a profound impact on the theory and practice of the European women's movement.

Similar interpretative problems have appeared more recently as scholars re-examine the historical evidence for France, Germany, Italy and other continental European countries prior to the First World War.[5] Indeed, since the mid-1970s, historians of women in the United States have developed a comparable revisionist critique for the history of American feminism. Its initial thrust was to locate the origins of feminist activism in early nineteenth-century female reform societies and educational activities that fostered the development of female consciousness, rather than exclusively in the movement for equal rights that grew out of the political movement to abolish slavery. More recent work has emphasized the community consciousness of the women in female reform societies, but with what seems to me (in comparison to Europe) to be a far more local rather than an emphatically national or state-associated perspective.[6] New historical scholarship on Great Britain reveals similar findings.[7] It remains the case that this newer historiography has yet to offset the impact of earlier notions in the perception of feminism held by the general public. Such findings nevertheless suggest that our understanding of feminism cannot be restricted, as some have claimed, purely and simply to an expression of 'bourgeois' or 'possessive' individualism. Nor can feminism be considered, as Richard Stites has suggested for Russia, merely as one component of 'women's liberation'.[8]

To complicate matters, historians of Europe discovered that the term 'feminism' itself barely existed before the twentieth century and that, from the time of its introduction, it was controversial. As my own research on France developed, I became interested in the early history of the word *féminisme*. My enquiry established that this word and its derivatives originated quite recently in France.[9] Although invention of the word *féminisme* has often erroneously been attributed to Charles Fourier in the 1830s, in fact its origins are still uncertain. It only began to be used widely in France in the early 1890s and then principally as a synonym for women's emancipation.

The first self-proclaimed *féministe* in France was the women's suffrage advocate Hubertine Auclert, who from at least 1882 on used the term self-descriptively in her periodical *La citoyenne*. Auclert's usage was picked up and juxtaposed with '*chauvinisme masculin*' in L. Cosson's 1883 book, *Essai sur la condition des femmes*.[10] The words *féministe* and *féminisme* gained currency in the French press following the first 'feminist' congress in Paris, in May 1892. This gathering was sponsored by Eugénie Potonie-Pierre and her colleagues in the women's group *Solidarité*, who shortly thereafter juxtaposed 'féminisme' with 'masculinisme' in an 1893 pamphlet entitled *Socialisme et sexualisme: programme du parti socialiste féminin*.[11] By 1894–5 the terms had crossed the Channel to Great Britain, and before the turn of the century they were appearing in Belgian French, Spanish, Italian, German, Greek and Russian published sources. At the September 1896 women's congress in Berlin, Potonie-Pierre (in a report on the position of women in France) applauded the press for launching the word *féminisme* after she and her friends had invented it and sent it into circulation.[12]

By the late 1890s the words had jumped the Atlantic to Argentina and the United States. Inez Haynes Irwin, who had been a Radcliffe student in 1896–7, reported that she first heard the word *féministe* from a classmate who had just returned from France. According to Kathy Peiss, however, the terms were not commonly used in periodical literature much before 1910.[13] Elvira V. Lopez completed her doctoral thesis, 'El movimiento feminista' (which drew largely on European sources), at the University of Buenos Aires in 1901; but the term 'feminist' had already been circulating for several years, both in Argentina and in Cuba.[14]

Then, as now, these words (like other nineteenth-century 'ism' words – conservativism, liberalism, socialism) were employed not only by proponents and adversaries of women's emancipation but also by observers of their struggles. Then, as now, many parties used the terms polemically, rather than analytically; then, as now, the words were not used by everyone to mean the same thing. And, as the study of their history reveals, even when they used the vocabulary of 'rights', they referred far more often to the 'rights of women' than to 'rights equal to those of men'. This is a subtle, but profound, distinction. Feminism connoted a far broader socio-political critique, a critique that was woman-centred and woman-celebratory in its onslaught on male privilege.

In *fin-de-siécle* France, problems of defining and claiming 'féminisme' and 'féministe' arose immediately. As was true of French politics generally, factions quickly emerged. Groups and individuals espousing divergent theories of feminism and agendas for change began to categorize themselves and their rivals through the practice of exclusionary classification, by the addition of qualifying modifiers as well as by the formation of separate organizations and publications. By 1900 a veritable taxonomy of self-described or imputed feminisms had sprung into being: 'familial feminists', 'integral feminists', 'Christian feminists', 'socialist feminists', 'radical feminists' and 'male feminists' among others. Already at that time, 'socialist feminists' had begun to cast aspersions on 'bourgeois feminists', thereby perpetuating a polemical division that had begun in Germany in 1894, when the newly founded *Bund Deutscher Frauenverein* excluded the women of the German Social Democratic Party. This distinction spread quickly throughout the network of socialist parties of the Second International, and dominated historical scholarship on socialism and feminism until very recently.

Not only adversaries but also partisans of various factions persistently posed the question of who could properly be called a feminist and who could not; their efforts quickly raised several related questions that have since become all too familiar, including the questions that to the historian appear the most perplexing of all: Which advocates of which resolution to the woman question held women's best interests at heart? When is a feminist really an anti-feminist? What must the fundamental criteria be? And, most important politically, *who* will decide?

These definitional problems were quickly compounded by another problematic discovery, stemming from the fact that French scholars were pioneers in what we now call women's studies'.[15] In French historiography of women's history since 1900, historians and scholars of literary history quickly took up the words 'feminism' and 'feminist', using them anachronistically and with great abandon, only rarely defining their terms or scrutinizing the content of the ideas so labelled. In the first decade of the twentieth century, learned books and articles in French appeared on feminism in classical antiquity, in the Middle Ages, in the Renaissance and especially in the period beginning in the seventeenth century.

English-language scholars quickly demonstrated that such careless habits could be contagious; scholarly treatises addressed *Feminism in Greek Literature: From Homer to Aristotle*; *Feminist Writers of the Seventeenth Century*; *Feminism in Eighteenth-Century England*; and historical topics. Even the late Joan Kelly, who openly acknowledged that the term 'feminism' was not in use before the nineteenth century, deployed it to encompass a broad range of pro-woman advocacy by European women between 1400 and 1800.[16]

This practice seems highly problematic; not only is it anachronistic, but it is conceptually anarchic. A close reading of some of these studies reveals that few authors use the terms to mean the same thing. Moreover, many are internally inconsistent. Only an unusually attentive and well-informed reader can discover the myriad ways in which such a practice effectively deflects analysis from what are, in fact, important historical issues. In the meantime, scholars continue to speak loosely of 'precursors' and 'forerunners' of feminism or of 'proto-feminists' and, nowadays, of 'feminist anti-feminism', 'anti-feminist feminism' and 'post-feminists'. How can one decide what is pre- and what is proto-, let alone anti- or post-, without first setting forth what is 'feminist'?

Scholars have in the meantime invented their own definitions of feminism. The extent to which this practice can lead to contradictory results is exemplified in two recent collections of British women's texts from the period 1500–1800. Moira Ferguson speaks of 'first feminists' from 1500 on, while Simon Shepherd, discussing several of the same writers examined by Ferguson, insists that readers will find no feminism in these texts.[17] Clearly, Ferguson's notion of feminism differs from Shepherd's. It is, of course, doubtful whether the most basic assumptions of sixteenth-century women writers about women's nature, and their relationship to men, to the family and to the structure and purpose of social order, would be even slightly acceptable to critics of women's status in England today. The 'feminism' of the sixteenth century would be even more different from our own, and the demands by women and men for change in women's status in that century would require interpretation within the context of the cultures in which they wrote. Nevertheless, there is one common thread running through their arguments: what they share with their successors is the impetus to critique and improve the disadvantaged status of women relative to men within their particular cultural situation. Even this rudimentary definition of feminism, however, is not sufficient for analytical purposes.

Nor do the rough-hewn historical categories of feminism in circulation today in the United States and Great Britain offer much insight into the historical dimensions of feminism. Contemporary scholars employ both dualistic and tripartite distinctions. Among the dualistic distinctions proposed in recent years are 'old' and 'new' feminisms, social and 'hard-core' feminisms, 'first-wave' and 'second-wave' feminisms, 'classical' and 'modern' feminisms, 'equal rights' and 'female superiority' or 'equal authority' feminisms, 'maximalist' and 'minimalist' feminisms, 'congruent' and 'complementary' feminisms and 'humanistic' and 'gynocentric' feminisms. Tripartite distinctions include the 'egalitarian', 'evangelical' and 'socialist' feminisms identified in the recent British past (that is, since 1800) by sociologist Olive Banks, and the 'liberal', 'Marxist' and 'radical' feminisms located by Zillah Eisenstein and others in the contemporary American scene.[18] Alison Jaggar and others identify a present-day 'socialist feminist' category, distinct and separate from Marxist feminism, about which a sizeable literature has developed.[19]

Admittedly, these latter categories have relevance and meaning within a circumscribed field of contemporary discourse shared by readers of scholarly women's studies journals. It is more doubtful that such distinctions make sense to the general public. It is certain that none of them serve the analytical needs of historians who want to understand feminism prior to the twentieth century or in other parts of the world. The history of feminism cannot be rendered intelligible by imposing on the European past over-simplified 'now/then' or other, more complex, but time-bound categories devised for analysis of the American or British present, or by subordinating feminism to the clash between liberals and Marxists since the 1890s. The centuries-old history of European feminism, in particular, cannot be clarified by resorting to American scholars' distinctions between 'feminism' and 'women's rights' or the 'women's movement'.[20] A more systematic approach is required. We must have a comprehensive definition that can bear the weight of the historical evidence and make sense of it.

'RELATIONAL' AND 'INDIVIDUALIST' ARGUMENTS

Recent scholarship on the history of feminism in Europe reveals that two distinct modes of argumentation have been used historically by women and their male allies on behalf of women's emancipation from male control. Both of these modes, which express analytically divergent ways of thinking about women and men and their respective places in human social organization, must be encompassed in any historically sensitive definition of feminism. I have characterized these two modes as 'relational' and 'individualist'. The term 'relational' seems advantageous (as compared, say, with 'familial' or 'maternalist') because it encompasses all relationship, implying at least the possibility of extension to other classes of people besides husbands, children and other immediate relatives. These two modes of argument are not, in my view, coterminous with, or substitutable for, the perplexing and unfortunate dichotomy 'equality versus difference' which currently occupies centre stage in feminist theory debates.[21]

This scholarship also strongly suggests that prior to the twentieth century relational feminism represented the dominant line of argument. Indeed, relational arguments dominated European continental debate on the woman question until very recently. Individualist feminism, with its transcendentalist roots, also has deep historical and philosophical roots in European culture, but even in British and American discourse it has become increasingly prominent only since the publication of John Stuart Mill's *The Subjection of Women* in 1869. It has reached its most expansive development in twentieth-century Anglo-American thought, to the point at which it blurs the contours of the other major argument and appropriates the label.

The new historical scholarship teaches us that to look only to individualist feminism is to miss the rich historical complexity of protest concerning women's subordination. Focusing on it alone blinds us to the range of effective arguments used to combat male privilege throughout the western world during the past few centuries, and even to arguments put forth today by women and men in economically less privileged countries, where women's aspirations to self-sovereignty are often subordinated to pressing short-term political and socio-economic necessities.

Viewed historically, arguments in the relational feminist tradition proposed a gender-based but egalitarian vision of social organization. They featured the primacy of a companionate, non-hierarchical, male–female couple as the basic unit of society, whereas individualist arguments posited the individual, irrespective of sex or gender, as the basic unit. Relational feminism emphasized women's rights *as women* (defined principally by their child-bearing and/or nurturing capacities) in relation to men. It insisted on *women's* distinctive contributions in these roles to the broader society and made claims on the commonwealth on the basis of these contributions. By contrast, the individualist feminist tradition of argumentation emphasized more abstract concepts of individual human rights and celebrated the quest for personal independence (or autonomy) in all aspects of life, while downplaying, deprecating or dismissing as insignificant all socially defined roles and minimizing discussion of sex-linked qualities or contributions, including child-bearing and its attendant responsibilities.

Even in Anglo-American thought prior to the twentieth century, these two modes of argument were not always as analytically distinct as I am portraying them here, and we are only beginning to examine their intertwining and interplay. In earlier centuries evidence of both these modes can often be located in the utterances of a single individual, or among members of a particular group, exemplifying perhaps that not uncommon human desire to have things both ways. Two telling examples within the Anglo-American tradition are provided by the late eighteenth-century British writer on women's rights, Mary Wollstonecraft, and the nineteenth-century American suffragist, Elizabeth Cady Stanton. Wollstonecraft coupled her call in 1792 for the 'vindication of the rights of women' with a clear delineation of women's role and responsibilities as mothers; Stanton argued in 1869 that 'because man and woman are the complement of one another, we need woman's thought in national affairs to make a safe and stable government', and in 1892 insisted, in quite different circumstances, on a woman's right to 'her birthright to self-sovereignty'.[22] In the thought of these two women, the notion of self-sovereignty was primarily a moral imperative rather than the categorical absolute it has since become. When the whole of their thought is analysed, relational arguments dominate. Much more comparative work needs to be done on the thought and writings of such women and men in history before we will have a conclusive picture of the interweaving of these two strands of argumentation in any given setting.

There are important sociological reasons for positing two and only two categories rather than 'varieties' or 'relative degrees' of feminism. These two modes of argument continue to be meaningful because they also reflect profound differences of opinion that have long existed within western discourse about basic structural questions of social organization and, specifically, about what the relationship of individuals and family groups to society and the state should be. Both modes must be accounted for if one is to understand feminism historically.

Moreover, the sociological content and logical conclusions of these two modes of argument have been significantly different. Relational feminism, with its couple-centred vision, has led historically to very different interpretations of women's circumstances and needs than has individualist feminism, especially in the arena of state action on behalf of mothers. In the experience of nineteenth-century France in particular, the key arguments of relational feminism culminated in the seemingly paradoxical doctrine of 'equality in difference', or equity as distinct from equality. The fundamental tenets included the notion that there were *both* physiological *and* cultural distinctions between the sexes, a concept of womanly or manly nature, of a sharply defined sexual division of labour, or roles, in the family and throughout society following from that 'difference' and that 'nature', and of the notion of the centrality of the complementary couple and/or the mother/child dyad to social analysis.

The socio-cultural significance of physiological difference between the sexes was asserted and contested in Europe from the eighteenth century on, particularly as medical men turned to diagnosing social as well as physical ills. But it was not invariably to women's detriment, as Nancy F. Cott and Carl N. Degler have recently argued in the case of the United States.[23] As these ideas were elaborated in conjunction with the discourse surrounding the democratic and industrial revolutions of the last two centuries, 're-lational feminism' could and did incorporate demands for women's right to work outside the household, to participate in all professions and to vote, alongside demands for equality in civil law concerning property and persons. This it did in tandem with older demands for equal access to formal education and for unimpeded moral and ethical development. In other words, relational feminism combined a case for moral equality of women and men with an explicit acknowledgement of differences in women's and men's sexual functions in society. Increasingly, relational feminists called for governmental programmes that would bolster and enhance women's performance of procreative functions even as they argued that other avenues for life-work must also be available to women.

I first ran across such arguments based on difference in the influential writings of Ernest Legouvé, a mid-nineteenth-century French 'male feminist' who spoke out in 1848 for dramatic reforms in women's legal status in marriage and in their education, while whole-heartedly embracing the notion of 'equal but different' spheres for women and men.[24] I soon found similar features in the arguments of women who were Legouvé's contemporaries. Like Amy Hackett's German feminists and like Sweden's Ellen Key, Legouvé clearly did not fit within the 'equal rights' or 'autonomy' models then being used to index feminism. Nor, as it turns out, did most nineteenth-century leaders of the French women's movement, so many of whom placed women's empowerment in their maternal role at the centre of their thinking.[25]

Recent scholarship bearing on the history of feminism elsewhere in Europe has convinced me not only that the French were not unique in this respect but that this mode of argument, often directly traceable to French influence, had a far-reaching impact on developments throughout Europe and the rest of the world. Relational feminist thinking informed most activities of the women's movements of France, Britain, the Scandinavian states, Germany and other European nations; it characterized virtually all the reform efforts during the Progressive Era that have heretofore been labelled 'social feminism' by historians of the United States.

Both the relational and the individualist modes of argument have historical roots in what historian Temma Kaplan has called 'female consciousness', or consciousness of the 'rights of gender'.[26] The evidence also suggests incontrovertibly that proponents of the relational position possessed a 'feminist consciousness': they viewed women's collective situation in the culture as unjust, they attributed it to social and political institutions established by men, and they believed that it could be changed by protest and political action.[27] Nevertheless they insisted that women had a special role, distinct from that of men. The premises of relational feminism were thus rooted in sexual dimorphism and based on a vision of specified, complementary responsibilities – a sexual division of labour – within an organized society that could even (and often did) override claims for personal liberty that extended beyond moral equivalency.

These premises provided the foundation for making the broadest of claims for women's empowerment and the most sweeping changes in the sexual balance of power. In the late nineteenth century, relational feminists presented an ever more vocal challenge to the militaristic nation-state by threatening to 'regender' it. As Hubertine Auclert put it in 1885, the état mère de famille (the motherly state) must replace the état Minotaur (the Minotaur state); Auclert charged that the latter's exclusive interest was the levy of monetary and blood taxes. Bertha von Suttner condemned men's exaltation of battles and death at the expense of both life and life's creation through love.[28]

These are not isolated examples. The history of feminism is inextricable from the time-honoured concerns of historiography: politics and power. Hence, the history of feminism poses essential questions – questions about gender – for the political and intellectual history of Europe and the modern western world, just as women's history poses essential questions for its social and economic history. Throughout Europe and the Americas, the history of feminism – both in the growth of theory and in political practice – has become increasingly and inextricably entwined with the controversies surrounding the growth and elaboration of secular nation-states, industrial capitalism and war and peace among nations.

Between 1890 and 1920, however, the political aims and goals of relational and individualist approaches began to diverge. They appeared increasingly irreconcilable, as different groups of women began to articulate differing claims. Especially in Britain and the United States, individualist feminism gained momentum as increasing numbers of highly educated, single women intent on achieving personal autonomy became visible for the first time, the participation of married women in the industrial labour force became a political issue, and – most significantly – birth rates began to fall.

In European circles – and, to some extent, in Anglo-American circles – the quest for 'equal rights' sufficient to realize an individual woman's autonomy, a self-reliance asserted rhetorically as a self-contained ideal, seemingly without reference to societal purpose or relationship to others, provoked controversy and dissent. European critics of individualist feminism, echoing Tocqueville's more general concerns about individualism, filed charges of 'egoism' against women they thought to have adopted a male model as the human norm.

In France this debate became tightly entwined with nation-centred political and cultural visions; critics of individualist feminism branded it as 'foreign', claiming that it epitomized an Anglo-American threat to French visions of womanliness. In the ensuing backlash, the terms 'féministe' and 'féminine' were set in opposition as factions found themselves at loggerheads over a variety of issues. The conundrum I posed at the beginning of this essay took shape: Who was a feminist, indeed? Who was the better feminist? Was it Maria Deraismes, who urged repeal of the Napoleonic law that forbade paternity suits by seduced and abandoned women so that they could sue their lovers for child support? Or was it Léonie Rouzade, who argued for state subsidies for mothers? Was it Augusta Moll-Weiss, founder of the *Ecole des Mères* (School for Mothers) in Paris, who in 1910 insisted that 'being a better housewife [by developing skills and expertise that free women's time from the drudgery of household chores] permits one to be a better feminist'? Or was it Madeleine Pelletier, the woman doctor who in 1908 opened her tract, *Woman in Combat for her Rights*, by asserting that 'the individual is an end in itself, whatever the sex'. She argued compellingly that women must be liberated not only from the legal and economic control of husbands and fathers but also from socially imposed roles and from separate spheres, and that women must be at liberty to realize their potential as individuals, without regard to their sex or their capacity to give birth.[29] The model posited by Pelletier for women's self-realization looked to contemporaries all too much like the male model. In France such an 'unfeminine' and individualist approach to the emancipation of women would never be well received.

Why not? It remained the case in *fin-de-siècle* France and, indeed, well into the twentieth century, that sexual dimorphism was a fundamental ingredient of French socio-political thought and that the family – not the individual – continued to comprise the core unit in their thinking. Early twentieth-century French feminist groups invariably critiqued male/female relationships with reference to the family and explicitly proposed a radically restructured, non-patriarchal family; they insisted, nevertheless, on the necessary complementarity of, distinction between and interdependence of the sexes. Social roles, based in 'natural' physiological differences and the then seemingly inevitable constraints on women of reproduction and parenting, were paramount but were not perceived by most advocates of radical change to conflict directly with a woman's self-realization or self-fulfilment as a *moral and intellectual* being or with their full participation in society. Sexual dimorphism and the specific responsibilities of motherhood remained central to the French vision of the socio-political order.

This is not to say that the critique levelled against the prevailing institutional form of marriage, objecting to men's legal control over the persons and properties of women, was not a radical critique, or that a few women did not express a desire for total economic emancipation from men and for sexual liberty as well. Like many liberal economic demands of the mid-nineteenth century, however, these latter demands were elaborated alternatively in terms of 'freedom *from* externally imposed restrictions' and 'freedom *to* become'. Freedom from restrictions was the language of classical economic and political liberalism, transposed to serve the emancipation of women in a world of socially constructed restrictions. Freedom to become signified a more philosophical, more transcendental, more internalized project in self-realization; it has since come to connote a project for autonomous behaviour that, by critiquing all socially constructed norms or goals, refuses to acknowledge limitation by them.

In France, the emergence of individualist feminism forced a paradigm shift in the campaign for women's emancipation. Many French women and men as well as other Europeans who in the 1890s could be considered 'relational feminists' objected to such uncompromising individualism, an individualism that seemed to portend bitter competition between the sexes. The French considered it to be a peculiarly Anglo-American (or Anglo-Saxon, as they called it) mutation of feminism. They viewed it as atomistic and, hence, socially destructive. They interpreted its end-product as 'un-womanly'. A grotesque caricature of the 'emancipated woman', the *fin-de-siècle* feminist, a functional male who was neither wife nor mother, quickly became a bogey. This caricature of 'unsexed womanhood' contributed, perhaps more than anything else, to the development of an innovative and potentially divisive line of argument for women's rights based on 'woman-liness' and motherhood, which exhibited itself in virtually all French agitation for women's emancipation prior to the Second World War.

By the early twentieth century, therefore, most French feminists had rejected competitive individualism as anti-French, in keeping with their love-hate relationship with the Anglo-American world. From 1900 until the fall of the Third Republic in 1940, French feminism was closely associated with republican nationalism and its discourse became closely intertwined with the pro-family and pro-natalist concerns of the regime. As in the nineteenth century, its advocates continued to emphasize sexual difference, a sexual division of labour, motherhood and education for motherhood, and state subsidies for mothers, but they also demanded enhanced legal, educational and economic rights, and the vote for women. French feminists, both secular and Catholic, bourgeois and socialist, advocated putting France's welfare and a reconstituted family ahead of individual or personal needs, in the name of national solidarity.

Was this feminism? The French thought so. At the same time that they argued for compulsory home economics and *puériculture* (scientific infant care), coupled with comprehensive maternity benefits, they scoffed at medals for motherhood and instead demanded state subsidies for all mothers. They also defended women's right to work and insisted that employed women be granted equal pay for equal work. Within their nationalistic frame of reference this did not constitute a contradictory position, just as Mary Wollstonecraft's insistence on competent motherhood as woman's first duty was not contradictory in its context. In the French context, the politics of motherhood in the national interest emerged as a consistent, though complex, feminist politics.[30]

Indeed, up to the time of publication of Simone de Beauvoir's *The Second Sex* in 1949, physiological difference and the sexual division of labour predicated on it were rarely identified by self-styled feminists as a primary instrument of women's oppression. On the contrary, from the early twentieth century on, French feminists have found it both strategically and tactically useful, given France's seemingly perilous demographic position among European nations, to emphasize and celebrate the uniqueness of womanhood, especially women's role and rights as mothers. They demanded radical socio-political reforms by the state that would transform the social institutions surrounding motherhood and thereby encourage natality and at the same time improve women's status. The confusion that abounds today in France about what can properly be considered 'feminism' is symptomatic of the extent to which today's French women's advocates ignore – for it seems to result more from ignorance and neglect than from overt rejection – the legacy of their own predecessors.

A HISTORICALLY BASED DEFINITION OF FEMINISM

The historical evidence presented above sustains two prior propositions on which I base a definition of feminism incorporating both the relational and individualist traditions. First, feminism must henceforth be viewed as a rapidly developing major critical ideology – by which I mean a comprehensive view of the world – in its own right. As an ideology, feminism incorporates a broad spectrum of ideas and possesses an international scope, one whose developmental stages have historically been dependent on and in tension with male-centred political and intellectual discourse but whose more recent manifestations transcend the latter. Thus, feminism must be viewed as not intrinsically a subset of any other western religious or secular ideology, whether Catholic or Protestant Christian, Judaic, liberal, socialist or Marxist (although historically a feminist critique has emerged within each of these traditions by initially posing the question: And what about women?). The historical evidence just reviewed also suggests that in order to comprehend fully the historical range and possibilities of feminism, we must locate the origins and growth of these ideas within a variety of cultural traditions, rather than postulating a hegemonic model for their development on the experience of any single national or socio-linguistic tradition – be it Anglo-American, or French, or German, or Italian, or Spanish, or Swedish, or any other. Put differently, feminism must itself be 'revisioned' by expanding our investigative horizons.

Seen in this way, feminism emerges as a concept that can encompass both an ideology and a movement for socio-political change based on a critical analysis of male privilege and women's subordination within any given society. As the starting point for the elaboration of ideology, of course, feminism posits gender, or the differential social construction of the behaviour of the sexes, based on their physiological differences, as the primary category of analysis. By so doing, feminism raises issues concerning personal autonomy or freedom but not without constant reference to basic issues of societal organization, which centre, in western societies, on the long-standing debate over the family and its relationship to the state, and on the historically inequitable distribution of political, social and economic power between the sexes that underlies this debate. Feminism opposes women's subordination to men in the family and society, along with men's claims to define what is best for women without consulting them; it thereby offers a frontal challenge to patriarchal thought, social organization and control mechanisms. It seeks to destroy masculinist hierarchy but not sexual dualism.

Feminism is necessarily pro-woman. However, it does not follow that it must be anti-man; indeed, in time past, some of the most important advocates of women's cause have been men. Feminism makes claims for a rebalancing between women and men of the social, economic and political power within a given society, on behalf of both sexes in the name of their common humanity, but with respect for their differences. The challenge is fundamentally a humanistic one, raising basic issues concerning individual freedom and responsibility as well as the collective responsibility of individuals to others in society and modes of dealing with others. Even so, feminism has been, and remains today, a political challenge to male authority and hierarchy in the most profoundly transformational sense. As a historical movement in the western world, the fortunes of feminism have varied widely from one society to another, depending on the possibilities available within a given society for the expression of dissent through word or deed.

Based on this definition of feminism, I would consider as feminists any persons, female or male, whose ideas and actions (in so far as they can be documented) show them to meet three criteria: (a) they recognize the validity of women's own interpretations of their lived experience and needs and acknowledge the values women claim publicly as their own (as distinct from an aesthetic ideal of womanhood invented by men) in assessing their status in society relative to men; (b) they exhibit consciousness of, discomfort at or even anger over institutionalized injustice (or inequity) towards women as a group by men as a group in a given society; and (c) they advocate the elimination of that injustice by challenging, through efforts to alter prevailing ideas and/or social institutions and practices, the coercive power, force or authority that upholds male prerogatives in that particular culture. Thus, to be a feminist is necessarily to be at odds with male-dominated culture and society.

The specific claims that have been made by feminists at particular times and in specific places in European history range from arguments for ending the maligning of women in print, for educational opportunity, for changes in man-made laws governing marriage, for control of property and one's own person and for valuation of women's unpaid labour along with opportunities for economic self-reliance; to demands for admission to the liberal professions, for readjustment of inequitable sexual mores and ending prostitution and other forms of sexual exploitation, for control over women's health, birthing and child-rearing practices, for state financial aid to mothers and for representation in political and religious organizations (symbolized in western societies not only by the vote but also by access to public office). Such claims can all be seen as culturally specific subsets of a broader challenge to male pretensions to monopolize societal authority, that is, to patriarchy. At the same time, each of these claims addresses a structural issue, a problematic practice with political dimensions, which transcends the boundaries of the western world and has applicability to the experience of women in other societies.

TOWARD A NEW FEMINIST POLITICS

This definition of feminism suggests not only a reconsideration of the relational feminist tradition in history but a contemporary reappropriation of its most distinctive contribution in the interest of a new feminist politics. The relational mode of approaching women's emancipation, by honouring women's own interpretations of 'difference' in its manifold complexity, may hold the key to overcoming contemporary resistance to feminism. It seems to me that most of those women who say today, 'I'm not a feminist, but . . .' would in fact identify themselves as relational feminists, once made aware of the depth and extent of this tradition. It is to the logical and societal consequences of individualist feminist arguments – the individual as an end in itself – that they object.

Yet within present-day Anglo-American feminist circles, resistance to this type of relational thinking and its implications is not negligible. Arguments based on sexual difference, women's maternal roles or nurturant thinking, or especially the suggestion that physiological or hormonal differences between the sexes, or female sexuality itself, might have socio-political implications, continue to make many current partisans uneasy. Some would prefer to disassociate themselves from such arguments, even at the expense of obscuring the historical importance of relational feminist arguments in the western tradition. Others resist the arguments for moral and/or spiritual distinctiveness, especially those that historically pointed to a mission of moral reform and unremunerated benevolence for women based on their capacity to nurture.

At bottom, the real problem late twentieth-century feminist theorists have had with relational feminist arguments both historically and today is that such arguments seem to cut both ways; even as they support a case for women's distinctiveness and complementarity of the sexes, they have been and can be appropriated by political adversaries and twisted to endorse male privilege. It is no secret to those who study women's history that certain aspects of arguments grounded in women's special nature, physiological and psychological distinctiveness, the centrality of motherhood and a sharp sexual division of labour within the family and society have in the past been co-opted by those hostile to women's emancipation. This threat remains.

A closer reading of women's history and the history of the woman question in western thought shows, however, that throughout the nineteenth century and well into the twentieth arguments for women's emancipation grounded in sexual difference and relational feminist claims could be and were used most effectively by women and men alike to achieve far-reaching rearrangements in the gender-based system, even in the face of heated opposition and attempts at co-optation. One has only to invoke the achievement of Alva Myrdal and her associates in Sweden, who did not abandon the terrain of sexual difference but built upon it during a time of population crisis, to turn objections against women's employment into arguments for women's right to motherhood even as they continued to work. Such a relational approach must not be dismissed as historically wrong-headed, or too dangerous, or as irrelevant to the needs of women in today's world, especially now that women have access to political power and authority. Instead, we should be trying harder to reappropriate relational feminism and make it work to our advantage. Surely, the best way to fight appropriation and wilful misinterpretation of one's claims is to speak unambiguously and to maintain the initiative in countering opposition. Moreover, if we reject relational feminism because it can be misappropriated, then we must reject individualist feminism on the same grounds.

The individualist approach also has been and is even now being used against us. In the United States it was successfully turned against us in achieving defeat of the Equal Rights Amendment at the state level. By attacking gender roles, by denying the significance of physiological difference, by condemning existing familial institutions as hopelessly patriarchal and by contesting motherhood, individualist feminists of the 1970s formulated claims for personal autonomy, choice and self-realization for women that simply placed the socio-political context, as well as the relational realities of most women's lives, outside discussion and left this terrain to be effectively claimed by opponents who succeeded in mobilizing public fear.

It has been one of the paradoxes of the contemporary Anglo-American women's movement that women's claims for a radical and thoroughgoing individual equality of rights with men would, if realized, preclude the possibility that there may be value for women in sexual distinctions. After all, solidarity among women is based not solely on recognition of a common oppression but also, historically speaking, on a celebration of shared and differential experience as members of the same sex, the child-bearing and nurturing sex. Feminist scholar-activists have discovered, for instance, that women's cultural experience of motherhood as negative and restricting is historically specific and, given a different shape, the experience can potentially offer women much satisfaction. However, we must find the initiative to reshape the world to our own purposes, by 'rethinking' the male-dominated family and its politics in a manner that incorporates, rather than neglects, the socio-political dimensions of women's experience. Reintegrating individualistic claims for women's self-realization and choices, with its emphasis on rights, into the more socially conscious relational framework, with its emphasis on mutual responsibilities, may provide a more fruitful model for contemporary feminist politics, one that can accommodate diversity among women better than either of the two historical approaches can separately.

It is historically significant that Anglo-American feminist theorists are today embarked on a reassessment and a cautious rehabilitation of relational feminist ideas about 'difference', womanliness, sexuality and motherhood itself. This reassessment has been inspired to some extent by borrowings from recent continental European feminist theory, though with little knowledge of the centuries-long development of European (especially French) feminism that could so enrich the undertaking. Ten years ago we knew all too little of that complex heritage; today, however, the range and diversity of the history of discourse about women and on women's behalf within western thought stand revealed. If we now fail to recognize the historical importance of this tradition and its arguments on behalf of the emancipation of women, and to encourage its assimilation and use, our appreciation of the range and vitality of western thought will be greatly impoverished, and our resources much diminished.

As we plot a future path, we must draw on the most valuable features of this historical tradition. What feminists today must do – and are now beginning to do – is to reappropriate the relational part of our intellectual heritage, which we now know to be grounded in the very heart of western thought on 'the woman question', to reclaim the power of difference, of womanliness as women define it, to reclaim its concern for broad socio-political goals and to reweave it once again with the appeal to the principle of human freedom that underlines the individualist tradition. We must collapse the dichotomy that has placed these two traditions at odds historically and chart a new political course. Armed with a richer history and a more comprehensive working definition of feminism, I suggest that, with compromises and concessions on both sides, we can make both modes of feminist discourse work together on behalf of an equitable world, a world in which women and men can be at once equal and different, a world free of male privilege and male hierarchy and authority over women.

NOTES

This essay is a much abbreviated and slightly amended version of 'Defining feminism: a comparative historical approach', *Signs: Journal of Women in Culture and Society*, 14(1), Autumn 1988, pp. 119–57. It is republished here with permission of the University of Chicago Press. In the interests of space, references have been severely truncated.

1 V. Woolf, *Three Guineas*, London, Hogarth Press, 1938, pp. 184, 250.
2 As in the collection J. Mitchell and A. Oakley (eds), *What Is Feminism?*, New York, Pantheon Books, 1986, which nevertheless attempts to grapple with historical questions. See, in particular, the thoughtful essays by Rosalind Delmar and Nancy Cott.
3 A. Hackett, 'The politics of feminism in Wilhelmine Germany 1890–1918', 2 vols, Ph.D. dissertation, Columbia University, 1976, p. v.
4 C. Register, 'Motherhood at center: Ellen Key's social vision', *Women's Studies International Forum*, 5(6), 1982, p. 602.
5 For an overview of European developments and further bibliographical references and documents see S. G. Bell and K. Offen (eds), *Women, the Family, and Freedom: The Debate in Documents, 1750–1950*, 2 vols, Stanford, Calif., Stanford University Press, 1983; and K. Offen, 'Liberty, equality, and justice for women: the theory and practice of feminism in nineteenth-century Europe', in R. Bridenthal, C. Koonz and S. Mosher Stuard (eds), *Becoming Visible: Women in European History*, 2nd edn, Boston, Mass., Houghton Mifflin, 1987, pp. 335–73. See especially the contributions of James C. Albisetti, Ann Taylor Allen and Catherine M. Prelinger for Germany, and Marilyn J. Boxer, Anne Cova and Claire G. Moses for France.
6 Influential contributors to this revisionist account of American feminist history include Barbara J. Berg, Nancy F. Cott, Estelle B. Freedman, Linda Gordon, Nancy Hewitt, William Leach, Mary P. Ryan, Anne Firor Scott, Kathryn Kish Sklar and Carroll Smith-Rosenberg.
7 See (among others) the publications of Jane Lewis, Barbara Caine, Leslie Parker Hume, Joyce Senders Pedersen and Jane Rendall.
8 R. Stites, *The Women's Liberation Movement in Russia: Nihilism, Feminism, and Bolshevism, 1860–1930*, Princeton, NJ, Princeton University Press, 1978.

9 See K. Offen, 'Sur les origines des mots "féminisme" et "féministe"', *Revue d'histoire moderne et contemporaine*, 34(3), July–September 1987, pp. 492–6. A slightly expanded English version appears in *Feminist Issues*, 8(2), Fall 1988, pp. 45–51.

10 *La citoyenne*, 64, 4 September–1 October 1882, p. 1; L. Cosson, *Essai sur la condition des femmes*, Paris, P. Dupont, 1883, pp. 59, 121, 125.

11 M. Deraismes, 'A propos du congrès de la Fédération des sociétés féministes', *Revue des revues*, August 1892, pp. 1–3.

12 R. Schoenflies *et al.*, *Der Internationale Kongress für Frauenwerke und Frauenbestrebungen: Berlin, 19–26 September 1896*, Berlin, Walther, 1897, p. 40.

13 See I. H. Irwin's 'Adventures of yesterday', pp. 209, 450, deposited at the Schlesinger Library, Radcliffe, and available on microfilm in the RPI microfilm collection, 'History of Women'; and Peiss, 'A great personal, joyous adventure: feminist ideology of the 1910s and its social context', in P. Lattin, J. Bischoff and L. Tafel (eds), *Feminist Research in the Eighties: Conference Proceedings*, De Kalb, Ill., Northern Illinois University Press, 1983.

14 On Argentine usage see A. Lavrin, 'The ideology of feminism in the southern cone, 1900–1940', Working Paper no. 169, Washington, DC, Latin American Program, Woodrow Wilson Center, 1986; and M. Molyneux, 'No God, no boss, no husband: anarchist feminism in nineteenth-century Argentina', *Latin American Perspectives*, 13(1), Winter 1986, pp. 119–45.

15 See M. J. Boxer, 'Women's studies in France circa 1902: a course on feminology', *International Supplement to the Women's Studies Quarterly*, 1, January 1982, pp. 26–27.

16 J. Kelly, 'Early feminist theory and the *Querelle des Femmes*', *Signs*, 8(1), Autumn 1982, pp. 4–28; reprinted in *Women, History, and Theory: The Essays of Joan Kelly*, Chicago, University of Chicago Press, 1984.

17 M. Ferguson (ed.), *First Feminists: British Women Writers, 1578–1799*, Bloomington, Ind., Indiana University Press, 1985; S. Shephard (ed.), *The Women's Sharp Revenge: Five Women's Pamphlets from the Renaissance*, New York, St Martin's Press, 1985.

18 See O. Banks, *Faces of Feminism: A Study of Feminism as a Social Movement*, New York, St Martin's Press, 1981; and Z. Eisenstein, *The Radical Future of Liberal Feminism*, New York, Longman, 1981.

19 See A. Jaggar, *Feminist Politics and Human Nature*, Totowa, NJ, Rowman & Allanheld, 1983.

20 See especially Gerda Lerner's influential essays and her book, *The Majority Finds its Past*, New York, Oxford University Press, 1979.

21 See K. Offen, 'Feminism and sexual difference in historical perspective', in D. Rhode (ed.), *Theoretical Perspectives on Sexual Difference*, New Haven, Conn., Yale University Press, 1990, pp. 13–20, 266–7.

22 M. Wollstonecraft, *Vindication of the Rights of Woman*, 1792; excerpts reprinted in Bell and Offen, *Women, the Family, and Freedom*, vol. 1, doc. 12; E. C. Stanton, speech before the Woman Suffrage Convention in Washington, DC, 18 January 1869, reprinted in Bell and Offen, ibid., vol. 1, doc. 137, pp. 494–5; 'Solitude of self: an address delivered by Elizabeth Cady Stanton before the United States Congressional Committee on the Judiciary, Monday, January 18, 1892', ed. Harriot Stanton Blatch, n.p., 1910, p. 5.

23 See N. F. Cott, 'Feminist theory and feminist movements: the past before us', in Mitchell and Oakley, *What Is Feminism?*, pp. 49–62; and C. N. Degler, 'Darwinians confront gender, or, there is more to it than history', in Rhode, *Theoretical Perspectives*, pp. 33–46, 267–9.

24 See K. Offen, 'Ernest Legouvé and the doctrine of "equality in difference" for women: a case study of male feminism in nineteenth-century French thought', *Journal of Modern History*, 58(2), June 1986, pp. 452–84.

25 See C. G. Moses, *French Feminism in the Nineteenth Century*, Albany, NY, State University of New York Press, 1984; and K. Offen, 'New documents for the history of French feminism during the early Third Republic', *History of European Ideas*, 8(4–5), 1987, pp. 621–4.

26 T. Kaplan, 'Female consciousness and collective action: the case of Barcelona, 1910–1918', *Signs*, 7(3), Spring 1982, pp. 545–66.

27 See in particular the recent work by French historian M. Riot-Sarcey: 'La conscience féministe des femmes de 1848: Jeanne Deroin, Désirée Gay', in *Un fabuleux destin, Flora Tristan: actes du premier colloque international Flora Tristan (Dijon, 3 et 4 mars 1984)*, Dijon, Editions Universitaires de Dijon, 1985, and with E. Varikas, 'Feminist consciousness in the nineteenth century: a pariah consciousness?', *Praxis International*, 5(4), January 1986, pp. 443–65.

28 H. Auclert, 'Programme électoral des femmes', *La citoyenne*, August 1885; B. von Suttner, *Das Maschinenzeitalter*, 1899 (orig. publ. 1889), trans. S. G. Bell, in Bell and Offen, *Women, the Family, and Freedom*, vol. 2, doc. 12.

28 A. Moll Weiss, 'La ménagère et le féminisme', *Revue internationale de sociologie*, 18(7), July 1910, pp. 499–503; M. Pelletier, *La femme en lutte pour ses droits*, Paris, Giard & Brière, 1908.

30 See K. Offen, 'Body politics: women, work, and the politics of motherhood in France, 1920–1950', in G. Bock and P. Thane (eds), *Maternity and Gender Policies: Women and the Rise of the European Welfare States*, London, Routledge, 1991.

Chapter 5

Equality and difference in National Socialist racism

Gisela Bock

This essay aims to shed light on the conceptual couple 'equality' and 'difference' by looking from a historian's point of view at National Socialism in Germany. Two implications of this approach are particularly important. First, the crucial core of National Socialism and its crimes was racism, in both theory and practice. In this context, therefore, 'equality' and 'difference' concern not only gender relations, but also race relations, and the groups that were discriminated against on racial grounds included both women and men. Second, while racism was not confined to National Socialism or Germany, but was an international phenomenon, National Socialism carried all forms of racism to unprecedented extremes. This was possible because National Socialism politicized racism by extending it from the social to the political sphere, transforming it into race policy; and where 'politics are centered around the concept of race, the Jews will be at the center of hostility'.[1] Racism was from the beginning institutionalized within the state, so that measures ranging from the legislative to the bureaucratic could be marshalled in support of the persecution of Jews and the policy of compulsory sterilization, beginning in 1933, and ultimately in support of the massacres which started six years later. The following reflections will therefore be concerned with the political sphere and with this pair of issues – racist sterilization and racist massacre – which were forms of compulsory intervention in the body and in life. To put them in perspective, I will first outline some of the current opinions held by historians and non-historians on the topic of women and National Socialism, particularly those regarding gender difference and gender equality. In the second section of the essay I shall deal with various gender dimensions of National Socialist policies on procreation and welfare, and in the third with some gender dimensions of National Socialist genocide.

VISIONS OF WOMEN AND NATIONAL SOCIALISM

According to one opinion, National Socialism favoured women. A first version of this view holds that, before 1933, 'equality' was emphasized, particularly by the women's movement, 'difference' was played down, and having children was scorned. National Socialism is supposed to have made child-bearing respectable again, to have rewarded mothers and upgraded the family, to have promoted not an illusory and undesirable 'equality' of women with men but their 'equal value'. Another version of the same position underlines a different link between the earlier women's movement and Nazi gender policies. The former supported women's distinctiveness and 'separate sphere', the centrality of maternity and demands for the improvement of the situation of mothers; National Socialism is said to have taken over this radical feminist programme.[2] A further and influential version argues that, regardless of countervailing ideologies, National Socialism produced for women 'a new status of relative if unconventional equality'. Women experienced improved job opportunities and rising wages and benefited from social policies related to maternity; their loss of political status did not differ from the same loss as experienced by men.[3]

A second opinion, for many years the prevailing one among feminists and non-feminists alike, evokes a similar picture but evaluates it differently, seeing it not as pro-women, but as anti-women. It deplores the fact that, before 1933, the women's movement had proclaimed the value of motherhood, corporal as well as spiritual, and argues that National Socialism adopted largely the same view. National Socialism is thus interpreted as having valorized motherhood in both moral and material terms, thereby reducing women to mothers. This is held to have been achieved in several ways: by the use of propaganda, by incentives such as child allowances and various other subsidies given to mothers, and by coercive means (*Gebärzwang*) such as firing women *en masse* from their jobs, excluding them from the universities, outlawing birth-control, tightening up the anti-abortion law and vastly increasing the number of convictions for abortion. These measures, designed to keep women out of the labour force and to encourage them to bear as many children as possible, are seen as constituting a policy of extreme pro-natalism and a cult of motherhood, which are in turn interpreted as the essential and distinctive features of National Socialist sexism and of the regime's victimization of women.

Both these opinions are problematic, particularly with respect to the issues of maternity and female 'difference'. Their proponents often confuse propaganda with actual policies, take account of only selected parts of this propaganda and misrepresent historical facts. For example, the National Socialist image of women limited them much less to a 'separate sphere', to motherhood and housewifery, than, for instance, the image of women dominant in the United States of the 1930s.[4] Despite a number of Nazi and non-Nazi voices in 1933–4, women were not fired *en masse* during the National Socialist era and the number of employed women increased, particularly in the industrial labour force and among married mothers. The decline in the number of women university students was not so much due to the regime's intervention as to economic developments – except for the exclusion of Jews of both sexes.[5] Financial incentives were paid not to women, but to men. The number of convictions for abortion did not increase, but decreased by one-sixth by comparison with the Weimar Republic period.[6]

Most important, however, is the fact that millions of women and men under the National Socialist regime were discouraged from having children at all. The National Socialist state did not abolish birth-control, but took it over. In 1933, prior to the introduction of any pro-natalist measures, it introduced a law ordering compulsory sterilization of those considered to be of 'inferior value', thus embarking on a policy of anti-natalism. This anti-natalist policy was designed to improve the 'quality' of the population, to bring about 'race regeneration' and 'racial uplift' (*rassische Aufartung*). In 1933–4, an enormous propaganda campaign attempted to render this policy popular, and around one and a half million people were officially declared to be 'unworthy of procreating' (*fortpflanzungsunwürdig*). In 1935, abortion on medical and eugenic grounds was included in the sterilization law. In the same year, two laws introduced marriage prohibitions, one against marriages between Jews and non-Jews, the other between the eugenically 'inferior' and other (non-sterilized) Germans, with the aim of preventing 'racially inferior' offspring. From 1939 on, this anti-natalist policy receded into the background as mass murder and genocide took over. The female among the victims of these policies include otherwise very diverse groups. Between 1933 and 1945, almost 200,000 women were sterilized on eugenic grounds, one per cent of those of child-bearing age. The number of those prevented from marrying is as yet unknown. From 1933, about 200,000 German Jewish women were exiled, and after 1941 almost 100,000 of them were killed. From 1939, probably over 80,000 female inmates of mostly psychiatric institutions were killed, including all those who were Jewish. Over two million foreign women performed forced labour during the war, and hundreds of thousands of them had to undergo involuntary abortions and sterilizations. Several million non-German Jewish women were killed in the massacres during the Second World War, as were an unknown number of other women, mostly gypsies and Slavs.

In view of these figures and policies concerning the female victims of National Socialist racism, the assertion that the essence and distinctiveness of National Socialist policy towards women consisted in 'pro-natalism and a cult of motherhood' must be called into question. Equally problematic is the further assertion, common to both the opinions I have outlined, that in the National Socialist state gender relations were based not on 'equality' but on 'difference' between the sexes and that men and women were treated differently. On the one hand, within the groups that were racially discriminated against, both men and women of the racially discriminated groups were considered to be 'alien' and 'different' (*anders, fremd, artfremd*); they were treated as 'unequal' and above all as 'inferior' (*minderwertig*). On the other hand, both men and women of the racially privileged groups were considered and treated as 'equal' (*gleich*, *gleichartig*, *artgleich*) and above all as 'superior' (*wertvoll*). The race theorists of National Socialism held gender relations, and specifically conceptions of 'equality' and 'difference', to be different in different ethnic groups. Thus in their view only the women of 'superior' ethnic groups were 'different' from men and fit to occupy 'separate spheres'. The 'inferior' women and men, by contrast, whether Jews, blacks or gypsies, were held to display 'sexual levelling' (*sexuelle Applanation*). According to one of these authors, 'the division into manly and womanly characteristics is a specific feature of the Nordic race, so that this race most purely embodies the manly and womanly essence', and Nordic men and women 'differ more sharply from each other' than the men and the women of other races.[7] Finally, and most importantly, National Socialist policy-makers by no means treated 'racially inferior' women 'differently' from the men of their groups, but 'equally'. Both men and women became victims of forced sterilization, forced labour and massacre. For these women, there was no 'separate sphere'.

In order to revise prevailing opinions, we must include and place at the centre of our analysis racism both as theory and as practice. However, when we turn to research on National Socialist racism, on anti-Jewish and anti-gypsy policies, and on sterilization and euthanasia, we usually find that any discussion of gender relations is conspicuously absent.[8] Occasionally, we even find eminent historians of the genocide supporting, without any qualification, the view that 'women's emancipation' was considerably accelerated under the National Socialist regime.[9] Moreover, we find in this body of scholarship another common opinion which argues or implies that, in the context of National Socialist racism, the issue of women and gender relations is irrelevant or even inadmissible, because, on the one hand, not 'all women' became victims of National Socialist racism and, on the other, both men and women were equally its victims, numerically as well as in virtue of the equal treatment they received at its hands.[10] Racist policies, it is sometimes said, were not directed against women; their female victims became victims not 'as women', but irrespective of their sex, as gender-neutral members of certain racial groups. Yet the view that women's history is irrelevant to the history of racism is merely the obverse of the opinions already mentioned, which imply that the history of racism is irrelevant to the history of women. It condemns half the victims of racism to historical invisibility. But it also poses a series of questions: Does 'gender equality' or 'equal treatment' of the sexes among the victims actually mean gender neutrality? What has 'equality' come to mean in this context? Would a focus on the female victims of racism be legitimate only if all or most of its victims had been female, or if all women had been its victims (instead of a minority of hundreds of thousands of German and millions of non-German women), or if victimized women had been treated differently from victimized men?

There have indeed been attempts to overcome the limitations inherent in so much recent scholarship and to link women's history to National Socialist race policy and genocide. One resulting view focuses not on the female victims of National Socialist racism, nor on the minority of women who played an active part in the promotion of race policies, but on the majority of the women who belonged to the groups considered to be racially 'superior'. According to this view, these women were guilty of and responsible for genocide not just generally, because of the German nation's collective guilt, but specifically and individually 'as women' – as mothers, wives and home-keepers. Their guilt is held to stem from the fact that they lived and believed in their female 'difference' and in the value of their 'separate sphere', thereby sharing and supporting Nazism's conception and treatment of women. Far from victimizing women, Nazi pro-natalism and its cult of motherhood drew upon women's own aspirations to be, and be valued as, mothers. Women willingly 'lent the healthy gloss of motherhood', of human and family values, to cover up a criminal regime and are therefore seen to be at the 'very centre' of 'Nazi evil'. The elaboration of ideas of gender difference, maternity and separate spheres by males, females and feminists since the late eighteenth century is said to have paved the way for the National Socialist massacres; the prescription of 'polarized identities for males and females' – among the victims as well as among those who were not – is held to be at the roots of the massacres. Precisely because of their 'difference' as a sex, German non-Jewish women are held to have been 'equally' guilty of genocide, 'no less than men' who are usually at the centre of historical studies of the Holocaust.[11]

This concept of equal guilt deriving from sexual 'difference' confronts us with another difficult sense of 'equality'. No less important in this context is the problematic fact that this view is based on the traditional picture of Nazism as a pro-natalist regime which fostered a cult of motherhood – an assumption which we have already seen to be fraught with contradiction and difficulty. A still further contradiction relates to the issue of women's power which is of course central to the argument of women being at the very centre of the Nazi crimes. On the one hand, female difference – expressed in motherhood and the separate sphere – is held to be the source of power-lessness, not even implying some 'invisible power' of women. On the other hand, it is held to have been a source of women's power to bring about genocide.[12] Another influential version of this view attempts to overcome the contradiction by claiming that, indeed, female 'difference' implied female power, the 'power of the mothers'; such 'power of the mothers' is then held to have been at the roots of genocide.[13] Although neither sources nor historical scholarship support this assumption, its function is obvious. It revives the old myth of Nazi 'pro-natalism and cult of motherhood', which is so thoroughly jeopardized by even a superficial glance at the depressing and contradicting facts of racism and genocide, by presenting it as a female version of genocide. Despite the problems of this approach, it poses important questions: What really was women's contribution to and guilt and responsibility for National Socialist race policy and genocide? Was it specific to the female sex and therefore grounded in female 'difference'? If not, was it equal to the contribution of men, and in what way? If so, how 'separate' actually were the 'separate spheres' under National Socialism?

I shall explore some of these issues by focusing on some gender and race dimensions of National Socialist policies of sterilization, of welfare and of massacre. The exploration will conform to a methodological requirement which I consider indispensable: that in any adequate analysis of National Socialist racism, its agents and its victims must be central. No generalization can be valid unless it is also valid for these groups. It will emerge that National Socialist racism was by no means gender neutral any more than National Socialist sexism was race neutral. On both levels, in the sources as well as in historical analysis, the conceptual couple equality/difference has an essential place. At the same time, however, it is context dependent.

ANTI-NATALISM AND THE 'PRIMACY OF THE STATE IN THE SPHERE OF LIFE'

'Superiority' and 'inferiority', *Wert* and *Minderwertigkeit*, were the main categories common to all forms of Nazi racism. These terms were, moreover, intimately linked to the language of 'equality' and 'inequality'. The sterilization law of 1933, like the anti-Jewish laws, put into practice the classical racist demand, proclaimed in Germany specifically by the advocates of eugenic sterilization: 'Unequal value, unequal rights' (*ungleicher Wert, ungleiche Rechte*).[14] According to section 14 of the law, sterilization was forbidden to the 'healthy' members of both sexes, while according to section 12 it was compulsory for their 'inferior' members. In addition, these notions were linked to the language of the 'private' and the 'political'. The sterilization law was officially proclaimed, upon its enactment, as enforcing the 'primacy of the state over the sphere of life, marriage and family' (*Primat des Staates auf dem Gebiet des Lebens, der Ehe und der Familie*). It was thus through the policy of birth-prevention that the private sphere came to be subordinated to and ruled by the political sphere. The sterilization law was, according to its official commentators, an expression of the view that 'the private is political', and that any decision about the dividing line between private and political is in itself political.[15] Finally, this policy was linked to the concept of 'biology' which assumed a variety of meanings in this discourse. It referred not to the different bodies of men and women, but to a superior or inferior 'biological value' which was, for women and men alike, genetically transmitted. 'Biology' also, and most importantly, meant bodily intervention for the sake of social change. In this respect, the sterilization law went even further than the anti-Jewish laws of 1933, since it ordered compulsory bodily intervention and was thereby the first of the Nazi measures that sought to 'solve' social and cultural problems by what were referred to as 'biological' means. It was in these terms, rather than in the language of gender, that in 1936 Himmler praised the sterilization law to the Hitler Youth: 'Germans . . . have once again learned . . . to recognize bodies and to bring up this God-given body and our God-given blood and race according to its value or lack of value.'[16]

Forced and mass sterilization was pursued for the sake of 'uplifting the race' or 'the people', of 'eradicating inferior hereditary traits' by preventing 'inferior' people from having children and passing on their traits to posterity. The Nazi sterilization law, which was the culmination of the preceding international movement of eugenics or race hygiene, was an integral component of National Socialist racism as defined by the regime itself:

> The German race question consists primarily in the Jewish question. In second place, yet no less important, there is the gypsy question . . . [But] degenerative effects on the racial body may arise not only from outside, from members of alien races, but also from inside, through unrestricted procreation of inferior hereditary material.[17]

The sterilization law established psychiatric grounds for sterilization, particularly feeble-mindedness, schizophrenia, epilepsy and manic-depressive derangement. It did not specifically mention Jews, gypsies, blacks or Poles and therefore seemed to be ethnically neutral. Interestingly, Hitler objected briefly to sterilizing persons of non-German ethnicity, on the grounds that they deserved no 'uplift' of their race. But this objection was soon overcome, and 'inferior' Germans and emotionally or mentally disabled persons of other ethnic groups were subjected to the law on equal terms. (After 1945, this fact was appealed to by those who claimed, defending the sterilization policy, that it had nothing to do with racism.)

None the less, ethnicity made a difference. Psychiatric theory and practice established various links between ethnicity and psychiatric constitution, for example that western Jews were more prone to schizophrenia than 'normal' people and eastern Jews more prone to 'feeble-mindedness'. Gypsies were likely to be classified as 'feeble-minded', and black people were thought to be more prone to both feeble-mindedness and schizophrenia. In 1937, all Afro-Germans who could be found were sterilized. Like many gypsies, they were sterilized both within and outside the 1933 law. In 1941 – the year when the deadly deportations from Germany to occupied Poland began – a Berlin Jewish woman was sterilized because she had been diagnosed as schizophrenic, a derangement 'proven' by the fact that she had 'depressions' and had attempted to commit suicide. From March 1942, Jews were exempted from the sterilization law, but by then the massacres did to them what sterilization would have done to their offspring – prevented them from living.[18]

Because neither women nor men were mentioned in the sterilization law it seemed to be gender neutral and to affect the sexes equally. Yet even this apparent gender neutrality was not self-evident but the subject of controversy. Interestingly, there was up to 1933 a public debate as to whether it might be unjust or unwise to sterilize women and men in equal numbers, since the operation on women (salpingectomy, including full anaesthesia, abdominal incision and the concomitant risk) was so much more dramatic than that on men (vasectomy), and the higher rate of complication and death might provoke resistance. In 1933, however, the Propaganda Ministry announced that just as many women as men would have to be sterilized, regardless of their sex, for reasons of 'justice' and the 'logic' of hereditary transmission. In fact, the 400,000 sterilization victims were about half women, half men.

None the less, gender made a difference, and the sterilization policy was anything but gender neutral. Compulsory and mass sterilization of women meant violent intervention not only with the female body but also with female life. Probably about 5,000 people died as a result of sterilization, and whereas women made up 50 per cent of those sterilized, they made up about 90 per cent of those who died in the process. Many of them died because they resisted right up to the operating table or because they rejected what had happened even afterwards.[19] An unknown number, mainly women, committed suicide. Hence, the first National Socialist massacre, scientifically planned and bureaucratically executed for the sake of 'racial uplift', was the result of anti-natalism, and its victims were mostly women. Historians have not noted it because women's bodily difference seemed to be unimportant, even in the case of a policy of bodily intervention.

There were also other respects in which sterilization was not gender neutral. Childlessness, like having children, had a different meaning for women and for men. Their reactions and forms of resistance to sterilization consequently differed in many ways. Women as well as men protested against their stigmatization as 'second-class people' – in thousands of letters preserved among the documents of the sterilization courts – but women complained of the resulting childlessness more often than men. This was especially true for young women (the minimum age for being sterilized was 14). Many women attempted to become pregnant before sterilization. Their resistance was sufficiently important for the authorities to give the phenomenon a special name: 'protest pregnancies' (*Trotzschwangerschaften*). One girl emphasized that she had got pregnant in order 'to show the state that I won't go along with that'. These protest pregnancies were a major reason for the expansion of the sterilization law in 1935 into an abortion law, after which abortions could be performed on the same eugenic grounds as sterilizations. (This law also allowed abortion on the ground of a woman's state of health.) When abortions were performed for eugenic reasons, sterilization also was compulsory, and the number of such cases was about 30,000.[20]

Physically, sterilization means the separation of sexuality and procreation, and it had different meanings for women and men. A particularly important issue for male victims was the fear of castration, and here the medical authorities attempted to explain the difference and allay their anxieties. One doctor wrote about sterilized men in 1935: 'Happy that nothing can happen to them any more, that neither condoms nor douches are necessary, they fulfil their marital duties without restraint.' With respect to women a quite different aspect of sexuality was discussed in the professional press. Tens of thousands of women who, as one of them asserted, did 'not care at all about men' and had never had sexual intercourse, were sterilized because, according to the opinions of the all-male jurists and doctors, the possibility of pregnancy through rape had to be taken into consideration.[21] Therefore, the commentary to the law explicitly laid down that 'a different assessment of the danger of procreation is necessary for men and for women', and in the sterilization verdicts the following phrase, supported by government decree in 1936, regularly appeared. 'In the case of the female hereditarily sick, the possibility of abuse against her will must be taken into account.' Frequently, compulsory sterilization was advocated as a means of preventing the 'consequences' of a potential rape, namely pregnancy. The risk of 'inferior' women being raped was thus taken to be so high as to be a ground for the sterilization of women. At the same time, sterilized women often became objects of sexual abuse.

Those to be sterilized were denounced mostly by doctors, psychiatrists and the heads of psychiatric institutions who handed to the authorities 80 per cent of the almost 400,000 denunciations in 1934 and 1935. Members of the same professional groups drew up the decisive applications for sterilizing specific persons; the most active agents here were 'state doctors', occupants of a position created in 1934 specifically for the purpose of searching for sterilization candidates. Sterilizations (and marriage prohibitions) were decided upon by about 250 specially created courts in which the judges were exclusively male doctors, psychiatrists, anthropologists, experts in human genetics and jurists. This brought with it a highly important innovation: state power to decide on the subject of procreation was conferred on male doctors and scientists. However, women were also involved in the procedure. For instance, some social workers and female doctors (mostly, but not exclusively, those in the respective Nazi organizations) were among those who denounced possible candidates; their number seems to have declined as the 'state doctors' took over most of this activity.[22]

The courts decided on psychiatric diagnoses, using different criteria for women and men. Those for women measured their 'departure from the norm' against norms for the female sex, and those for men against norms for the male sex. To determine female 'inferiority', heterosexual behaviour was regularly investigated, and negatively evaluated when women frequently changed sexual partners or had more than one illegitimate child. The comparable behaviour of men was less investigated, and any findings carried little weight in the sterilization verdict. Women, not men, were tested on their inclination and capacity for housework and child-rearing (tests which were also applied to childless women). Women as well as men were assessed as to their inclination and capacity for extra-domestic employment. All these criteria were particularly prominent in the most crucial diagnosis, that of 'feeble-mindedness'. Indeed, whereas this diagnosis was the reason given for almost two-thirds of all sterilizations, women constituted almost two-thirds of the group sterilized on these grounds. About 10 per cent of the trials ended with acquittal;[23] women were let off when they could prove, to the satisfaction of the doctors and lawyers in court, who often came to inspect them at home and consulted their superiors at the extra-domestic workplace, that they did their work adequately inside as well as outside the home.

Unlike the later policy of extermination, the sterilization policy was not carried on secretly, but almost entirely in public view. In contrast to the impression given by many studies of women under National Socialism, the population was virtually bombarded with anti-natalist propaganda from 1933 on (before the Nazi rise to power, public sterilization propaganda was largely limited to the professional press). When in 1933–4 the Propaganda Ministry organized an aggressive campaign on 'population policy', Catholics were prevented from participating because of their pro-natalist and anti-sterilization stance, and the Catholic mothers' leagues were suppressed in 1935 on account of their anti-sterilization activities. Whereas in 1933 the 'women's page' of the *Völkischer Beobachter*, the official Nazi daily, dedicated 15 per cent of its space to the topic 'motherhood', it was reduced to 5 per cent by 1938.[24] National Socialism by no means wanted children at any cost and never propagated the slogan 'Kinder, Küche, Kirche' which has frequently, but wrongly, been ascribed to it;[25] equally, the biblical injunction 'Be fruitful and multiply' was explicitly rejected.[26] The Propaganda Ministry sharply denounced the misunderstanding that 'the state allegedly wants children at any cost' and reminded citizens that the goal was 'racially worthy, physically and mentally unaffected children of German families'. Official and influential authors estimated only a minority of somewhere between 10 and 30 per cent of German women to be 'worthy of procreating', and an equal percentage to be 'unworthy of procreating' (*fortpflanzungsunwürdig*).[27]

Often, propaganda was specifically addressed to the female sex, because it seemed to require more effort to make women understand the new anti-natalism than to get it across to men.[28] In 1934 the *Völkischer Beobachter* argued against women who 'see the value of their existence in having children' and proclaimed the sterilization law as the 'beginning of a new era' for women. Millions of pamphlets explained to women that 'the state's goal' was not prolific propagation but 'regeneration', and that they should present themselves and their children to the sterilization authorities if they felt that anything was wrong with them. Maternalism (*Mütterlichkeit*) became the target of vigorous polemics, many of them in journals for women and by female authors. According to one such writer, a medical doctor, there was 'a great danger arising from women precisely because of their maternalism', since 'it acts, like any egoism, against the race'. The 'unfortunate struggle between the sexes' was to be replaced by their common struggle for the 'future generation'. The traditional view that 'woman, because of all her physical and mental characteristics, is particularly close to all living beings, and has a particular inclination towards all life' was sharply criticized because it would encourage women to practise 'the worst sin against nature' ('nature' was understood as 'eradicating' the weak if left undisturbed by humane and charitable intervention).[29] Gertrud Scholtz-Klink, the 'Reich Women's Leader' who advocated sterilization and spoke against Catholic women workers' rejection of this policy, agreed with male Nazis on another aspect of 'female nature'. Like them, she insisted on the profound racial difference between 'German and un-German science', but denied that any differences of gender were relevant in this field: 'There is nothing like a specifically "female" knowledge, any more than a specifically "female" method', and 'no gender-based scholarship'.[30]

Such Nazi visions of nature, women and anti-natalism contrasted sharply with the widespread maternalism of the moderate majority and a radical minority of the earlier women's movement. But ironically, whereas many historians have interpreted this maternalism as a precursor of the Nazi conceptions of gender, the voices of some radical feminists who, before 1933, advocated the sterilization of the 'inferior' (hoping thereby to render birth-control acceptable and respectable) are not usually regarded as precursors of Nazi policies.[31] Whatever the precise historical relationship turns out to be, it seems probable that the earlier feminist views on these issues – both maternalism and anti-natalism – did not influence the rise of National Socialist conceptions and policies. As to the latter, it is evident that never before had there been a state which, like the National Socialist regime, pursued an anti-natalist policy of such dimensions and efficiency in theory, in propaganda and in practice.

What, then, is the substance of Nazi pro-natalism and its alleged cult of motherhood? How did National Socialism conceive of gender relations in this area, and how is this area linked to anti-natalism and to race policy in general? Clearly, more 'German and healthy' babies were desired, but propaganda on this issue never failed to stress the contrasting policy of anti-natalism. In an important public speech of June 1933, the Minister of the Interior explained the hoped-for numerical relation between pro- and anti-natalism: 300,000 more children per year should be born (30 per cent of the birth rate), but 12 million Germans (20 per cent of the population) were

suspected of being 'inferior'.[32] More importantly, no terror or compulsion
was employed and no new bureaucracy developed for pro-natalist purposes.
Rather, Nazism relied here on volition, tradition and a range of welfare
measures such as marriage loans (1933), tax rebates for the head of household in respect of wife and children (1934, 1939) and child allowances
(1936). While these benefits did not succeed in raising the birth rate (its rise
between 1933 and 1938 was rather due to increasing and then full employment), they resembled those introduced in most European countries as an
integral component of the emerging welfare states, in contexts where pro-
natalism was sometimes less, sometimes more rampant than in Nazi
Germany.

National Socialist family subsidies nevertheless differed from those in
other European countries in two significant respects: they were shot through
with sexism and with racism. In connection with the first issue, studies of
Nazi pro-natalism have overlooked the role of men, just as studies of Nazi
anti-natalism have overlooked the role of women. As in the other masculinist dictatorships, Italy and Spain, Nazi state welfare privileged fathers over
mothers, and glorified fatherhood as 'nature'; one Reich minister declared:
'The concept of fatherhood has been handed down through age-old processes of natural law', and 'the concept of the father is unambiguous and
must be placed at the centre of financial measures for the family'. Race
theorists insisted on the 'patriarchal spirit of the Nordic race'. Unlike female
'nature', male 'nature' seemed to require economic rewards. As the male
head of the Nazi Party's organization Mother and Child emphasized:

> There is no more beautiful image of selfless service than that of a mother
> with her children ... who never thinks whether she is going to get
> anything in return ... At the very moment at which she began to calculate
> returns, she would cease to be a good mother.[33]

Begetting children was considered more valuable than bearing and rearing
them, and child allowances were paid to fathers, not to mothers; unmarried
mothers obtained them only if the father of their child was known to the
authorities. This gender policy differed sharply from that prevailing in the
European democracies, where child allowances were paid to mothers, if
only in response to the tenacious struggles of maternalist feminism.[34]

The second characteristic feature of Nazi family subsidies, its connection
with racism, was unique, differing even from practice in the other dictatorships. All those classified as 'inferior' – such as eugenically 'unfit' parents
and children, Jews, gypsies and labourers from eastern Europe – were
denied benefits and discouraged from having children.

Thus, while state welfare for families and procreation was not in itself
sexist or racist, National Socialism nevertheless linked the emergence of
modern state welfare to sexism and racism by privileging men over women
and 'valuable German' men over 'racially inferior' men. Welfare policy met

its limits in race policy; the latter had priority over the former. Pro-natalism focused on fathers, and was shaped by the requirements of anti-natalism for the sake of 'racial uplift'. Hence, the unique and specific gender dimension of National Socialist population policy consisted not in 'pro-natalism and a cult of motherhood', but in anti-natalism and a cult of fatherhood and masculinity; whereas the latter was largely traditional, state anti-natalism was entirely novel. A historical continuity leads from there to the escalation of racism in the 1940s.

GENDER DIMENSIONS OF GENOCIDE

National Socialist race policy was directed, in both principle and practice, not only against men, but equally against women. Yet despite the equal treatment meted out to victims of both sexes, race policy was in many respects directed against women precisely as women. This is obvious in the case of racist anti-natalism, since when it comes to giving life human activities are obviously gender based, and the anti-natalist 'primacy of the state in the sphere of life' assumed new features in the 1940s. But gender issues and gender difference were also important when it came to the 'primacy of the state in the sphere of death', particularly to genocide.

When war was declared in 1939, the practice of legalized sterilization was curtailed in order to liberate workforces for war and massacre. Anti-natalism was now directed almost exclusively against women, particularly against those who had to perform forced labour and those in the concentration camps. Early in the war, Polish women who became pregnant were sent back east, and it seems that many took deliberate advantage of this policy in order to avoid forced labour. Their gesture was babies against war-work. But from 1941, when war was declared on Russia, the policy changed and pregnant Polish and Russian women had to stay in Germany. They were encouraged, and often forced, to undergo abortion and sterilization, and often had their children taken away from them. Pregnant Russian women were put to work at 'men's jobs' in the munitions industry so as to increase the chance that they would miscarry: a policy of war-work against babies. Around the same time, sterilization experiments were pursued under Himmler's command, particularly in Auschwitz and Ravensbrück, on Jews and gypsies. Originally they were meant for the future sterilization of those *Judenmischlinge* who were exempted from extermination, and the experiments were performed on both women and men. But they soon focused on women, who received injections into the uterus performed by doctors with previous experience of sterilization. Their aim now was to develop a technique for the mass sterilization of women who were considered 'inferior' on both ethnic and eugenic grounds. Jewish and gypsy women in the camps were used for the experimentation of a policy that in future was to overtake hundreds of thousands of ethnically and eugenically 'inferior' women all over Europe.[35] In all these instances, female difference was used to prevent maternity.

The pre-war sterilization policy was also a 'forerunner of mass murder',[36] of genocide as well as of 'euthanasia' (called Aktion T4), the massacre of the ill in which up to 200,000 ill, old and disabled people were killed between 1939 and 1945. Most of them were inmates of psychiatric clinics, women as well as men, and they included all Jews in such institutions. To kill them, gas was used for the first time. Anti-natalism anticipated certain features of this massacre in that, first, it had grown out of a mentality which saw sterilization not as a private and free choice, but as a 'humane' alternative to killing for the sake of the *Volkskörper*, as an 'elimination without massacre',[37] as a political substitute for 'nature' which 'naturally' (that is, without modern charity and medicine) prevented 'unfit' people from surviving. Second, it was through the policy of sterilization that the experts and authorities had already become used to dealing with bodily intervention and death, particularly in the case of women. Third, the very first victims of this massacre were 5,000 disabled children aged 3 and under, precisely those whose mothers (and fathers) could not previously be identified as sterilization and abortion candidates (either because of the limits of bureaucracy or because the child's handicap was not hereditary). They were searched out through the channels of the sterilization bureaucracy. Finally, the activists of T4 – mostly doctors and other medical personnel – had also been advocates and practitioners of compulsory sterilization, and many of them also played an important role in the genocide of the Jews.

Late in 1941, the T4 gas chambers and the male members of the teams who operated them were transferred from Germany to the death camps in the occupied east where they served for the systematic killing of millions of Jews and gypsies, women as well as men. This transfer was not just one of technology but had several significant gender dimensions. Before gas was used, hundreds of thousands of Jews had already been killed, mostly by mass shooting. The SS men involved seem to have experienced considerable 'psychological difficulties', particularly in shooting women and children, as was acknowledged, for instance, by the commandant of Auschwitz. Even Himmler became nervous while watching executions which included the killing of women and children. Soon after, gas technology was introduced not only as a means to accelerate killing, but also as 'a "suitable" method', a 'humane' alternative to overt bloodshed, which would relieve the largely gender-specific scruples of the killers. Some of the first mobile gas vans used for killing Jews were used exclusively on women and children. Women were the majority of those who were delivered from the ghettos to be killed in the gas chambers of the death camps in occupied Poland. Nazi doctors in the death camps, who had turned from healers into killers, were able to function – sometimes over years – largely because of male bonding, heavy drinking and their adaptation to an 'overall Nazi male ideal'.[38]

'Men, women and children' was the frequent description of the victims in many contemporary documents. In Auschwitz it was mostly Jewish women, and particularly those with children, who were selected for death as soon as they arrived in the camp ('every Jewish child meant automatic death to its mother'), whereas most able-bodied Jewish men were sent to forced labour. Almost two-thirds of the German Jews deported to and killed in the death camps were women, as were 56 per cent of the gypsies who were sent into the Auschwitz gas chambers.[39] The precise number of women among the other millions of dead will probably remain unknown. Hannah Arendt described the situation, the 'image of hell', as a massacre where no difference was made 'between men and women', a 'monstrous equality without fraternity or humanity', the 'darkest and deepest abyss of primal equality'.[40]

Historians have not yet explored this kind of 'equality' nor the meaning of the fact that the initiators, decision-makers and actors involved in these massacres were men, and that at least half of their victims were women. But the male massacre experts were by no means blind to such gender dimensions and did not consider this 'equal treatment' of the sexes among their victims as self-evident or self-explanatory. Rather, they felt that such murderous violence against women needed to be especially legitimized and its necessity particularly emphasized. Goebbels, in a widely broadcast radio speech of 1941 which explained why the Jews had to wear the Star of David, emphasized that Jewish women had to wear it too because they were just as dangerous as Jewish men, even though they 'may look utterly fragile and pitiful'.[41] But in Himmler's view, the justification for killing Jewish women was gender difference. In 1943, he felt the need to respond to a 'question which is certainly on people's minds. The question is: You know, I do understand that they kill adult Jews, but women and children . . . ?' He addressed his SS men and other high officials, summarizing previous reflections and urging his audience 'only to listen but never to speak about what I am going to tell you here':

We came to the question: what about the women and children? I have decided to find a clear solution here too. In fact I did not regard myself as justified in exterminating the men – let us say killing them or having them killed – while letting avengers in the shape of children grow up.

Hence, Jewish women were killed as women, as child-bearers and mothers of their people. But Himmler went further, placing female victims at the centre of his own definition of genocide:

When I was forced somewhere in some village to act against partisans and against Jewish commissars . . . then as a principle I gave the order to kill the women and children of those partisans and commissars too . . . Believe you me, that order was not so easy to give or so simple to carry out as it was logically thought out and can be stated in this hall. But we must constantly recognize that we are engaged in a primitive, primordial, natural race struggle.[42]

In this kind of 'logical thought',[43] in this – successful – attempt to override male scruples about a war of men against women, the most extreme form of the National Socialist 'natural' *Rassenkampf* was defined as a deadly struggle of men not just against men – as in a traditional military campaign – but particularly against women as mothers.

Occasionally, historians have perceived the centrality of the massacre of all Jewish women, boys and elderly men to the *Rassenkampf*; others consider it as self-evident and unworthy of specific mention.[44] Still others have singled out, as the most important gender dimension of the Holocaust, the notion that non-Jewish women participated in it by believing in female difference, particularly in motherhood, and by being mothers and wives. There were, in fact, many women who actively participated in Nazi race policies, but they do not correspond to this notion. They were a minority among the perpetrators and a minority among women at large, though a remarkably tough and efficient one, as their victims often emphasized. The more active among them were usually unmarried and without children; they were drawn from all social classes except the highest ones; and their participation in racist policies was mostly, as was often the case with comparable men, a function of their job or profession. Whereas the sterilization policy was entirely directed by men, some female social workers and medical doctors helped select the candidates. In the six T4 killing centres, female nurses assisted male doctors in selecting and killing. Female clerical workers worked alongside men in the offices and bureaucracies which dealt with race policies and genocide. Some women academics co-operated with their male superiors in gypsy studies and laid the groundwork for the selection and extermination of gypsies. Female camp guards who supervised women in the concentration camps came mostly from lower-class backgrounds and had volunteered for the job because it promised some upward mobility. Of all the women activists, they were closest to the centre of the killing operations and the most responsible for their functioning.[45] National Socialist racism was not only institutionalized as state policy, but also professionalized. Female participation in it, and responsibility for it, did not depend on a commitment to female difference, separate spheres and motherhood, but on the extra-domestic adaptation of women to male-dominated and professionalized race policy. These women did not act as mothers, nor did they believe in maternalism as a feature of the female sex.

CONCLUSION

In this essay I have aimed to show why a range of prevailing opinions about the place of women in National Socialism are problematic. Many of their problems are due to traditional and simplified conceptions of the meaning of gender equality and gender difference for the National Socialist regime, particularly in the context of its racism, and for the history of women under this regime. I have attempted to focus not only on some top Nazis' ritualized pronouncements on women, conjuring up 'the nobility of motherhood', but on the conceptions which were relevant to actual policy-making; not only on the majority of 'healthy German' women, but on the minorities which became victims of race policy – and which were soon to become much more than just a minority. Some of the results are summarized here.

The notions of gender equality and gender difference are context depen-dent. The context on which they depended in National Socialist theory and practice was, first of all, its racism. Race policy was what gave National Socialism its novelty and specificity. Moreover, this context is important because it applied the concepts 'equality' and 'difference' not only to gender relations, but also to race relations. Concepts and policies which focused on race relations also shaped National Socialism's visions of women and gender relations. Therefore, the latter were not traditional, simple and coherent, but in many ways novel, multiple and contradictory.

There is no essential continuity between early twentieth-century feminist maternalism and National Socialist visions of women. Whereas in the femin-ist view, female 'difference' was the ground on which claims for women's 'equality' were based, National Socialist notions of race-based gender 'equality' and 'difference' were the ground on which 'racially inferior' women received a treatment which was equal to that of the men of their groups – persecution, sterilization and death. Moreover, the National Socialist notions allowed a number of 'racially superior' women to partici-pate in the development of the theory and practice of race policy. They did not act as mothers and wives, but acted on equal terms with the male agents of racism and in virtue of their extra-domestic roles. Hence, neither the female victims nor the female agents of National Socialist race policy inhab-ited a separate sphere dedicated to female 'difference'. Yet precisely this novel and 'monstrous equality' requires to be explored in terms of gender.

No image of essential female difference and no cult of motherhood were at the core of the National Socialist view and treatment of the female sex, nor was the image of women as mothers, where it appeared, specific to National Socialism. From its beginnings, National Socialism had broken with these images in many ways, most of all in its race policy. The essential and specific gender dimension of National Socialist birth policy did not consist in pro-natalism and a cult of motherhood, but in anti-natalism and a cult of fatherhood and masculinity.

In particular, it is impossible to conceive a more profound contrast than that between Himmler's view of Jewish women doomed to death by virtue of being (potential) mothers, and the visions of motherhood developed by the strong German Jewish feminist movement before 1933, at a time when it constituted a pillar of the moderate German women's movement. Jewish feminists had often pointed to the parallels between women's emancipation and Jewish emancipation, and had claimed the right to be different both as women and as Jews. One of their crucial concerns, similar to that of other contemporary women's movements, was the value of motherhood; this was perceived as one form of female 'difference' which had not been sufficiently protected and empowered and which had not yet had a chance to develop its own cultural forms. Like all the other western women's movements of that period, the German Jewish one had searched for a desirable relation between the recognition of women's equality and that of women's difference.[46]

National Socialism put an end to such efforts, a fact which suggests that modern racism and modern sexism have a parallel structure (even though Nazi sexism was largely traditional, whereas Nazi racism was both novel and deadly). Both deduce, from selected 'differences' among human beings, their 'inequality' in the sense of a hierarchy of values; and both measure 'inferiority' against the cultural norms of an allegedly 'superior' group. They deny the actually or allegedly different group not only the right to be 'equal', but also the right to be different without being punished for it: to live 'differently' in physical, emotional, mental – in short, in cultural – respects. As long as equality is understood as 'sameness' and difference as 'inferiority' – in terms of gender as well as of race – there is no space for human plurality, for the right and liberty to be different.

NOTES

1 H. Arendt, *The Jew as Pariah: Jewish Identity and Politics in the Modern Age*, ed. R. H. Feldman, New York, Grover Press, 1978, p. 160. She emphasized the importance of the fact that for National Socialism, anti-Semitism and racism were not only social but eminently political issues; see H. Arendt, *The Origins of Totalitarianism*, New York, Harcourt, Brace & World, 1966.
2 For references to this view see K. Offen, 'Defining feminism: a comparative historical approach', *Signs*, 14, 1988, p. 154.
3 D. Schoenbaum, *Hitler's Social Revolution: Class and Status in Nazi Germany, 1933–1939*, Garden City, NY, Doubleday, 1967, pp. 191–2.
4 L. J. Rupp, *Mobilizing Women for War: German and American Propaganda, 1939–1945*, Princeton, NJ, Princeton University Press, 1978, esp. chs 2, 3.
5 C. Huerkamp, 'Jüdische Akademikerinnen in Deutschland 1900–1938', forthcoming in *Geschichte und Gesellschaft*, 1993. For women's employment see D. Winkler, *Frauenarbeit im 'Dritten Reich'*, Hamburg, Hofmann & Campe, 1977; R. Hachtmann, *Industriearbeit im Dritten Reich*, Göttingen, Vandenhoeck & Ruprecht, 1989. For a comparable situation in the United States see A. Kessler-Harris, 'Gender ideology in historical reconstruction: a case study from the 1930s', *Gender and History*, 1, 1989, pp. 31–49.
6 G. Bock, *Zwangssterilisation im Nationalsozialismus: Studien zur Rassenpolitik und Frauenpolitik*, Opladen, Westdeutscher Verlag, 1986, pp. 160–1, 170–3.
7 H. F. K. Günther, 'Rassenkunde des jüdischen Volkes', appendix to H. F. K. Günther, *Rassenkunde des deutschen Volkes*, Munich, Lehmann, 1923, pp. 421–2; P. Schultze-Naumburg, 'Das Eheproblem in der nordischen Rasse', *Die Sonne*, 9(1), 1932, p. 25.

8 An exception is T. Wobbe (ed.), *Nach Osten: Die Verbrechen des Nationalsozialismus und die Verfolgung von Frauen*, Frankfurt, Neue Kritik, 1992.

9 S. Friedländer, 'Überlegungen zur Historisierung des Nationalsozialismus', in D. Diner (ed.), *Ist der Nationalsozialismus Geschichte? Zu Historisierung und Historikerstreit*, Frankfurt, Fischer, 1987, p. 35.

10 See the discussion in M. Broszat (ed.), *Deutschlands Weg in die Diktatur: Internationale Konferenz zur nationalsozialistischen Machtübernahme im Reichstagsgebäude zu Berlin. Referate und Diskussionen*, Berlin, Siedler, 1984, pp. 237–53.

11 C. Koonz, *Mothers in the Fatherland*, New York, St Martin's Press, 1987, pp. 6, 17, 405, 419.

12 ibid., pp. 181–3, 218–19.

13 K. Windaus-Walser, 'Gnade der weiblichen Geburt?', *Feministische Studien*, 1, 1988, p. 131.

14 H. Burkhardt, *Der rassenhygienische Gedanke und seine Grundlagen*, Munich, Reinhardt, 1930, p. 93.

15 A. Gütt, E. Rüdin and F. Ruttke, *Gesetz zur Verhütung erbkranken Nachwuchses vom 14. Juli 1933*, Munich, Lehmann, 1934, pp. 5, 176.

16 *Heinrich Himmler: Geheimreden 1933 bis 1945 und andere Ansprachen*, ed. B. F. Smith and A. F. Peterson, Frankfurt, Propyläen, 1974, pp. 54–5.

17 W. Feldscher (Ministry of the Interior), *Rassen- und Erbpflege im deutschen Recht*, Berlin, Deutscher Rechtsverlag, 1943, pp. 26, 118. See also K.-D. Bracher, 'Stufen der Machtergreifung', in K.-D. Bracher, W. Sauer and G. Schultz, *Die nationalsozialistische Machtergreifung*, Opladen, Westdeutscher Verlag, 1960, pp. 284–6; D. Majer, *'Fremdvölkische' im Dritten Reich*, Boppard, Boldt, 1981, pp. 103 ff., 180–1.

18 R. Pommerin, *'Sterilisierung der Rheinlandbastarde': Das Schicksal einer farbigen deutschen Minderheit 1918–1937*, Düsseldorf, Droste, 1979; Bock, *Zwangssterilisation*, pp. 358–60.

19 Information on these issues is available, among other sources, in around 200 doctoral dissertations accepted by medical faculties in the 1930s and 1940s which dealt with the sterilization mostly of women; see Bock, *Zwangssterilisation*, pp. 181–2, 372–81.

20 See ibid., pp. 384–8.

21 The available sources do not tell if some among these women were lesbians. Among thousands of cases, I have found only one where this was an issue. For the documents see ibid., pp. 389–401.

22 ibid., chs. 4 and 5.

23 Hundreds of thousands of denunciations were not passed on to the sterilization courts, but were included in the 'hereditary census' of the German people; its files, which were said to comprise 10 million entries by 1941, focused on persons with 'negative hereditary traits'. Many of the cases not handed to the courts were postponed for the time after the war.

24 H. Kessler, *'Die deutsche Frau': Nationalsozialistische Frauenpropaganda im Völkischen Beobachter*, Cologne, Pahl-Rugenstein, 1981, pp. 42 ff., 86 ff.

25 B. Friedan, *The Feminine Mystique*, New York, Dell, 1963, p. 32; T. Childers, *The Nazi Voter: The Social Foundation of Fascism in Germany, 1919–1933*, Chapel Hill, NC, North Carolina University Press, 1983, pp. 174, 189.

26 One example is E. Rüdin (ed.), *Erbpflege und Rassenhygiene im völkischen Staat*, Munich, Lehmann, 1934, pp. 8–9.

27 For documents see Bock, *Zwangssterilisation*, pp. 24–5, 122–5, 456–61 (instructions from the Propaganda Ministry, the views of the blood-and-soil ideo-

logue Richard Walther Darré, the head of the party's Race Office Walter Groß, *et al.*).
28 There were some good reasons for this belief. For instance, in 1934 the Kassel Secret Police reported that women were particularly hostile towards the sterilization law (Deutsches Zentralarchiv Potsdam, 15.01/26060, f. 297).
29 *Völkischer Beobachter*, 31 January 1934; E. von Barsewisch, *Die Aufgaben der Frau für die Aufartung (=Schriften des Reichsausschusses für Volksgesundheitsdienst, no.5)*, Berlin, Reichsdruckerei, 1933, pp. 13–14; A. Bluhm, 'Das Gesetz zur Verhütung erbkranken Nachwuchses', *Die Frau*, 41, 1934, pp. 529–38. For the journals of women's organizations see Bock, *Zwangssterilisation*, pp. 130–1; for this propaganda see also Christa Wolf, *Kindheitsmuster*, Darmstadt, Luchterhand, pp. 58–62.
30 G. Scholtz-Klink, *Die Frau im Dritten Reich: Eine Dokumentation*, Tübingen, Grabert, 1978, pp. 364, 402, 379. For her speech see Bock, *Zwangssterilisation*, p. 208.
31 See A. T. Allen, 'German radical feminism and eugenics, 1900–1918', *German Studies Review*, 11, 1989, pp. 45–6.
32 W. Frick, *Bevölkerungs- und Rassenpolitik (Schriften zur politischen Bildung, no. 12/1)*, Langensalza, Beyer, 1933.
33 H. Frank, lecture to the committee for race and population policy in the Ministry of the Interior, 1937 (Bundesarchiv Koblenz, R 61/130); Günther, *Rassenkunde*, pp. 274 ff., 345–6; Erich Hilgenfeldt to Bormann, reporting a conversation with Himmler in 1942 (Bundesarchiv Koblenz, NS 18/2427).
34 G. Bock and P. Thane (eds), *Maternity and Gender Policies: Women and the Rise of the European Welfare States, 1880s–1950s*, London, Routledge, 1991.
35 Bock, *Zwangssterilisation*, pp. 440–56.
36 R. J. Lifton, *The Nazi Doctors. Medical Killing and the Psychology of Genocide*, New York, Basic Books, 1986, p. 23.
37 H.-W. Schmuhl, *Rassenhygiene, Nationalsozialismus, Euthanasie: Von der Verhütung zur Vernichtung 'lebensunwerten' Lebens 1890–1945*, Göttingen, Vandenhoeck & Ruprecht, 1987, p. 40.
38 Lifton, *Nazi Doctors*, pp. 159, 462 (quotes); R. Hilberg, *The Destruction of the European Jews*, 3 vols, rev. and definitive edn, New York, Holmes & Meier, 1985, vol. 1, pp. 332–4; vol. 2, pp. 690–1; vol. 3, p. 871; J. M. Ringelheim, 'Verschleppung, Tod und Uberleben: Nationalsozialistische Politik gegen Frauen und Männer im besetzten Polen', in Wobbe, *Nach Osten*.
39 L. Adelsberger, *Auschwitz: Ein Tatsachenbericht*, Berlin, Lettner, 1956, p. 127 (quote); J. Ficowski, 'Die Vernichtung', in Tilman Zülch (ed.), *In Auschwitz vergast, bis heute verfolgt: Zur Situation der Roma (Zigeuner) in Deutschland und Europa*, Reinbek, Rowohlt, 1979, pp. 135–6; M. Richarz, *Jüdisches Leben in Deutschland*, vol. 3, Stuttgart, Deutsche Verlagsanstalt, 1982, p. 61; E. Kogon *et al.* (ed), *Nationalsozialistische Massentötungen durch Giftgas*, Frankfurt, S. Fischer, 1986, pp. 88–97, 105–8, 122, 131, 134, 158, 210–15.
40 H. Arendt, 'The image of hell', *Commentary*, 2–3, 1946, pp. 291–5. For her reflections on the concept 'equality' see also her *Origins of Totalitarianism*, chs 1, 9.
41 Quoted in H. G. Adler, *Der verwaltete Mensch: Studien zur Deportation der Juden aus Deutschland*, Tübingen, Mohr, 1974, pp. 63–4.
42 *Heinrich Himmler*, pp. 169, 201.
43 Himmer's 'logic' resembled that which had led to the sterilization of equal numbers of women and men which proved so fatal for women. This kind of 'logic' has been brilliantly analysed by Arendt, *Origins of Totalitarianism*, ch. 13.
44 E. Jäckel, 'Die elende Praxis der Untersteller', in *Historikerstreit*, Munich, Piper,

1987, pp. 118/19; E. Nolte, 'Die Sache auf den Kopf gestellt', ibid., p. 229, argues that mentioning women here 'merely unfolds what can be more briefly expressed with the term "race murder"'.

45 For a different view – that these women 'did not affect the workings of the Nazi state' – see Koonz, *Mothers*, p. 405.

46 M. A. Kaplan, *The Jewish Feminist Movement in Germany: The Campaigns of the Jüdischer Frauenbund, 1904–1938*, Westport, Conn., Greenwood Press, 1979; Offen, 'Defining feminism', in this volume; Bock and Thane, *Maternity*; A. T. Allen, *Feminism and Motherhood in Germany, 1800–1914*, New Brunswick, N.J., Rutgers University Press, 1991.

Chapter 6

The power and powerlessness of women

Jean Bethke Elshtain

Before I begin, let me indicate that it is *not* the task of the political theorist to tell people 'what is to be done'; rather, our vocation, as Hannah Arendt articulated it, is to *think* what we are doing. And, I would add, to serve as a moral witness to the perils and possibilities of our times.

What follows is a reflection on power and powerlessness, on the who and the what of it, or at least a bit of it. I begin with a conundrum: women are and have been powerful; women are and have been powerless. There is no contradiction here. Instead we find a resonant paradox, an ambiguity that seeps through all reflective attempts to confront 'the powerlessness of women'. In recent decades, to be sure, important commentators reflecting various feminist positions often ignored or denied associations of women with images of authority, potency and power, concentrating instead on women's historic oppression, 'second-class citizenship' and, in the view of some, universal victimization.

There were many rhetorical and political reasons for this focus in recounting the story of women in culture and history. But in telling only one side of the story the commentators to whom I shall offer a counterpoint sometimes wound up portraying women as so uniformly and universally downtrodden, demeaned, infantilized and coerced that men came to seem invincible, individually and collectively terrifying in their power and their intent to oppress. It was hard to see how women might emerge from the shadows, confronted, as they were, by such an implacably hostile external force. The 'oppressed group model', as Kathleen Jones has described it,

> tended to present a one-dimensional view of women's experiences that denied categorically that there was anything redemptive, or politically valuable about them. Ironically, this view incorporated the devaluation of women's experiences, and accepted the patriarchal reading of the significance of women's lives it claimed to be criticizing.[1]

Yet women themselves really knew – and *know* – better, whatever the reigning ideology might dictate. We know that we are not wholly without resources as we bring our personal and political authority to bear on complex social situations. We know that we have various 'means' to attain at least some of our desired 'ends'. We know that our foremothers bequeathed to us much more than a sustained tale of woe. We contemporary women are the heirs of centuries of women's stories and strengths, all the many narratives of perseverance and survival, of determination to 'go on' through tragedies and defeats. We know our mothers and grandmothers often had laughter in their hearts, songs on their lips and pride in their identities. Knowing this, we cannot accept any account that demeans women in the name of taking the measure of our powerlessness.

A confession: It is difficult for me to think of women as powerless in any total sense. I am a child of the rural American west, the state of Colorado. If one has seen either one's grandmother or mother or aunts drive a tractor, load cattle for market, organize a charity drive, manage the household finances, kill a rattlesnake, start a small business, purchase a truck, act as a midwife, make clothing out of flour sacks, preserve fruits and vegetables for a family for the winter, break ice in sub-zero weather so the cattle can drink, stand for election to the governing body of the local school district, get a high-school diploma through an extension course, become a citizen at the age of 65, make determined stands on a number of issues ranging from where the family will live to what job the husband-father should take and what would be too disruptive to the family, one shares with the American writer Alice Walker a tradition that assumes women are capable. Yet we also know that our foremothers did not – save for a few extraordinary and rare royal leaders – run countries, fight wars, explore and conquer new lands, make the laws and enforce them, nor determine the shape of official, bureaucratic arrangements in the modern world. They were neither industrialists nor generals, presidents nor judges, political theorists nor polity founders. Women do not figure in the canon of Hegel's 'world historic figures'.

Our legacy is riddled with ambiguities. Our thinking about this legacy must grapple with a double-edge: power and powerlessness. In this discussion I shall not go over by now familiar ground, all the data on earning disparities, sexual victimization, lopsided poverty and institutional invisibility. I assume that we all know these social facts. I presume the reader shares some general recognition of the structural dimensions of women's social and economic powerlessness. But this is just the beginning of the story. Facts never 'speak for themselves'. We use them to tell stories. We locate them inside wider webs of meaning and significance. Our conceptual frameworks turn on the way we understand key terms, most importantly 'power' itself.

DEFINING POWER: WHY POLITICAL SCIENTISTS HAVE MISSED SO MUCH

I teach in a Department of Political Science. But I describe myself as 'a political theorist, *not* a political scientist'. The self-understanding embedded in my ongoing effort to distance myself from the label 'political scientist' is no mere quirk. For those among my colleagues in the United States who assume the authority of 'science' believe that terms of political discourse, including power, can be defined and understood 'operationally'. To this end, such inescapable concepts as 'power' get reduced to stipulative defi-nitions that enable the researcher, so the story goes, to formulate and to test hypotheses on whether, and to what extent, power is operative in a particu-lar instance.

Thus the definition of power developed initially in mainstream American political science got reduced to the formula: X has power over Y if he can get Y to do something Y would not otherwise do. We can observe Y's behaviour and assess the force X brought to bear. The locus for such observations is extant 'decision-making', political institutions, whether national, state or local governing bodies, or organized associations that aim to influence such bodies – corporations, unions, 'interest groups'. Power is a form of com-pulsion exerted by the already (relatively) powerful upon one another within official political institutions designed to promote the aims and interests of competing groups. It is of, by and for elites.

Power as a form of direct pressure on a social actor to perform a specific action here becomes a 'thing in itself', measurable like amps on an electricity meter. There is no room in this discourse for moral debate or judgement. Interesting and important as such debates might be, they have no legitimate role to play in scientific politics. Values are one thing; facts and nothing-but-the-facts are another. Within the larger political vision presumed by this one-dimensional view of power, women got construed as apolitical beings by definition. The argument was really quite simple. Women and men have different social roles. The social role of women promotes a value-system based upon women's 'life experiences' inside non-political areas of social relations – marriage, the family, religious and communal associations. Not occupying decision-making roles and arenas, women are severed from the give and take of interest-group politics and its rule-governed power broker-age. Women are neither the X's with power-over nor the Y's whose behav-iour is compelled. Women do not figure in the geometry of power relations. Even voting by women is essentially an apolitical activity, a means whereby women, who tend to be moralists hence conservative, support those political parties that appear to confirm their values rather than promote their interests. Promoting interests is a political activity; preserving values is non-political.

Pinioned inside this discourse of tautologically confirmed and confirming meanings, women faced a perpetual double bind. Concerns which arose from their position in the private sphere, including the health, education and welfare of children, were construed as mere expressions of personal values and moralistic concern. But hard-nosed realistic talk about power from women meant they had forfeited the right to represent to or within the public sphere the private world they had by definition forsaken when they chose to locate themselves as political beings.[2]

Recognizing the conceptual shortcomings and political complacency of this once prevailing view, a few rebellious analysts worked to broaden the scope of analysis by extending the meaning of power. One important attempt along these lines, by two political scientists, yielded an alternative formula. Power, they argued, is not limited to X making a decision that compels Y but in X's devoting himself to limiting the scope of political decision-making to consideration of only those issues he finds non-threatening. Power may be operative when no specific behaviour or action is discernible, for one tacit aim of those who wield official power is to *preclude* action and to forestall debate. Thus it is that some issues are organized into politics and some are not. Those that are not remain 'private discontents' outside the purview of public policy. The unacknowledged face of power enables the powerful to deny that politics is involved in many situations and outcomes, because no overt, public conflict has occurred.

This second, more complex definition of power, although it retained an institutional focus on decision-makers, opened up some important questions. It directed the attention of researchers to how and why some questions get defined as 'political' while others do not. It helped analysts see that every social order is sustained in ways sometimes hidden from public scrutiny and accountability. It disrupted the complacency with which mainstream political scientists justified non-participation in political life by assuring themselves that those who did not participate in politics were those for whom participation was not a value. That is, ignorant, indifferent or satisfied persons or groups preferred the value of non-participation by definition. If they reckoned participation highly, they would participate. There are, after all, no legal barriers to running for office, joining a party, becoming a lobbyist, promoting one's interests. Even among men *homo politicus* is a relatively rare animal. The majority of working-class men, for example, are not politically active because their values dictate non-participation. The same is true of all but a few women – their values locate them outside the realm of politics proper. Not necessarily so, suggested proponents of the two-dimensional understanding of power.

All this seems very abstract, 'academic' indeed. But academic debates exert real effects on the lives of real people, given the power to 'name' and to define that we lodge in experts. To insist that women play and have played no political role from a standpoint that offers a full-blown rationalization for their – and others' – non-participation is to justify a social order while claiming merely to describe it. Thus it is that congealed political realities get refracted through thought in a mutually reinforcing relationship. Those defined outside the boundaries of concern confront not only institutional barriers but unreflective analyses that 'name' them in ways they themselves have not chosen. Perhaps I have said enough to signal my dissatisfaction with understandings inherited from positivist political science if we would think in supple ways about women's power and powerlessness. Does political theory, that enterprise with which I associate myself, do any better?

THINKING ABOUT POWER THEORETICALLY

Rousseau, it seems, knew something. For it was Rousseau who proclaimed that those who separate politics from morals must fail to understand both. A detour through the past in the form of those texts that comprise the canon of western political thought yields many riches. This tradition is not of a piece, encompassing Aristotle and Aquinas, Augustine and John Stuart Mill, Machiavelli and Marx. It offers multiple understandings of power, its meaning, its range of application, its legitimate and illegitimate uses, its relation to authority, justice and political order. A few western political theorists took up 'the woman question' explicitly; most did not. But even those who did not still instruct us through their omissions and their sometimes tortuous attempts to explain and justify the political powerlessness of women or, perhaps better, women's non-political being and identity.

I cannot recount this centuries-long tale here.[3] Most important for our consideration are the many 'power' words in classical languages, a plethora of contrasting, sometimes overlapping, sometimes competing meanings. For power had not yet been shrunk down to meet the requirements of secularized and scientized analysis. Thus we find *imperium*, *virtus*, *arete*, *potestas*, *potentia*, *dynamis* and more.[4] Power is construed variously as creative energy, as ritual, as force, as legality. The dictionary (*OED*) reflects this kaleidoscopic conceptual inheritance. 'Power' occupies a full column divided into three major categories of usage: as 'a quality or property', as 'the ability to do something or anything, or to act upon a person or thing' or as 'a particular faculty of body or mind', 'the ability to act or affect something strongly; physical or mental strength; vigour, energy, force of character'.

Within the relational, contextual and shifting boundaries of power as used and understood in political and social life historically, women can be seen as having the ability to act upon a person or thing, particularly children, hence as powerful. Besides, individual women certainly possessed faculties of body or mind that offered them 'the ability to affect something strongly'. We know this from folklore and sober history alike.

Yet neither women as a group nor individual women could leap over embedded constraints on the form and scope of their power. Women could be saints but not popes, queens but not legislators, angels of mercy but not warriors of death. Whether our historic forebears regarded such constraints as unacceptable is not an easy question. Not holding our ideas of power and equality, not being members of a modern secular society that celebrates individual choice and downgrades community obligation, what strikes us as intolerable no doubt seemed to the overwhelming majority of our pre-modern ancestors part of nature's plan and God's design. Women were authoritative in ways men were not; men governed in ways women did not. (It is important to remember that male 'choices' and roles were restricted and constrained too, although, from our vantage point, men in general and men of the ruling stratum in particular appear to have had a good deal more pomp in their circumstances than similarly placed women.)

If one takes an even longer view of the story of power, before Plato, Aristotle and the self-conscious beginnings of political thought, sacred, mythopoeic usages predominate. For power is indispensable to various ways of thinking about things – not only politics but God and the sacred. Political meanings in the west got layered upon older, mythic understandings, potent images of ritual, taboo, the demonic, the sacred. 'Thine', says the Old Testament, 'is . . . the power, and the glory'. This is reflected in the *OED*, in which power as a characteristic of political or national strength is a usage dating from 1701; a 'late use', claims the dictionary, and one preceded by 'a celestial or spiritual being having control or influence; a divinity'.

Whether and to what extent women were powerful or powerless, silenced or heard, revered or reviled in past societies, western and non-western, is an assignment for a lifetime. We do know certain things, however. Every human society differentiates maleness from femaleness and widely differing societies have located complementary forms of power in the two sexes. Historic and ethnographic evidence suggests that women's economic and political power and authority are most likely to occur where one finds a 'magico-religious association between maternity and fertility of the soil', thus associating women 'with social continuity and social good'.[5] Cultural anthropologists argue that, in societies like the Iroquois, for example, where women wielded great power in some areas as men did in others, to view male and female authority as sexually unequal reflects a western, state bias. Dozens of societies, they insist, were worlds in which neither sex was wholly dominant over the other, but each prevailed in demarcated areas of social life.

'Were' may be inapposite here. Recent scholarship suggests that such societies, whose lives run as subtexts within the dominant narrative order, retain this mode of complementarity. In her introduction to Marla N. Powers, *Oglala Women: Myth, Ritual and Reality*, Catharine Stimpson writes:

Powers argues that Oglala society rebukes the theory that gender is a hierarchy universally demanding female subordination, a theory that women's studies has frequently found plausible. Particularly today, Oglala women may devise a fiction of male superiority. In actuality, relations between female and male tend to be 'complementary,' with female and male roles having equal strength and power. For the Oglalas and for their traditions, sexual difference breeds mutual respect.[6]

One thread that seems to run through the tangle of historic and ethnographic evidence is a picture of *formal* male power being balanced or even undermined by *informal* female power. Myths of male dominance are often maintained when males do not actually dominate in the secure ways the myths proclaim. In peasant societies, for example, beneath the appearance of total male dominance lies a complex reality in which women exercise effective control over many aspects of community life and men are not allowed to interfere.[7]

In societies, past and present, in which 'the home' is the hub of human life, an arena of economic production as well as human procreation, a school, a hospice, a clinic, a symbolically and actually potent place, women are often the repositories of several understandings of power associated with that sphere. Such female power is complementary to the more institutionalized, 'political' and juridical authority of men. As one cultural anthropologist writes: 'The roles and power ascribed to women are informal and uninstitutionalized in contrast with the culturally legitimated statuses and authority attributed to men.'[8]

What are we to make of all this? We cannot return to pre-secular, pre-modern ways of life. But we can see that secular male dominance is most visible in societies in which complementarity of powers has given way to an enhancement and expansion of institutionalized male authority accompanied by a simultaneous diminution of women's domestic, sacral and informal authority. As the world of female power recedes, the sphere of male power encroaches, absorbing more and more features of social life into the orbit of the juridico-political, the bureaucratized, the 'legitimately' powerful: the state. Women are left with few apparent options: to acquiesce in their historic loss of symbolic-domestic authority; to manipulate their diminished social role as mothers inside increasingly powerless families; or to join forces with the men, assuming masculine roles and identities and competing for power on established, institutionalized terms. For if one embraces a strong version of the teleology of historic progress we have inherited from the Enlightenment, with its attendant ontology that locates 'women' on the negative side of the ledger along with nature, emotion and passion, one has little choice but to leap into the arms of the hegemonic discourse and to embrace the already established vision of the free, rational, wholly independent male self and his powers and power.

If none of these options seems particularly attractive, perhaps we must rethink the terms of our current situation. I am searching for a language that helps us to see that dependence and independence, powerlessness and power, are deeply related and that not all forms of dependence or human vulnerability can or should be jettisoned or rationalized out of our theories and our ways of being in the world. Knowing that women have been powerful in many times and places, recognizing that women have not been uniformly subjugated and powerless, we are invited to search for new forms of public and private power. As our focus shifts from obsession with images of female victimization, we recognize the often terrible costs of being the institutionally and politically powerful sex. For is it not ironic that the dominant sex has also been the most expendable – that, historically, male bodies were sent into battle to kill and to die in order that female bodies of their own group be protected? Do we not convey a peculiar double message to our own 18-year-old sons whose social power and social vulnerability are signalled by registration for the draft?

Such recognitions spawn competing responses. To many contemporary feminists, being powerful means assuming legitimate authority as well as male political and military responsibility. They proclaim a 'right to fight'. Other feminists seek to create a society modelled on female principles, one in which all male-constituted social and political forms are destroyed and a wholly new order dominated by women prevails: matriarchy must supplant patriarchy. Many women who do not identify as feminists yearn for a return to traditional complementarities in which they were provided for, looked after and sheltered from the grim realities of the 'rat race' and the shocks of political combat. (This dream can be dreamt only by middle- to upper-middle-class women. Poor women, black women, working-class women were never sheltered in this way.) But western political theory, that is to say, ideas within the grasp of those of us constituted in part by the social absorption and authorization of categories central to the tradition I here evoke, may harbour the tentative promise of another way.

TOWARDS A REFLECTIVE UNDERSTANDING OF POWER AND POWERLESSNESS

Potestas, one Latin term for power, especially political power, control, supremacy or dominion. *Potentia*, another Latin term for power understood as might or ability, efficacy, potency, especially 'unofficial and sinister'. Fascinatingly, these contrasting usages demarcate historically roughly the boundaries of male and female forms of power.[9] Males have been the official wielders of institutional power and dominion; women the unofficial (hence potentially uncontrollable) repositories of non-legitimate, 'non-political' power. *Potentia* may conjure up the sinister, threatening and deviant, occupying a boundary that touches on the polluted, the uncanny, the potentially disordered.

But suppose we put another spin on this matter. Suppose that what we, you and I, have to fear is not so much the uncontrolled, because uninstitutionalized, power of the now-powerless but the over-controlled ministrations of the institutionally powerful. Suppose the institutional forms designed to limit, contain and curb excesses of power are themselves increasingly powerless. Suppose the powerful are daily disempowered by the very magnitude of the force at their disposal. Suppose what has become of dominion is not so much the power to act as a compulsion to react.

No doubt this supposes too much. But suppose my suppositions are even partly true. What are the implications? The most dire, perhaps, is that highly institutionalized forms of government, increasingly bureaucratized and dominated by technologies that facilitate centralized control, daily erode space for genuine political action, for beginning something anew, for creating and sustaining social forms that allow human beings to be at home in the world. Worshipping penultimate power and fantasies of perfect control, we find ourselves dominated by our 'tools', our instrumentalities of violence, genuflecting at the restlessly moving altar of consumerist fantasy, obsessively seeking 'more' and 'better' and 'the best'.

Psychiatrists speak of 'nuclearism'. Some scientists foresee the coming of a 'nuclear winter' and others conjure with the stuff of life itself: genetic engineering, it is called. Missiles proliferate. Enmities are shored up by the daily repetition of warlike rhetoric. Acid rain falls. Toxic waste stagnates. Species are added to the endangered list. Teenagers in North America commit suicide in epidemic proportions. Who are we? What have we become? Powerful/powerless: does it matter? Are we not more and more 'equalized' as potential victims of the historic quest for power as control in the west?

The answer is a 'yes' that must be deployed with caution. To give in too fully to the apocalyptic mode tempts us to allow full play to our most deeply rooted apprehensions, thereby blinding us to possibilities that may lie within our reach. Ends – it has become a truism – are also beginnings. I am searching for an alternative here – a vision of power as productive, as an incitement to both discourse and action. An enticing project for feminist theory and women's studies might be to trace historically or, better, genealogically paradigms of 'the female' and 'the mother' that have served as catalysts for action and sources of female authority, on the one hand, and, on the other, those paradigms that constrained, inviting privatization and pettiness of purpose. And then, of course, one must go on to offer critical reflection on these exemplars. One example would be the strength of the reincoded image of the Spartan mother which has located women in the social and political world and served as a source of meaning and civic power, but, simultaneously, reinscribed the centrality of war-making, what I tag 'armed civic virtue' in my recent book, *Women and War*, in the grand narrative of the west.[10]

A central feature of the engendered power I am urging upon us is that it have within it the means to put earthly force and dominion on trial and evaluate it with reference to certain moral ends. This means, minimally, that the realm of necessity, the world of everyday human meaning and life, no longer be either despised or defined as the unworthy mirror to the freedom of politics. In classical antiquity, the exclusionary *polis* and coercively universal empire got supplanted by the ideal of a universalist egalitarianism to be instantiated in particular, redefined communities. Although this heady moral revolution failed to secure earthly peace and justice, its promise of a peaceable kingdom lives on wherever men and women refuse to make peace with making war; wherever love and care are gifts freely given, not revocable allowances that may be stingily recalled; wherever the power to forgive is reckoned at least on a par with the power to punish.

Some interesting historic parallels are called to mind by this historic fragment: if the early Christian man or woman was a 'fool' to the received 'wisdom' of the powerful and worldly, women have been constituted an 'everlasting irony' in the bosom of social life (Hegel); a potential threat to 'that which makes the city one' (Plato); a temptation to forsake civic virtue (Rousseau); a brake on the process of civilization given their devotion to the particular (Freud). Perhaps women are the 'fools' in western political thought and practice whose official powerlessness grants them a paradoxical freedom: freedom from full assimilation into the prevailing public identity whose aims, in our day, are efficiency and control. This freedom may invite despair as one's dreams of becoming a surgeon, a president or an electrical engineer evaporate in the harsh realities of competitive and male-dominated worlds. This freedom may invite bitter disgust as one fears daily that one's children may lack food and clothing and even minimal safety. Nevertheless ... if at least partial exclusion from wholesale absorption into the terms of institutional power is maintained, space for critical reflection and challenge to that power is more likely to be sustained.

Power and politics, yes, but what forms of power, what sorts of politics? I will phrase this as a difficulty, another conundrum if you will, borrowed from the Czech resister and writer Vaclav Havel: the politics of the power of the powerless, or resistance in the face of the radical absence of choice. What Havel and the brilliant Polish dissident and theorist of Solidarnosc, Adam Michnik, have to offer to a consideration of gender and power is just this: they remind us that to continue to think boringly in the inherited categories of right/left, progressive/regressive is, in Havel's words, to give one a 'sense of emerging from the depth of the last century'. He writes: 'It seems to me that these thoroughly ideological and many times mystified categories have long since been beside the point.'[11] Certainly such binary opposites must fail to capture the complexity of feminist reflection and cannot come close to the content of our actual beliefs and actions.

In language that makes contact with contemporary feminist awareness of, and emphasis upon, difference and plurality, Havel insists that between the aims of what he calls the 'post-totalitarian system' or what I dub, more generally, monological statism, there lies a

> yawning abyss: while life, in its essence, moves towards plurality, diversity, independent self-constitution and self-organization, the post-totalitarian system demands conformity, uniformity, and discipline . . . the post-totalitarian system . . . is utterly obsessed with the need to bind everything in a single order.[12]

Human identity is surrendered to the homogenized identity of the system. Havel calls this 'social auto-totality', a system that depends on demoralization and cannot survive without it.

What parts of the movements in Prague and Gdansk have in common with some strands of contemporary feminist and post-modernist discourse is to eschew categories with which many remain all too comfortable, to refuse to privilege the state and, in a sense, to worship the state by continuing unambiguously to valorize its sovereignty. As feminists explore and search for forms of power that do not replicate 'business as usual', one powerful reality must be kept in mind: war is immanent within the form of the modern nation-state. To hope that one might use the state as a vast instrumentality to be turned to 'our' good ends and purposes unambiguously is to be naïve and, paradoxically, to find oneself supporting practices that subvert the democratic-egalitarian core of feminism.

Also, with their insistence that a movement's style of action, including a refusal to deploy base methods in order to be effective and to respect the dignity of those they oppose, feminists and those involved in comparable political movements make contact with a political vision that acknowledges the vulnerability of, and need to nurture, all new beginnings, including those of a political sort. This may seem a weak and problematic creed if one is to protest at the current breaking of bodies and minds, literally and figuratively, in the politics of our troubled epoch, but it is, I believe, the point from which we should begin.

I discovered or, perhaps, *learned* this lesson anew in the hours I spent with members of the Mothers of the Plaza de Mayo in Buenos Aires, Argentina, in August 1986. The Mothers, by their public presence and courageous action, shattered the systematic deceit that had shrouded the disappearances of their children; they transgressed official orders by marching in the plaza. 'Las locas', the madwomen, they were called – beyond the pale, outside the boundaries of legitimate politics. Yes, we are crazy, they said, turning the epithet on its head. They reversed the strategy of the authorities and fashioned it into a political weapon. The language they spoke was double: the language of the anguish of a mother's loss and the language of human rights.

Here are fragments of one of our exchanges:

J.B.E.:   Do you expect to go on indefinitely?

Maria Adela de Antokaletz: What we want and think is that the Mothers of the Plaza de Mayo must endure for ever, much more than in our own lifetimes. It has to do with having a guardian position on society in order to watch so this will not happen again. Not here, not anywhere.

Renée S. de Epelbaum: To watch and to denounce. Perhaps it won't be necessary for us to go to the plaza if the criminals are punished. But we want to witness, to denounce every violation of human rights. Because, you know, at the beginning, we only wanted our children. But, as time passed, we got a different comprehension of what was going on in the world. Today I was listening to the radio and there was somebody who sings very well who was singing about children, about babies starving. This is also a violation of human rights. Perhaps it is not much that we can do, but people for human dignity and human rights must realize justice where they can.

And Maria Adela de Antokaletz went on to tell me, to emphasize, that the struggle they had carried out had always had a 'clear moral purpose' and had 'always been non-violent and carried out with dignity'. What Solidarnosc as a movement shares with the Mothers (and, by implication, with the feminism towards which I am moving) is a repudiation of the false transcendence of violence; a rejection of any order built on doubles and mirrors by which one keeps alive that by which one feels threatened. The aim of Las Madres and Solidarnosc was to liberate themselves by refusing to sacralize any new victims. 'Neither maggots nor angels', Adam Michnik says – no one is utterly repulsive; no one utterly good.[13] They revealed the reincoded seductions of mimetic violence in order to break its spell. There is a truth here: not a big, booming, grandly teleological Truth, but a truth that does not allow him or her who has grasped it to serve as judge and executioner. And there is something of the nature of the Fool as well, one who refuses to conform to the wisdom of the world, whose folly reveals the established lunacy of princes, whose identities are a break against deadening normalizations.

The last voice to be heard in this overlong meditation will be a woman's, but one who saw herself first and foremost as a citizen and a political philosopher: these essentially defined her, Hannah Arendt proclaimed, but gender did not. Yet Arendt challenges received notions of political beginnings presented as the actions of male hordes of contractualists, warring or pillaging until compelled by fear or self-interest to seek civic order. Such accounts of political founding deny the realities of human social beginnings from the bodies of women and from the fragile bodies of children. Not so Arendt, who embraces a metaphor of birth. Seeking the ontological root of hope, the human capacity that sustains political being and our capacity to act, Arendt finds it 'in the fact of natality'. Her metaphor, most fully elaborated in the following passage from *The Human Condition*, is worth quoting in full:

> The miracle that saves the world, the realm of human affairs, from its normal, 'natural' ruin is ultimately the fact of natality, in which the faculty of action is ontologically rooted. It is, in other words, the birth of new men and the new beginning, the action they are capable of by virtue of being born. Only the full experience of this capacity can bestow upon human affairs faith and hope, those two essential characteristics of human existence . . . It is this faith in and hope for the world that found perhaps its most glorious and most succinct expression in the few words with which the Gospels announced their 'glad tidings': 'A child has been born unto us.'[14]

The infant, like all beginnings, is vulnerable. We nurture that beginning, neither knowing, nor being able to control, the 'end' of the story. Birth is a 'miracle' that renews and irreversibly alters the world. Arendt's configuration stirs recognition of our own vulnerabilities and necessary dependency on others. And it offers, as well, a form of reason that rejects subduing and mastering others as essential to the attainment of one's own power and status as a human being.

Women, in and through their powerlessness, understand what it means to be vulnerable. Their openness to beginnings, even under conditions of hardship and privation, terror and torture, has daily renewed the world, making possible future beginnings. The challenge for women at this fateful juncture is to keep alive memories of vulnerability as they struggle to overcome structurally sanctioned inefficacy and to reaffirm rather than repudiate interdependencies as they seek a measure of institutional 'legitimacy'. That I here call for a heroism that cannot reasonably be morally binding (for none of us is required to perform repeated acts of supererogation) may be true. That I impose a weighty political burden on women, and that this is in some sense unfair, is no doubt also true. That women alone cannot give civic birth to a transformed politics is undoubtedly the case. But women, from a double vision that straddles powerlessness and power, are in a powerful position to insist with Albert Camus that one must never avert one's eyes from the suffering of children and, seeing that suffering, one is required to act.

What images of power, then, locate us as beings who are called to reflection and action, beings receptive to others yet firm in our sense of ourselves? There is a lot about human beings that is messy and uncontrolled, helpless before the wintry blasts, but there is also something about us that searches for reason and meaning and requires action. Our understanding of power must grasp the complexities of our all-too-human nature.

Now: what has all this to do with the theme of this volume, namely, gender, equality and difference? I must build the argument piece by piece. To assume, with the 'oppressed group model', that powerlessness is a given of women as a universal class or category, and that this powerlessness is well nigh absolute in relation to the all-powerful class or category male, is simultaneously to affirm an image of women's 'difference' as a mark of inequality. The 'equal', in such a scheme, can only be construed as 'the same as' the powerful class or group. Equality, that is, is a relation that pertains only among the powerful and only in relation to a universally unequal, powerless class whose difference condemns them to an inequality that is systematically and officially denied.

But if one shifts the terms of the discussion a bit by moving away from the presumption of an absolute dichotomy between powerful/powerless, one's views on equality/difference must also shift. As one focuses on the many forms and faces of power, one comes to understand power as a set of relations. As the late Michel Foucault insisted, power should not be construed as some totalistic, oppressive system that bears down from 'on high' and exists to forbid and to prohibit. Such an absolutely crystallized power system of pure and continuing force has never existed. Even in the most dire situations, there is more nuance and fluidity. Indeed, with Hannah Arendt one must insist that control by brute force is a move away from power into some other mode and that mode is necessarily terribly unstable and destructive. Thinking of power as both *potestas* and *potentia*, as institutions that attempt to congeal certain relations of power, even as power of a more dynamic, potentially subversive sort, works in ways never fully controllable by *potestas*, opens up considerations of equality and difference, helping us to see that these terms cannot and should not be posed as absolute antinomies.

Just as power can take a number of forms and is not always repressive, just as power relations are reversible and revisable, so the difference/equality debate is notoriously unstable and endlessly contestable. Programmatic definitions are almost always worthless. The best way to proceed is through concrete example and interpretation. If one begins by refusing to accept an antithesis between equality and difference, the debate opens up in interesting ways. To be sure, the officially, juridically powerful have been in a stronger position to dominate the discourse of equality – what must one be to be 'equal'? – than those not similarly placed. Then the question is: must the new woman become the old man in order to be 'equal'? Only if one assumes that equality is necessarily a discourse of 'the same', of 'the male', and one in turn valorizes 'difference' as the discourse of women.

As I struggled with this matter conceptually, a very specific instance of the interplay of the discourse of equality and difference came to me. I thought of my own retarded daughter, now a young adult, so the reader should consider that the mark of 'difference' at work here is that of developmentally disabled or different. I can track four stages in the discourse of equality and difference as it pertains to the developmentally disabled. (a) The retarded are outside the discourse of equality altogether, having been marginalized and 'named' by the more powerful as lacking the qualities necessary to have any part in the world of equality and inequality, the world of juridical and civic relations. Their 'difference' by definition disqualifies them. (b) The retarded are drawn within the circle of concern of those who do have a civic identity, who are part of the discourse of equality. They become the recipients of concern. Their welfare must be seen to. But they are not yet participants in the discourse of equality. (c) The retarded, in and through their representatives, make claims upon the 'equal', arguing that they, too, have the 'qualifications' to be part of the discourse. They, too, can vote, hold jobs, etc. They are included in the discourse, but only in so far as they can make the case that they are not as 'different' as was once assumed. (d) Finally, the retarded find their own voice and insist that, in fact, they can never be the normalized subject of the discourse of equality in its canonized form but this difference does not sever them from equality. They struggle to make the case for equality with respect for difference. The language shifts – to developmentally different. Equality, or entering the discourse of equality, does not conduce here to homogeneity or 'the same'. Instead, equality remains a powerful term of political discourse and an instrument for social change and justice, one of the strongest weapons the (relatively) powerless have at their disposal in order to make their case and define their claims.

Perhaps this little parable of the steps in the evolving discourse of difference/equality and powerlessness/power as they pertain to the mentally different holds lessons for feminist scholars. It suggests that reversals and the valorization of that which was marginalized proffer short-term satisfaction but little by way of concrete, political engagement and an incitement to social change and commitment. Instead, grappling with those powerful terms of political discourse that *necessarily* define politics in the west is an unavoidable task. Something else is here intimated about how we do our work. It is ironic that those who seek to dismantle the grand theoretical systems of the Enlightenment sometimes do so in an abstract, hyper-theoretical way. Far better, it seems to me, to theorize practices and to engage in theoretical practices. This helps us to keep our feet on the ground and to avoid the systematizing delusions that have plagued western philosophy. What is good, just, equal, respectful of difference and open to the play of power relations is determined in the actual daily practices of countless individuals. The intellectual is part of this process, not above it.

NOTES

1 K. B. Jones, 'Aspects of citizenship in a woman-friendly polity', unpublished MS, p. 9.
2 See e.g. S. M. Lipset, *Political Man: The Social Bases of Politics*, Garden City, NY, Doubleday Anchor, 1963, pp. 216–17.
3 In *Public Man, Private Woman: Women in Social and Political Thought*, Princeton, NJ, Princeton University Press, 1981, I offer the unabridged story.

4 D. Emmet, 'The concept of power', in J. K. Champlin (ed.), *Power*, New York, Atherton, 1971, pp. 78–106, illumines these many meanings.
5 P. R. Sandy, *Male Dominance and Female Power*, Cambridge, Cambridge University Press, 1981, p. 155.
6 C. Stimpson, 'Foreword' to M. N. Powers, *Oglala Women: Myth, Ritual and Reality*, Chicago, University of Chicago Press, 1987, p. xii.
7 See e.g. M. Segalen, *Love and Power in the Peasant Family*, Chicago, University of Chicago Press, 1983.
8 J. Taylor, *Eva Peron: The Myths of a Woman*, Chicago, University of Chicago Press, 1971, p. 13.
9 I am not suggesting that the Romans had this in mind explicitly; rather, I am claiming that the weight of ethnographic evidence pushes towards these contrasting definitions and locates males lopsidedly inside one, females inside the other.
10 See the full discussion in J. B. Elshtain, *Women and War*, New York, Basic Books, 1987.
11 Vaclav Havel *et al.*, *The Power of the Powerless: Citizens against the State in Central Eastern Europe*, Armonk, NY, M. E. Sharpe, 1985, p. 59.
12 ibid., p. 72.
13 See A. Michnik, *Letters from Prison and Other Essays*, Berkeley, Calif., University of California Press, 1985, p. 169.
14 H. Arendt, *The Human Condition*, Chicago, University of Chicago Press, 1958, p. 247.

Chapter 7

Female identity between sexuality and maternity

Silvia Vegetti Finzi

Il y a nulle parité entre les deux sexes quant à la conséquence du sexe. Le mâle n'est mâle qu'en certains instants, la femelle est femelle toute sa vie ou du moins toute sa jeunesse; tout la rapelle sans cesse à son sexe.

Jean-Jacques Rousseau, 1782[1]

First, are you our sort of a person?
Do you wear
A glass eye, false teeth or a crutch,
A brace or a hook,
Rubber breasts or a rubber crotch,
Stitches to show something's missing? No, no? Then
How can we give you a thing?

Sylvia Plath, 1961[2]

NATURAL RIGHTS AND FEMALE NATURE

The 'Declaration of the Rights of Man and of the Citizen', ratified on 26 August 1789 by the Assemblée Constituante of France, proclaimed for the first time that human rights were *natural* rights which predated, and existed independently of, any law passed by the state. Article 1 declared that 'men are born and remain free and equal in their rights'. No mention was made of women, but the term 'man' was understood to be gender-neutral and to include both sexes. Women were therefore being offered, in the name of equality, two possibilities that had not as yet been explored: freedom and citizenship. The offer, however, remained a merely formal one until a much later date, and even then was only partially translated into concrete and tangible rights. One need only remember that in July 1789 the French National Assembly had reconfirmed the Salic law, which denied women the right of inheritance,[3] and that the declared equality of rights did not bring with it the basic right of female suffrage.

'Egalité et liberté en droit' must, therefore, be seen as a legal expression

belonging to eighteenth-century Enlightenment philosophy, and epitomized by Diderot and d'Alembert in the *Encyclopédie*. 'Natural equality',
they had written, 'is the equality that belongs to all men by the grace of their
very nature. This equality is the principle and foundation on which freedom
rests.' The concept of 'nature' thus played an essential role in legitimizing
equality in this philosophical discourse and an indirect role in proclaiming
the right of one and all to freedom. Moreover, it was because women were
held to share this nature that they were entitled to freedom.

If one compares this conception of nature to the philosophical and scientific views which held sway in the early eighteenth century,[4] it is liable to
appear paradoxical. Rather than being used to theorize equality, the concept of nature was appealed to in the earlier period to establish a radical and
fundamental difference between woman and universal man, and to legitimize the exclusion of women from politics. According to both moral and
medical discourses, the place of women was determined by their distinctive
body, by the constraints of their reproductive function. Moreover, the laws
of nature seemed to determine the position of woman so strictly as to
preclude the possibility that her life could have any alternative meaning. Her
only choice was between being healthy and being sick, a choice in turn
determined by the capacity to stay more or less faithful to her own sex. If one
could speak of a female morality at all, it was a morality indissolubly linked
to woman's goal, to the economy of her reproductive body.

The term 'nature' was thus employed in two distinct and incompatible
ways. While it was used in the philosophy of the pre-revolutionary period to
explain sexual difference, it became in Enlightenment philosophy the basis
of a theory of juridical equality. One text in which the tension between these
two conceptions is particularly evident is Rousseau's *Du contrat social*,
where the term appears in both senses.

Rousseau begins from the assumption that the human condition is a
basically dependent one in which people are continually constrained by
physical necessity; but because he assumes that the laws of nature are
objective and impersonal, he does not regard this state of affairs as intrinsically bad or objectionable. Only human power can transform the
diversity and dependence of human existence into inequality. However, this
inequality can in turn be corrected by means of a social contract which serves
to establish something closely resembling our lost condition of natural
equality. As Rousseau put it:

> The fundamental contract, far from destroying natural equality, sub-
> stitutes a *moral and legitimate equality* where nature had introduced a
> physical inequality between men. Thus, although men might have been
> born unequal in strength and intelligence, they all become equal by
> conventions and by law.[5]

The condition produced by nature is therefore corrected by a 'natural law';

and the latter comes to be so fully identified with the former that Jouvenel, in his well-known *Essai sur la politique de Rousseau*, can say that a 'new nature' has been created.[6]

The 'new nature' of Rousseau's natural law was, above all, disembodied: the strength and intelligence of each person became irrelevant to the definition of their humanity. At the same time, sexual polarization disappeared, since, according to the contract, the citizen was a gender-neutral being. This secondary and denatured nature retained from the 'primary' nature only the idea of necessity. Instead of connoting different and complementary physical qualities, the expression 'human nature' came to indicate only a minimum common denominator of rationality. As a result, women continued to be different in their physical nature from men but came to be equal in their spiritual nature. Having been excluded from the *polis* on account of the excesses so typical of her sexuality,[7] woman suddenly found herself, for the first time in European history, co-opted into the political sphere of society.

As I have already pointed out, this co-opting, while it had a significant effect on female subjectivity which is still felt, remained more a theoretical commitment than a reality. If we take into consideration only the civil and political rights that women have really gained, we are forced to conclude that they have been the principal absentees in the historical events that are usually held to constitute the beginning of the modern world. The objections made by a group of women who intended to run for office in the Estates General of 1789, published in their *Cahier de doléances*, still hold today:

> Just as a nobleman cannot represent a plebeian and the latter cannot represent a nobleman, so a man, no matter how honest he may be, cannot represent a woman. Between the representatives and the represented there must be an absolute identity of interests.[8]

Or to take another case, Olympe de Gouges asserted in her *Declaration of the Rights of Woman and of the Female Citizen* that if women had the right to capital punishment they should also have the right to speak from the tribune. She herself was guillotined in 1793, and it has been pointed out with some bitterness that 'The only right conceded to women was the right to the guillotine.'[9]

These historical events seem to lend support to the idea, often advocated by the most radical contemporary feminist theorists, that women are not subject to the rules of citizenship because they are not represented by the social contract. Livia Turco, for example, the national representative for women's affairs in the Italian Social Democratic Party, has argued that 'There are no female citizens, because the real experiences of women take place outside the sphere of politics, in a universe considered to be quite "other" in comparison with the political one.'[10]

However, the non-citizenship of women is only a reality if we limit the effects of what has been termed a 'philosophical revolution' to the realm of politics. Actually, the French Revolution marked the birth of modern man and of his specific anthropological being. And when we consider the complexity of the transformations that have occurred in social relations, in relationships with the world at large and in relations of the individual to himself or herself, we can see that women played a crucial role in these processes. The new man seems to have shaped his own idealized identity by stylizing that 'other self' that is woman. Moreover, the emergence of the basic juridical idea of equality was accompanied by a redefinition of oppositional codes which persisted throughout the nineteenth century. Sexual difference (which had been theorized before the first half of the eighteenth century in terms of 'nature') was now redefined in sublimated forms which were far subtler than the earlier, rather coarse declarations of principle. Women became the ground on which the transformational ability of the bourgeois revolution was to be tested. At the same time, they ended up paying a heavy price for their exclusion from the rights of citizenship. For despite the fact that they were unable to exercise these rights, they were none the less constrained to carry the burden of duties imposed by a class which defined itself as universal.

In this essay, I shall reconsider women's membership of the new society that was shaped by the ideas of the French Revolution from the perspective of these duties. In particular, I shall reconsider the psychological duties which fell to women: the duties to interiorize certain norms, to discipline and regulate the self, which were in turn incorporated in practices which made women one of the foremost concerns of a discontented civilization. Let it not be forgotten that modern psychiatry evolved, above all, in relation to female mental illness, the psychic suffering of a subject forced to pay a high price in order to participate in a society which tended to obliterate her distinctiveness and incorporate her into a male world.[11]

THE PARADOX OF DEMOCRATIC SOCIETIES

The collapse of the *ancien régime* marked the demise of 'medieval' man; a man who belonged to a given lineage, usually to an agricultural society, and who was subject to a dense network of social controls which regulated his life and the flow of time. His place in this world was determined by his birth, and his entire existence consisted in collectively induced forms of behaviour, themselves the product of socially shared rules. The 'modern' man who succeeded him was (to sketch a cultural portrait) an individual independent of divine power, who no longer belonged to the community in which he originated and who enjoyed a high degree of political autonomy. In the 'citizen', Enlightenment culture thus produced an entirely new actor: a sovereign individual, the possessor of natural rights, master of himself and of his own life.

This individual could make himself in a way that had never been possible before. As the master of his own political identity, the citizen went through a process of conforming and adapting to society which could be carried out in the first person singular. As is evident in Rousseau's *Emile*, the construction of the new man was brought about through the regenerative powers of education. In order that he may derive the maximum benefit from this process, the little Emile is removed from the city and grows up in the countryside, in contact with nature. At his side there is only the teacher, who dedicates to his disciple all his time and energy. Even suckling is regulated by instructions that the tutor himself writes for the mother or wet-nurse – women are creatures to whom nature has assigned the task of bearing and nurturing the infant, but unfortunately they do not possess the competence to fulfil it. Emile, the model child, is an orphan. His parents are excluded from the scene of his education because they represent the past and the persisting social inequalities which education aims to overcome. Thus, the educational process requires a sole relationship between an adult and a child, both of the male sex, who have cut themselves off from their origins and rejected any female genealogy. The start of his education, therefore, represents Emile's real birth, and his teacher is his progenitor. At the conclusion of this symbolic 'pregnancy', the teacher deludes himself into believing that he himself has created Emile, without the intervention of a woman: 'Then . . . I will clasp him to my breast and cover him with tears of sympathy; I will say to him, you are my wealth, my child, my handiwork.'[12] The purpose and result of this project of rational education are to turn a man inwards into himself. This education does not take place in society, but it is directed towards society. Thus, after Emile completes his education, he returns to Paris, to live as a citizen among men of his own rank. Yet he continues to differ profoundly from his peers because he is faithful to himself, to an interior contract which he has made with the impersonal power of his teacher who represents, in Emile's mind, the moral law.

A backward movement has shifted his education from the city to the countryside, from the external world to the home, from the home to the mind, so that the teacher may install himself *inside* the mind of his disciple. The isolation in which Emile lives until his maturity provokes a dissolution of contracts with others and leaves room for him to make contracts with himself. The practice of 'turning inwards into oneself' in order to listen to the voice of wisdom and virtue in one's own soul is a first invitation towards a prevalently negative education, designed to overcome the edicts of traditional morality.

This new interiorized norm produces a self-limitation of behaviour which tends to make the controlling and repressive mechanisms of society superfluous. Moreover, the shift of mechanisms of behavioural control from exterior to interior (a move also exemplified by Protestant morality) provokes what the French historians Marcel Gauchet and Gladys Swain have called 'the paradox of democratic societies'.[13] The withdrawal from external controlling factors seems to bring about a radical, internal dependence. As Michel Foucault has shown,[14] the social emancipation of the individual seems to bring with it (as a consequence or as part of an exchange) a loss of psychic freedom. The new man whom Emile represents is free because he has been educated towards the internal exercise of civil liberty. But paradoxically, with the freedom gained in the *polis* came a whole series of self-imposed limitations, so that externally imposed repression reappeared as self-discipline and self-control. Madness, which had in the eighteenth century been regarded as a reversion to a natural state, came to be defined, for example by Esquirol at the beginning of the nineteenth century, as 'the sickness of civilization'.[15]

One might object that the interiorization of moral norms was a long process and less abrupt than this account implies. As Foucault's late works show,[16] 'ancient' man, the citizen of classical Greece, had elaborated a theory and practice of austerity, a moral subjectivity, to counter arbitrary desire and passion. Because the Athenian citizen had to exhibit his moral superiority and exemplary character in order to justify his social supremacy (instead of relying on claims to divine descent), he developed an ethos of self-control which would be continued by Christianity. There is thus a certain continuity between earlier cultures and the Enlightenment. Nevertheless, the juridical principles sanctioned by the French Revolution represented a basically new stance; whereas in classical antiquity the stylization of the self, the economy of pleasures and the control of the passions were aristocratic virtues reserved for the male adult citizen whose income allowed him to live without having to work, the post-revolutionary world brought into existence social rights and duties which purported to be universal in scope.[17] Because freedom was everyone's inalienable right, it could no longer be a social privilege; rather it possessed the impersonal necessity of a natural phenomenon. Since everyone received this right at birth, everyone was obliged to use it properly and to enter into a series of contracts with others, incurring in the process both cost and benefits. For the first time, the fundamental principles were truly *erga omnes*, applicable to female as well as male citizens. (There remained, of course, a gap between formal proclamations and corresponding practices; but even postulates have social effects on self-representations and on the shared symbolic world.)

The female citizen, now a potential holder of political rights to equality and freedom, thus found herself confronting the immense task of gaining what had been offered to her by the magnanimity of male thought, by the universal claim embodied in a philosophical project.

THE DOMESTICATION OF WOMEN

As the emerging middle classes developed their identity, they simultaneously presented themselves as an ideal to be emulated by other classes, a

132 Beyond Equality and Difference

parameter valid for all humanity. But within the middle classes, the difference between the sexes remained unchanged: 'To vaguely assert that the two sexes are equal and that their duties are the same, is to lose oneself in vain declamations.'[18] Rousseau investigates female education in the fifth book of *Emile*. Since women's role consists, as ever, in being a wife and mother, her education must be directed towards the fulfilment of these two duties:

> All education of women must be directed towards men. To please them, to be useful, to be loved and honoured by them, to raise them when they are young, to care for them when they are adult, to advise them, to console them, to render their life agreeable and pleasant – these are women's duties from their infancy on.[19]

Rousseau's portrait of Sophie, Emile's ideal wife, represents her as a relative creature, in that her features are complementary to the fundamental features of man:

> In the union between the sexes each of them concurs equally to the common goal, but not in the same manner. From this diversity originates the first difference which constitutes the moral relations between the one and the other. One must be active and strong, the other passive and weak. It is absolutely necessary that one wills and acts; it is sufficient that the other puts up but little resistance. If this principle is established, it follows that woman is made especially for pleasing man.[20]

In order to guarantee that the 'second nature' induced by education conforms to the essence of female nature, the mother must teach her daughter that 'dependence is the natural state of women'. Docility is her most important dowry since she is subjected to men for her entire life, first to her father, then to her husband. Moreover, once she becomes a mother, she must subject her desires to her child. The mother of a family, far from being a society woman, is confined to her home as a nun to the nunnery. Women's felicity resides in the government of the home, leaving the government of the external world to man.

The character of the modern middle-class family requires that, within this private, familiar space, women should be subjected to an intensive process of education. In contrast to the education of boys, that of girls is directed more towards the conservation of the past than to the prefiguring of the future. To a great extent, then, the social limitations and impositions to which the bourgeois woman is subject are therefore essentially those traditional customs passed down from generation to generation. A novel feature of these limitations is, however, that they become invisible. An all too early, close, intense and intrusive education – such as can only be exercised within the family and through the mother – permits the girl to be manipulated without her realizing it. A 'second nature', induced in this way, will appear to her as the free expression of her most authentic nature. As Rousseau emphasizes:

> The obedience and fidelity she owes to her husband, the tenderness and care that she owes to her children, are such natural consequences and so close to her condition that she will be in bad faith if she refuses to go along with the interior sentiment that guides her.[21]

Not only the educational goals set for males and females, but also the manner of their education, differ profoundly. The equality of rights which characterizes the citizen is contradicted by the existence of two human figures who are complementary but not equivalent. Whereas the nature of males is corrected by an education which aims to remedy the physical differences between them, female nature is merely perfected by education, as if it represented an inevitable destiny. In the case of the male, his (corrected) nature opens up a possibility, in the case of the female, a necessity.

The universality of the Enlightenment subject reveals itself as unrealizable in Rousseau's new pedagogics, which has to recognize the existence of two gendered subjects, Emile and Sophie. The first is the real protagonist of education and its utopian aspirations; the second is a secondary and marginal figure, moulded by educational processes which are as rigid as they are subtle. Moreover, they seem to be so obvious that there is no need to justify them by philosophical theories. The mother must reproduce society; the father must produce social change. None the less, the mother is not, as Rousseau wants to make us believe, external to the elaboration of the modern subject. She appears to be absent because the ways in which she manipulates her daughter are not theorized as educational innovations; instead they pass through modes of indirect, intimate and subterranean communication which are closer to the body than to discourse. They evade judgement and criticism, thus resisting changes of society and culture. Already in the first half of the eighteenth century, the bourgeois woman was exposed to a subtle restructuring of her body and thoughts, adjusted to her ultimate function as wife and mother.

The modern conception of woman in turn replaced an earlier aristocratic ideal which rapidly disintegrated as the nobility was discredited, unable any longer to serve as a point of reference.[22] Equally, the convent, which had for centuries been responsible for the education of young women, suffered the corrosive criticism of atheism.[23] In its place, the family took over the central role in the education of middle-class women; the doctor became its ideologue, the mother its executor.[24] But whereas, in the first half of the eighteenth century, medical science emphasized the weakness of the female body in order to discourage women's participation in political life, in the second half it is rather the excesses of the female body which are emphasized, its sexual exuberance, in order to justify a precise programme of women's 'domestication'.[25]

The dangers against which female education is called upon to struggle are, according to Rousseau, the vices of aristocracy: idleness, indocility, frivolity, infatuation. From infancy, every desire must be subjected to obedience. Obedience is a value in itself and departures from it must therefore be punished, even with absurd and contradictory orders. Rousseau underlines this in the case of girls:

> They must first be habituated to discipline, so that it never costs them anything to domesticate their fantasies in order to submit them to the will of others. If they like to work continuously, one must sometimes force them to do nothing.[26]

Whereas, in the case of the boy, the goal of self-mastery is internal liberty, in the case of the girl it is a total adherence to the will of another.

But in order to reach this goal, it is necessary to domesticate the early rebellious and excessive sexuality of women, a task reserved not for the teacher (the sublime figure who moulds the conscience, not the bodies, of his pupils), but for the doctor and the mother. This change in environment, manners and character in educational strategies is particularly well illustrated in de Bienville's *La nymphomanie* of 1771. Written by a doctor, but meant for mothers, this book contains a mixture of sanitary prescriptions and moral instructions that were to have a great success in the nineteenth century.[27] It is interesting to note that, whereas the text purports to be exhaustive in its coverage, it does not mention the schooling of girls, despite the fact that it was increasing in both quantity and quality. The reason for this omission is that the author regarded schooling as a marginal and negligible factor in his overall educational project, which was concerned with female sexuality – with the bodies and imaginations of young middle-class women. The topic was in part held to be important because the sexuality of aristocratic women had come to be seen as licentious – as shady and impulsive, subject to excessively vague and diffuse controls, given over to the extended family, open to strangers and too close to the servants.[28] By contrast, middle-class life was characterized by the privatization of the domestic world, the centrality of the mother-figure and the stringent reciprocal control of gestures and intentions.[29] If, in the past, woman's licentious behaviour had been stigmatized, it was now her very sexuality that was held to be potentially dangerous.

The shift from the first to the second of these models required that women's sexuality be diagnosed as pathological and, at the same time, that a connection (no matter how tenuous) be made between the reproductive and nervous systems, thus authorizing doctors to act simultaneously as gynaecologists, psychologists and pedagogues.[30] The role of the doctor was above all that of the theoretician, since the task of controlling the behaviour of young women fell to their mothers. Mothers were instructed by family doctors to keep a constant eye on their daughters' morality, to discover their thoughts, to select their stimuli as well as to discipline bodies and souls tempted by excess.

As a result of this climate of suspicion, female sexuality became the very essence of womanhood, to the point where all women's desires, fantasies, dreams and games appeared erotic. Woman was an 'erotic subject', as Lou Andreas-Salomé was later to point out,[31] an erotic subject who was throughout the nineteenth century rigorously disciplined in an attempt to bring about the interiorization of norms and conflicts, a sense of guilt and a fear of punishment. Physiological rhythms were slowly altered to fit social needs, passions were tamed into sentiments, and expressive communication became embedded in ever more neutral social codes.[32]

One of the consequences of letting women take care of other women was that change was disguised as 'tradition', a long, slow process described by the pedagogue and historian of education Egle Becchi:

It is not hard to understand, in broad outline, where this education was carried on and what means and goals were adopted by the women who were to influence the young girls and the other women they were educating. Without a doubt, the home was of central importance since in domestic life 'doing' and 'knowing what to do and how to do it' could remain unwritten rules which were none the less assimilated by means of example, by imitation, and in the interest of collaboration. All this came about with very few or even no words (as women are given over to chatter, their words have to be stigmatized) even though the work done in the home was basically aimed at the production of tangible and vital things.[33]

It was to this tradition that middle-class culture gave a decisive twist when doing became subordinated to being. The concern of mothers seems to have focused more on the daughter herself than on her skills, and this to such an extent that work was used as a means to discipline thought, as a means to fight dangerous erotic fantasies and as a means to instrumentalize the sublimation of drives.[34]

Since it was a mother's duty to keep an eye on the most secret behaviour and intentions of her daughter, the result was combat at close quarters. The mother opposed sexuality and maternity, by using the threat of maternity to repress the free exercise of erotic desire. From puberty on, women thus came to think of maternity as a punishment that befell them when they freely expressed their sexuality. Pre- and extra-conjugal sex was criminalized as the female sin *par excellence*, and illegitimate pregnancy was constantly evoked as both offence and punishment for an imprudent act.

Thus, the control of female eroticism was to some extent carried out by the same women who were being controlled. The walls of the home, which had for centuries functioned as the boundary within which female desire was limited and contained, were internalized and transformed into inhibition mechanisms which were later to come to light in psychoanalysis.

PSYCHOLOGICAL SEXUALITY AND SOCIAL MATERNITY

The recognition of female sexuality and the internalization of its control brought about both self-control and a first shaping of subjectivity. The body, robbed of desire, remained an inert object, a disturbing element that expressed itself in an estranged way through the symptoms of hysteria.

The psychiatric therapies used in the course of the nineteenth century to cure hysteria had only one thing in common – the assumption that the female body is an 'object' that can be treated independently of the person living in it. Institutionally organized knowledge described, and opposed to each other, two aspects of this reified body – the erotic and the maternal. The former belonged to the realm of psychiatry, the discipline which studied the pathology of the female eros. The latter belonged to the realm of gynae-cology, which controlled 'natural' reproductive processes. Once surrendered to the psychiatrist, the body was transformed into a map of erogenous zones in which actions and reactions were experimentally induced. By contrast, the body, manipulated by the obstetrician, was an internal organ – the uterus – an invisible, unpredictable and autonomous reproductive instrument. While the erotic dimension of woman had to be made to obey, her ability to procreate had to be kept efficient. In the first case nature had to be mastered, while in the second it had to be encouraged, sometimes violently, to fulfil its purpose.

Whereas the psychiatrist knew that he was working against the natural instincts of woman, the gynaecologist believed that he was aiding and abetting female nature. However, as is well known, the nature redefined by the new contract was a 'second-degree nature' in which the maternal power of woman was progressively socialized. Whereas psychiatry was rightfully included among the educational methods used to achieve 'moral' autonomy,[35] gynaecology was only indirectly related to these disciplinary practices.

First psychiatry and later psychoanalysis were two extreme forms of control and cure, which played similar roles in the process of opening up a cultural space in which female sexuality could be investigated. But whereas psychoanalysis recognized female erotic desire, rendering it acceptable and translatable into words, it excluded the exploration of maternal desire.[36] Maternity, having been disjoined from sexuality, was removed from the domain of discussion. In Freud, the female experience plays a marginal role and is viewed exclusively in relation to the model of male development; becoming the mother (of a male child) is seen as overcoming imaginary castration and penis envy. Freud does not, however, see that maternity may be a potentially rich aspect of women's body and mind, a complex of energies, figures, affects and attitudes which are possessed by one sex and constitute its difference. These dispositions need not necessarily be expressed by bringing a child into the world. They may also be employed in other projects of social, cultural, ethical or aesthetic life without, however, losing their distinctiveness. All this, however, has no place within Freudian anthropology, shaped as it is by the patriarchal tradition of occidental culture.

Maternity was also excluded, moreover, from the realm in which images of women were created. Even a feminine literary genre such as the romantic novel (written and consumed by women) produced a shared erotic imagery while hiding the problem of maternity in an undiscursive dimension of reality. Maternity was a non-textual experience. Love stories translated the middle-class culture of sentiments into a popular medium. The transformation of passion into a form of private suffering (a characteristic feature of these stories) provided women with models for the articulation of their own experiences. Moreover, the stereotypes in which the heroines of this feminine literature were imprisoned were all the more influential by virtue of the fact that this genre was, for many women, their first and only contact with culture. With the coming of the cinema a universally recognized grammar of love was disseminated: the love dream became the cultural model which best expressed the female erotic imagination.[37] At the same time, the representation of maternal passion remained linked to archaic cultural stereotypes: the woman/mother-figure suffered a kind of historical shipwreck and was destined to disappear along with economic underdevelopment.

UNREPRESENTED MOTHERHOOD

In our modern western society, maternity, taken as a global experience, does not have any cultural resonance. The ability to 'think motherhood' seems to have receded along with nature, or better still along with the feeling of 'being part of the cosmos'.[38] The model of the bourgeois male individual was unable to incorporate motherhood. 'Denatured' nature calls for sterilized social contracts rather than symbiotic relationships, complicities of bodies or embarrassing functional closeness. Even the relationship between mother and son, for example, has come to seem immodest in its ostentatious physicality.

Thus it was the child, rather than men and women, who became the leading actor in discussions of procreation as well as in the demographic policies and welfare projects formulated in the 1930s. At the same time, women were progressively reduced to 'reproductive machines' devoid of autonomy and intentionality. Their knowledge of 'what to do and how to do things' was taken away from them by health institutions and turned into a specialized branch of knowledge administered by medical doctors.[39] Only their final product remained visible, while the 'production process' was hidden away in conformity with capitalist modes of organizing labour.

However, although the rights of women to be represented and to shape their own lives as mothers were expropriated, women still continued to see motherhood as the central event of their lives. And they continued to communicate to each other their experiences and feelings about being or not being mothers, even though this form of communication remained marginal by comparison with the 'competent' discourses of obstetricians, paediatricians, educators and all the other experts who came along. Stigmatized as 'chatter', communication among women occurred only in moments carved out from a life spent in the home or neighbourhood. It was characterized by a minimal use of denotations and a wealth of connotations.

Rather like an underground river carrying unrecognizable detritus, this type of connotative communication mixed residual dialects, family terms and phonetic archaisms with inventions and linguistic contaminations. Children understood this primary language without self-consciously knowing it, and thus acquired a shared ability to express themselves, long before they learned the official language.[40] As in music, rhythm and intonation were important; and, as in the theatre, gesture and mimicry were central. In this language, narrative time, reiterative and repetitive, has the character of fairy tales. And the narrative voice often shifts from the first person singular, from speaking about oneself, to the voice of a vague, hard-to-identify person who is none the less emblematic of a given experience. Elisabetta Rasy has defined 'chatter' as 'expulsion from the interior'. In her view:

> This way of communicating, while evading the dictates of meaning and the consequences of what is said, allows women to experience an area of vital irresponsibility – free from the very physiology that it punctuates – where they can seek the impossible harmony between the interior demands and the exterior process of becoming.[41]

The female use of speech, mediated more by voice than by language, demands something closer to participation than to actual understanding. The strength of this type of communication resides in its ability to create a time and place that are not split, a 'transitional space' of communicative fluidity.[42] Its truthfulness resides in the effort to express an uncoded interior life. Speaker and listener are no longer at the opposite ends of an imaginary telephone call, but are intertwined and interfused with each other by virtue of the suggested but unmentioned fact of belonging to the same sex.

As long as there were places reserved for the women to meet, there was also a social acceptance of a female community which never demanded to be heard, to change things or to interact with the male world. Conversations carried on because women experienced pleasure in inventing and because the undertow of the conversation, by making the implicit explicit, renewed the links between speakers, their bodily feelings and imaginations. Favourite subjects were pregnancy, birth, sickness, love and death. These topics, rooted simultaneously in the intimacy of lived experience and in the cyclic time of the life course, formed a last refuge in which mothers could speak of motherhood.

Women's right to express themselves as citizens and holders of civil rights imposed a condition: that their specific voice should give way to the dominant symbolic discourse. As women began to gain access to strong and socially recognized forms of communication, chattering suddenly became obscene in its deliberate physicality, in its shameless immediacy. It lost its legitimacy and the traditional settings in which it was practised, and as a result fell into disuse and even disrepute.

The point of reverting to this lost form of communication is not to evoke nostalgia for the past or to bemoan the marginalization of women, but rather to ask whether anything of it survives which could be updated and used to enlarge our understanding of male/female differences. At the same time, however, the revival of chatter serves as a criticism of dominant discourse and a reminder of the price that women pay for their inclusion in this social symbolism. Once women gave up their own distinctive type of communication, they began to present themselves in male, individualistic terms; they moved from perceiving the interior to representing the exterior. Having lost their sense of themselves as belonging to nature, their synchrony with astral time, their mutual bonds forged through suffering, there was nothing else left but to give themselves meaning through the presumed obviousness of the ego. If we can identify motherhood with 'women's unthought', this is because it has been excluded from self-government and has not been retrieved from the unconscious by psychoanalysis.[43]

EXPLORING MOTHERHOOD

Freudian research began, as is well known, by investigating hysteria. Hysterical symptoms were explained in the context of a self-regulating process in which they were taken to be a sign of an excess. Within this framework, the repressed experience appears as one side of the psyche, divided from itself by its own stylization. *Civilization and its Discontents* can be read as a psychic report on the effects of a political act – the 'Declaration of the Rights of Man'. The asset side of the report does not include motherhood, a term excluded from the psychoanalytic encyclopaedia.

If female sexuality is 'the problem' of psychoanalysis, the core that makes this discipline work and yet keeps it in check, motherhood is nevertheless kept at arm's length and given over to the falsifying self-evidence of banal reflections. The separation of sexuality and fertility, let alone the separation of fertility and procreation, has meant that only in the past few years has attention focused on the need to rethink motherhood. The poverty of both theory and experience in this domain is painfully obvious.

This absence of any adequate theory of maternity is sufficiently serious in itself. But the problem is exacerbated by recent scientific developments. While women are now working on a historical, psychological and political rehabilitation of natural motherhood,[44] they are doing so at a time when it is fast becoming outdated. For we are witnessing a phase of transition from the instrumental control of the reproductive process to its replacement by artificial techniques, the danger of new reproductive technologies expropriating procreation. They aim at producing an entirely extra-corporal generation through laboratory processes. Progress in this field is fast and in a certain way anticipates our capacity for intellectual and effective exploration.

These biomedical techniques seem to have adopted the familiar impersonal and imperative nature of a vital process. Their effects reveal a perverse omnipotence that cannot be identified with the subjectivity of any individual. They are as acephalous in their advance as the life they try to mimic. At the same time, they indulge in a combinatory game of possibilities which reactivates the mythical imagination, with which they share the pleasures of omnipotence and the anonymity of conception.

Genetic technologies act like the 'temporal arm' of a fantastic and myth-creating way of thinking, which has always been considered harmless because it was beyond the bounds of possibility.[45] Faced with this way of thinking, our rational modes of thought are quite impotent, because the individual subject – a projective portrait of western anthropology – does not know what stance to take or how to relate to it. In a certain sense, biotechniques represent the eruption of an element relegated by culture to the background, and hitherto regarded as of little relevance. For this reason, it is important that we reinstate it in our imagery and translate it into the symbolic dimension, without losing sight of its specific characteristics.

Psychoanalysis can offer us metaphorical support in this undertaking, of the kind indicated by Freud when he pointed out that

> The individual leads in actual fact a double life, one in which he is an end to himself and another in which he is a link in a chain which he serves, against his will or at least independently of his will. The individual himself considers sexuality as one of his own objectives but, from another point of view, he is only the appendix of his seminal plasma, to which he lends his powers in exchange for a recompense of pleasure. He is the mortal vehicle of a – possibly – immortal substance much like the holder of an entail who benefits temporarily from an institution which will continue to exist after his death.[46]

Women have not usually thought of their desire for motherhood as the expression of two factors, psychological and biological. They have placed maternity in the realm of autobiography without realizing that this is not the only sphere in which it belongs. They have seen their child-bearing as a narcissistic achievement and have reacted to unwanted pregnancies without understanding their meaning, without asking themselves, what design is there behind an unwanted child? Motherhood has become the female sub-conscious of our epoch. Today, it is more procreation than sexuality which creates problems. Sterility originating in psychosomatic disturbances of women has become ever more common.[47] Such symptoms reveal that, for women, it is around maternity that a 'new discontent with civilization' has developed.

Only by producing a model of motherhood that takes into account both its biological and psychological aspects will we be able to understand the natural maternity of women as well as technological (re-)production by scientific means. To deny the maternal component of gender identity risks pushing it into the realm of the repressed and seeing it reappear in the psyche in the troubling form of a symptom. It is not that one must be a mother in order to be a woman, as traditional culture insisted. What is necessary is to reflect on maternity, to be aware of it so as to be able to use its creative and expressive potential.[48] This potential may be expressed by giving birth to children or in other ways, but it must be known and controlled. Our reproductive distinctiveness is too great and rich to be reduced to an *option* of self-realization or turned into a sublimated availability.

Before it is too late, women's reflections on maternity and its transmission must be elaborated, so that we may develop a responsible stance towards the anonymous and impersonal proliferation of technologies. But to reflect on maternity is not to enter in triumph, because it requires, as we have seen, a preliminary accepting of its foreignness, the construction of an identity that extends beyond the boundaries of the ego, and the narcissistic sacrifice of our presumed self-sufficiency. We know that, historically, motherhood has been used to deny women citizenship and to confine them to the private sphere. Recognizing motherhood therefore entails a redefining of the political sphere and a renegotiation of the powers of science. It is not easy to carry out a critique that at every step runs the risk of stumbling into the pitfalls of anarchy or of anti-scientific obscurantism.[49] It is tempting to wait for things to change by themselves, to wait for technology to find its own limits by realizing its own ends. But there is no morality whatever in technologies which pursue all the available possibilities and cannot predict what will come of them.

Faced with what seems an inevitable progression, we need a strong and alternative point of view from which we can construct a conception of difference without being considered inferior. Such difference, however, cannot be expressed in a simple statement, nor merely in a critical and deconstructive attitude.[50] Instead, it is necessary to reconstruct the external and internal history which has made us what we are. In the course of this transition, other possibilities, other and unintended ways of being and of communicating, will become visible. In the process of denouncing the hypocrisies of culture (such as the equality of all citizens), new spaces for emancipation and liberation will open up. Each criticism may bring about the activation of an alternative. In this sense, historicizing psychoanalysis involves positing new objects of investigation. Among them are the objectives of learning to root our thoughts in the body, to reassemble what male culture has taken apart (such as the antinomies nature/culture, public/private, body/soul, maternity/paternity, language/generation, which all sustain women's inferiority in regard to men) and to overcome the prohibitions and intimations of patriarchy, as a first step towards achieving a female sexual subjectivity.

There is in us a potential, blocked and impoverished by centuries of anathema, that needs to be revived, valorized and reinscribed in a society which will recognize, as an asset, the existence (in the world) of two sexes. The exploration of what is possible is more than a cognitive undertaking because it requires us to assume responsibility and take an ethical stand. A female ethics must confront an immense historical task: it must find ways of expressing a subject which has passed through the crisis of the Enlightenment promise of rational control of the world as well as the crisis of the psychoanalytic utopia of mastering oneself, the predominance of the ego over the id. I do not believe, as did Antigone, that there is a natural law which will guarantee justice.[51] I do think, however, that ethics must embrace a larger sphere than that historically constituted by the *polis* and the citizen. A new gendered ethics[52] must also concern private relationships, of woman with herself as well as with others. The goal is to achieve an equilibrium of mutual recognition where difference does not imply hierarchy and where exchange does not imply the logic of domination.

NOTES

1 J.-J. Rousseau, *Emile ou de l'éducation*, 1782, in J.-J. Rousseau, *Oeuvres complètes*, Paris, Gallimard, 1969, vol. 4, p. 697.
2 S. Plath, 'The applicant', 1961, in S. Plath, *Ariel*, New York, Harper & Row, 1965, p. 4.
3 See C. Fauré, *Les déclarations des droits de l'homme de 1789*, Paris, 1988.
4 See esp. P. Hoffman, *La femme dans la pensée des lumières*, Paris, Ophrys, 1978.
5 J.-J. Rousseau, *Du contrat social*, in Rousseau, *Oeuvres*, vol. 3, p. 367 (my emphasis).
6 B. de Jouvenel, *Essai sur la politique de Rousseau*, Geneva, Bourquin, 1947.
7 Aristotle, *Politics*. I, 5–9. See S. Campese and S. Gastaldi, *La donna e i filosofi*, Bologna, Zanichelli, 1977; S. Campese, P. Manuli and G. Sissa, *Madre materia: sociologia e biologia della donna greca*, Turin, Boringhieri, 1983; M. Vegetti, *Il coltello e lo stilo*, Milan, Il Saggiatore, 1987; P. DuBois, *Sowing the Body: Psychoanalysis and Ancient Representations of Women*, Chicago, University of Chicago Press, 1988.
8 Quoted from L. Villari, 'Preface' to J. Michelet, *Le donne della rivoluzione*, (trans. from French, Milan, Bompiani, 1918), p. 8.

9 A. del Re, 'Storia di Olimpia de Gouges', *Il bimestrale*, supplement of *Il manifesto*, 31 January 1989.
10 L. Turco, 'Noi, le donne di Botteghe Oscure', *Repubblica*, 2 December 1988. See also Libreria delle Donne di Milano, *Non credere di avere dei diritti*, Turin, Rosenberg & Sellier, 1987 (English trans. 1991).
11 See e.g. S. Vegetti Finzi, *Storia della psicoanalisi*, Milan, Mondadori, 1991, and 'Miti del femminile ed immagini della natura', in *Studi freudiani*, Milan, Guerine, 1989, pp. 147–65.
12 Rousseau, *Emile*, p. 649.
13 M. Gauchet and G. Swain, *La pratique de l'esprit humain*, Paris, Gallimard, 1984.
14 M. Foucault, *La volonté de savoir*, Paris, Gallimard, 1976.
15 J. E. D. Esquirol, *Des passions*, Paris, 1805. See also M. Galzigna, *La malattia morale: alle origini della psichiatria moderna*, Venice, Marsilio, 1989.
16 M. Foucault, *L'usage des plaisirs*, Paris, Gallimard, 1984, and *Le souci de soi*, Paris, Gallimard, 1984.
17 M. Vegetti, 'Foucault e gli antichi', in P. Aldo Rovatti (ed.), *Effetto Foucault*, Milan, Feltrinelli, 1986, pp. 39–45.
18 Rousseau, *Emile*, p. 698.
19 ibid., p. 703.
20 ibid., p. 693.
21 ibid., p. 731.
22 See P. Ariès, *L'enfant et la vie familiale sous l'ancien régime*, Paris, Plon, 1960.
23 See J. Bowen, *Storia dell'educazione occidentale*, trans. from English, Milan, Mondadori, 1983, vol. III, pp. 275 ff.
24 For the alliance between the family doctor and the mother see J. Donzelot, *La police des familles*, Paris, Editions de Minuit, 1977.
25 See M. Dupont-Chatelain, *Les encyclopédistes et les femmes*, Geneva, Slatkine Reprints, 1970; R. Graham, 'Rousseau's sexism revolutionized', in P. F. R. Morton (ed.), *Woman in the Eighteenth Century and Other Essays*, Hakkert, 1976, pp. 127–39; P. D. Jamack, 'The paradox of Sophie and Julie: contemporary response to Rousseau's ideal wife and ideal mother', in E. Jacobs (ed.), *Woman and Society in Eighteenth-Century France*, London, Athlone Press, 1979, pp. 152–65.
26 Rousseau, *Emile*, p. 709.
27 J. D. T. de Bienville, *La nymphomanie ou traité de la fureur utérine*, Amsterdam, 1771; Italian trans. *La ninfomania*, ed. with introductions by A. G. Michler and S. Vegetti Finzi, Milan, Feltrinelli, 1986 (the following quotes are from this edition). The treatise was translated into many languages and often reprinted: Amsterdam 1772, London 1775, Brussels 1775, London 1776, Amsterdam 1778 and 1784, Venice 1783, Lausanne 1788, London 1789 and 1840, Paris 1886, Rome 1960, Paris 1980.
28 See the clinical cases described by de Bienville, ibid.
29 See P. Ariès and G. Duby, *Histoire de la vie privée*, vol. IV: *De la révolution à la grande guerre*, Paris, Seuil, 1986; P. Gay, *The Bourgeois Experience: Victoria to Freud*, vol. I, *Education of the Senses*, Oxford, Oxford University Press, 1984; L. Stone, *The Family, Sex and Marriage in England 1500–1800*, Harmondsworth, Penguin, 1977.
30 J. D. T. de Bienville, 'Delle parti organiche della donna', in de Bienville, *La ninfomania*, pp. 69–83.
31 L. Andreas-Salomé, *La materia erotica: scritti di psicoanalisi, 1914–1928*, trans. from German, Rome, Edizioni delle Donne, 1977.

32 M. Foucault, *Naissance de la clinique: une archéologie du regard medical*, Paris, Presses Universitaires Françaises, 1963, and *Surveiller et punir*, Paris, Gallimard, 1975; Foucault, *La volonté de savoir*; G. Bock and Giuliana Nobili Schiera (eds), *Il corpo delle donne: immagini e realtà storiche*, Ancona-Bologna, Transeuropa, 1988; O. Moscucci, *The Science of Woman, 1800–1929*, Cambridge, Cambridge University Press, 1990; E. Shorter, *A History of Women's Bodies*, New York, Basic Books, 1982.

33 E. Becchi, 'Introduction', in E. Becchi (ed.), *Storia della educazione*, Florence, La Nuova Italia, 1987, p. 20.

34 See S. Vegetti Finzi, 'Alla ricerca di una soggettività femminile', in M. C. Marcuzzo and A. Rossi-Doria (eds), *La ricerca delle donne: studi femministi in Italia*, Turin, Rosenberg & Sellier, 1987, pp. 228–48.

35 Galzigna, *La malattia morale*.

36 See S. Vegetti Finzi, *Il bambino della notte: divenire donna, divenire madre*, Milan, Mondadori, 1990 (forthcoming English trans. London and New York, Guildford Press, 1992); Vegetti Finzi, *Storia della psicoanalisi*; J. Mitchell, *Psychoanalysis and Feminism*, New York, Pantheon, 1974; J. Forrester, *Language and the Origins of Psychoanalysis*, London, Macmillan, 1980; M. Edelson, *Language and Interpretation in Psychoanalysis*, New Haven, Conn., Yale University Press, 1975.

37 See L. Melandri, *Come nasce il sogno d'amore*, Milan, Rizzoli, 1988.

38 See C. Merchant, *The Death of Nature: Women, Ecology and the Scientific Revolution*, San Francisco, Harper & Row, 1980, and E. Donini's introduction to the Italian translation, Milan, Garzanti, 1988.

39 C. Pancino, *Il bambino e l'acqua sporca: storia dell'assistenza al parto dalle mammane alle ostetriche, secoli XV–XIX*, Milan, F. Angeli, 1984; G. Colombo, F. Pizzini and A. Regalia, *Mettere al mondo: la produzione sociale del parto*, Milan, F. Angeli, 1984; *Le culture del parto*, Milan, Feltrinelli, 1985.

40 F. Dolto, *La cause des enfants*, Paris, Laffont, 1985.

41 E. Rasy, *La lingua della nutrice: percorsi e tracce della espressione femminile*, with an introduction by J. Kristeva, Rome, Edizioni delle Donne, 1978, p. 65; see also P. Violi, *L'infinito singolare*, Verona, Essedue, 1986.

42 The term 'transitional' is meant in the sense attributed to it by D. W. Winnicott, *Playing and Reality*, London, Tavistock, 1971.

43 With the outstanding exception of H. Deutsch, *The Psychology of Women*, 2 vols, New York, Grune & Stratton, 1944–5.

44 E.g. A. Rich, *Of Woman Born*, New York, Norton, 1976; N. Chodorow, *The Reproduction of Mothering*, Berkeley, Calif., University of California Press, 1978; D. Dinnerstein, *The Mermaid and the Minotaur*, New York, Harper & Row, 1976; C. Pateman, *The Sexual Contract*, Cambridge, Polity Press, 1988; F. Ferraro and A. Nunziante-Cesaro, *Lo spazio cavo e il corpo saturato*, Milan, F. Angeli, 1985; Vegetti Finzi, *Il bambino della notte*; S. Tubert, *La sexualidad feminina y su construcciòn imaginaria*, Madrid, El Arquero, 1988; E. Dio Bleichmar, *El feminismo espontaneo de la histeria: estudio de los trastornos narcisistas de la feminidad*, Madrid, Adotraf, 1985.

45 See S. Vegetti Finzi, 'Tecnologie del desiderio, logiche dell'immaginario', in A. Di Meo and C. Mancina (eds), *Bioetica*, Bari, Laterza, 1989, pp. 271–86.

46 S. Freud, 'Zur Einführung des Narzissmus' (1914), in S. Freud, *Gesammelte Werke*, vol. 10, Frankfurt, S. Fischer, 1967, p. 143.

47 The Argentine psychoanalyst Marie Langer maintains that the lack of female representation of maternity is related to the repressed image that women have of

themselves, and that it is the cause of many psychosomatic disturbances of women: M. Langer, *Maternidad y sexo*, Buenos Aires, Nova, 1964.
48 For some approaches see note 44 above.
49 For women's relationship to biology see L. Birke, *Women, Feminism and Biology: The Feminist Challenge*, Brighton, Wheatsheaf, 1986; E. Donini, *La nube e il limite*, Turin, Rosenberg & Sellier, 1990; J. Rothschild, *Machina ex Dea: Feminist Perspectives on Technology*, Oxford, Pergamon, 1983; E. Fox-Keller, *Reflections on Gender and Science*, New Haven, Conn., Yale University Press, 1985. See also *Sortir de la maternité du laboratoire*, Actes du forum international sur les nouvelles technologies de la réproduction, organisé par le conseil du statut de la femme tenu à Montréal, 1987, esp. pp. 24–32 (contribution by G. Corea and FINRRAGE); J. Testart *et al.*, *Le magasin des enfants*, Paris, François Bourin, 1990.
50 See J. Kristeva, 'Woman can never be defined', in E. Marks (ed.), *New French Feminism*, New York, Schocken, 1981; L. Alcoff, 'Cultural feminism versus post-structuralism: the identity crisis in feminist theory', *Signs*, 13(3), 1988, pp. 405–36; J. W. Scott, 'Deconstructing equality-versus-difference: or, the uses of poststructuralist theory for feminism', *Feminist Studies,* 14(1), 1988, pp. 33–50; C. Weedon, *Feminist Practice and Poststructuralist Theory*, Oxford, Blackwell, 1987.
51 Sophocles, *Antigone*, with an introduction by R. Rossanda, Milan, Feltrinelli, 1987.
52 See S. Vegetti Finzi, 'Etica della maternità', in Vegetti Finzi, *Il bambino della notte*, pp. 247–61; Vegetti Finzi, 'Tecnologie'; L. Irigaray, *Ethique de la différence sexuelle*, Paris, Editions de Minuit, 1984; C. Gilligan, *In a Different Voice: Psychological Theory and Women's Development*, Cambridge, Mass., Harvard University Press; Diotima, *Il pensiero della differenza sessuale*, Milan, La Tartaruga, 1987; T. de Lauretis, *Alice Doesn't: Feminism, Semiotics, Cinema*, Bloomington, Ind., Indiana University Press; J. Benjamin, *The Bonds of Love*, New York, Pantheon, 1988.

Part III

Justice, the female self and the politics of subjectivity

Chapter 8

The politics of paradigms: gender difference and gender disadvantage

Deborah L. Rhode

Traditional approaches to gender difference have alternated between exaggeration and denial. On most issues of public policy, denial has been the preferred strategy; women's special interests have remained unacknowledged and unaddressed. By contrast, policy initiatives that have spoken to gender difference have often overstated its nature and amplified its adverse consequences. Feminist responses have frequently remained entrapped in similar patterns. Many theoretical approaches that have sought to celebrate women's distinctive attributes have homogenized and essentialized their content, while strategies of denial have ignored women's particular needs and circumstances.

The following analysis surveys the limitations of traditional frameworks from both a theoretical and a policy-oriented perspective. After first reviewing certain consistent inadequacies in legal and legislative approaches, it proposes an alternative strategy, one that focuses less on gender difference and more on gender disadvantage. Such an alternative would demand close attention to context and to the diversity of women's interests over time and across boundaries such as race, class, ethnicity and sexual orientation.

Discussion then turns to related issues in feminist theory and to limitations in conventional strategies that celebrate or deny difference. Again, the alternative proposed here is a less dualistic, more contextual approach. Under this framework, the focus is less on difference *per se* than on the process by which sex-linked attributes acquire cultural meaning and significance. Such a perspective focuses not simply on women's differences from men, but also on their differences from each other, and on the ways that social context mediates gender relationships.

Before discussing the merits of these alternative approaches, one threshold observation is in order. How we talk about paradigms in itself presupposes a choice of paradigms. My choice is to resist the temptations of theoretical purity. Rather than thinking in terms of either/or – sameness vs difference, difference vs disadvantage – we should focus on issues of when and why. If the subject is gender, we cannot entirely escape conventional questions of difference. We can, however, resist their limitations on fundamental issues of feminist theory and practice.[1]

I

Feminism in general, and the American women's movement in particular, emerged against a backdrop of social, economic and political inequalities between the sexes. The prevailing assumption was that woman's nature was to nurture. Gender inequality appeared biologically grounded, spiritually ordained and culturally essential.[2] Woman's brain was too small, her powers of reasoning too limited and her 'tender susceptibility' too unsuited for demanding pursuits.[3]

According to scientific wisdom, women who diverted scarce physical resources from reproductive to productive pursuits risked permanent sterility.[4] Legal decision-makers similarly perceived a 'law of Nature and the Creator' that decreed domesticity as destiny and that justified females' exclusion from professional, political and civic responsibilities.[5] Although the precise method of divine communication was never fully revealed, its message was widely acknowledged. Until the last century, women lacked the right to vote, to enter contracts, to hold property or to stand for political office.[6]

Yet if the exaggeration of gender difference served to legitimate gender hierarchy, the denial of gender difference had similar consequences. Women's special vulnerability to sexual violence, harassment and economic dependence was, for the most part, politely overlooked. Among married couples, rarely did the force of law intervene against the consequences of force. Spousal 'chastisement', or 'domestic disturbances', the law's euphemisms for wife-beating, almost never resulted in formal sanctions.[7] Harassment had no conceptual cubby-hole, and social welfare policies did little to address the causes or consequences of female poverty.[8] Although legal decision-makers often talked of 'we the people', they were not in fact using the term generically. Women were largely unacknowledged in official texts, uninvited in their formulation and, before the last quarter-century, largely uninvolved in their interpretation.

Early feminist responses to gender inequality challenged but also presupposed its underlying assumptions. One strategy was to deny the extent or essential nature of gender difference. Beginning in the late nineteenth century, many activists joined Elizabeth Cady Stanton in dismissing as 'mysterious Twaddle' the 'sentimental talk about the male and female element'.[9] By contrast, other feminists premised their arguments for women's equality on women's difference. Jane Addams, one of the early American proponents of this position, cast mothers as 'municipal housekeepers', and many European theorists sounded similar themes.[10] With

In some respects, the ambivalence about difference had its advantages. On issues of equal rights, feminists could embrace either perspective and arrive at similar conclusions. To the extent women were the same as men, both should enjoy the same status; to the extent women were different, their distinctive perspectives and concerns deserved a role in public life. Yet this dual strategy also carried a cost. The preoccupation with women's differences from men obscured women's differences from each other, and deflected attention from the class, racial and ethnic bias of the early feminist agenda.[12] Claims about women's special moral sensibility over-simplified and over-claimed its importance, while ignoring its constraints. Moreover on some issues, such as protective statutes, competing views of difference could not happily coexist. As a consequence, feminists too often found themselves fighting with each other over the value of protection rather than uniting to challenge the conditions that made protection so valuable.

Such issues arose in the United States around the turn of this century as increasing numbers of state legislatures began passing regulations governing maximum hours, minimum wages and working conditions. Controversies increased after a pair of Supreme Court decisions struck down such regulations for male workers as a violation of their freedom to contract, but upheld restrictions for female employees in light of their special vulnerabilities and reproductive responsibilities.[13] Even after the Supreme Court reversed its holding as to male workers, the disputes over gender-specific protections persisted. In part, the debate centred on concerns about the fate of such protections under a proposed Constitutional Equal Rights Amendment. Underlying that issue were deeper questions about mandates of formal equality in circumstances of social inequality. Those same questions have resurfaced in the last decade, as the American women's movement divided over the merits of state legislation requiring employers to grant job-protected maternity leave but not paternity, parental or temporary medical disability leaves.

Then, as now, feminists who supported gender-specific policies began from the premise that women are different and that their special needs justify special regulatory intervention. Earlier in the century, the focus was on female employees' unequal labour-force status and unequal domestic burdens. Most women workers were crowded into low-paying jobs with few advancement opportunities and little likelihood of improving their status through unionization. Female employees were also far more likely than their male counterparts to assume major family responsibilities, and the combination of those duties with prevailing twelve- to fourteen-hour work shifts imposed enormous hardships. For most of these women, statutory regulation of hours and wages meant a substantial improvement in their quality of life.[14]

Yet as feminists who opposed gender-specific statutes also noted, such protections made women more expensive, and often protected them out of any jobs desirable to male competitors. The ideology of gender difference served to rationalize gender exclusions in occupations ranging from bartending and shoeshining to military service. In some contexts, regulation also increased female unemployment and reinforced assumptions about the appropriateness of unequal family roles.[15]

Although both sides of the protective labour debate claimed to speak for women, women's interests were more divided than partisans acknowledged. Those who denied the significance of gender difference frequently understated the obstacles to securing sex-neutral mandates and the value of sex-specific regulation. For the majority of workers, clustered in female-dominated jobs, such regulation brought significant improvements. Yet those who stressed accommodation of gender difference often underestimated its price. Special protection for women restricted their employment opportunities, and thus reinforced the social inequalities that protection was meant to address. Moreover, the ideology of paternalism spilled over to other welfare, family and criminal law contexts in which paternalism was less advantageous.[16]

The contemporary debate about gender difference and public policy involves similar complexities. In the United States, major attention has focused on issues involving pregnancy and parental leaves, and on women's exclusion from occupational settings thought to present special demands or risks, such as military service or toxic work-sites. Here again, sex-linked differences have been both overlooked and overvalued. On some issues, courts have transformed biological distinctions into cultural imperatives. On other questions, women's special needs have remained unmet.

What makes the United States pregnancy cases particularly instructive as sex discrimination opinions is the Supreme Court's initial unwillingness to treat them as such. During the mid-1970s, a majority of Justices upheld policies providing employee benefits for virtually all medical treatment except that related to childbirth. Yet in the first of these cases, the court relegated the entire discussion of discrimination to a footnote. There the majority announced its somewhat novel conclusion that pregnancy policies did not even involve 'gender as such'. Rather, employers were simply drawing a distinction between – in the court's memorable phrase – 'pregnant women' and 'non-pregnant persons'.[17] Preoccupied with issues of difference rather than disadvantage, the majority perceived no issue of discrimination; since pregnancy was a 'unique' and 'additional' disability for women, employers were entitled to exclude it from insurance coverage.[18]

Never did the majority explain why only pregnancy was 'unique', while men's disabilities, such as prostatectomies, were fully covered. Rather, the court's characterization assumed what should have been at issue and made the assumption from a male reference point. Men's physiology set the standard against which women's claims appeared only additional.

Following this line of cases, intense lobbying prompted passage of the federal Pregnancy Discrimination Act, which provided that pregnancy should be treated 'the same as' other medical risks for employment-related purposes.[19] This remains, however, one of the many contexts in which denials of difference serve only to reinforce the disadvantages that have accompanied it. The Act requires equality in form, not equality in fact. It demands only that employers treat pregnancy like other disabilities. It does not affirmatively require adequate disability policies. In the absence of statutory mandates, such policies have been slow to develop. Recent data have indicated that about three-fifths of female workers were not entitled to wage replacement, and a third could not count on returning to their same job after a normal period of leave. The United States has remained alone among major industrialized nations in failing to provide such benefits.[20]

In response to such inadequacies, many feminists have supported requirements that employers provide pregnancy leave whether or not leave is available for other disabilities or caretaking needs. Those who justify such policies generally begin from the premise that women are unequally situated with respect to reproduction. While no-leave policies pose hardships for both sexes concerning the disabilities they share, such policies present an additional burden for women. As a matter of principle, pregnancy should not have to seem just like other disabilities to obtain protection. As a practical matter, until legislatures are prepared to mandate adequate benefits for all workers, partial coverage seems like an appropriate goal.[21]

The danger, however, as other feminists have noted, is that settling for the proverbial half a loaf could erode efforts for more comprehensive approaches. Legislation that makes women more expensive also creates incentives for covert discrimination. Many feminists are unwilling to see women once again 'protected out' of jobs desirable to men.[22] To require maternity, but not paternity or parental leaves, is to reinforce a division of child-rearing responsibilities that has been more separate than equal. Difference-oriented approaches in various employment contexts have led to the establishment of special 'mummy tracks' that often turn into mummy traps.[23]

On these sorts of issues, a focus on differences is utterly unilluminating and misrepresents the controversy it seeks to resolve. Women are both the same and different. They are different in their needs at childbirth but the same in their needs for broader medical, child-rearing and caretaking policies. To know which side of the sameness/difference dichotomy to emphasize in legal contexts requires some further analytic tool.

The advantage of talking in terms of disadvantage is that it emphasizes a different set of questions and encourages a more contextual analysis. The issue is not difference *per se*, but the consequences of addressing it in a particular way under particular social and historical circumstances. Such a framework demands acknowledgement of the variation in women's interests across race, class and ethnicity, and recognizes that trade-offs may be necessary in terms of short- and long-term objectives.

From this perspective, the preferable strategy for resolving issues such as employee leave policy should be to press for the broadest possible coverage for all workers. While the importance of pregnancy benefits should not be overlooked, neither should they be overemphasized. More employers provide job-protected childbirth leave than other forms of assistance that are equally critical to workers and their dependants. Pregnancy-related policies affect most women workers for relatively brief intervals. The absence of broader disability, health, child-rearing and caretaking assistance remains a chronic problem for the vast majority of employees, male and female, throughout their working lives.[24] In such contexts, both men and women stand to gain if we press for more by refusing to settle for less. The stakes are not just equality for women but the quality of life for all individuals.[25]

Similar observations are applicable in a wide variety of other policy contexts. Many of the inadequacies in contemporary equal protection law stem from its preoccupation with difference. Traditional frameworks require only similar treatment for those similarly situated; sex discrimination is permissible if the sexes differ in ways relevant to a valid regulatory objective. Yet what differences matter and what objectives are legitimate remain open to dispute, and the responses have been less than satisfying. For example, women's continued exclusion from military leadership, combat and draft registration systems reflects continued stereotypes about gender difference. Despite women's demonstrated competence in police, prison and combat-related work, the assumption persists that they cannot or should not be trusted in the most demanding military positions.[26] So too, female workers have lost employment because of their different susceptibility to reproductive hazards and their different family obligations. Relatively little effort has been directed towards restructuring workplaces to minimize hazards or accommodate caretaking demands.[27]

To make significant progress will require an alternative form of analysis, one less fixated on difference and more attentive to the disadvantages that it has entailed. The most pressing problems now facing women do not generally find them 'similarly situated' to men: poverty, sexual violence, reproductive freedom, family responsibilities. The discourse of difference will sometimes have a place, but it should begin analysis, not end it. As deconstructionists remind us, women are always already the same and different: the same in their humanity, different in their anatomy. Whichever category we privilege in our legal discourse, the other will always be waiting to disrupt it.[28] By constantly presenting gender issues in difference-oriented frameworks, conventional legal discourse implicitly biases analysis. To pronounce women either the same or different from men allows men to remain the standard.

Under the disadvantage framework proposed here, a determination that the sexes are not 'similarly situated' only begins discussion. Analysis would then turn on whether legal recognition of sex-based differences is more likely to reduce or to reinforce sex-based disparities in political power, social status and economic security. Such an approach would entail a more search-ing review than has generally been apparent in cases involving gender. Its focus would extend beyond the rationality of differential treatment and the legitimacy of governmental ends. Rather, this alternative would require that governmental objectives include a substantive commitment to gender equality – to a society in which women as a group are not disadvantaged in controlling their own destiny. So, for example, in employment settings, the issue becomes not whether gender is relevant to the job as currently struc-tured, but how the workplace can be restructured to make gender less relevant. What sort of public and private sector initiatives are necessary to avoid penalizing parenthood? What changes in working schedules, hiring and promotion criteria, leave policies and child-care options are necessary to reconcile home and family responsibilities?

This alternative strategy will demand substantial changes in our legal paradigms and social priorities. It will also require a deeper understanding of the harms of sex-based classifications and the complexity of strategies designed to address them. Shifting focus from gender difference to gender disadvantage will not always supply definitive answers but it can at least suggest the right questions. It can also point up the limitations of traditional strategies, which have too often offered only access to, not alteration of, existing social institutions.

This is not to discount the difficulties in applying a disadvantage frame-work. Such an approach confronts many of the same difficulties in assessing women's interests that plague other paradigms. The strategy proposed here at least minimizes these difficulties by limiting its aspirations and acknowl-edging its complexities. The point is not to advocate some grand theoretical structure, but rather to suggest an approach that will be useful in particular contexts under particular social conditions. We need not commit ourselves to some abstract assessment of the origins or extent of gender difference. Nor do we need to determine what women's 'authentic' interests may be; we know more than enough about what they will not be to provide a current legal agenda. Changes in law will not of themselves ensure our arrival at any predetermined destination, but they can change our pace and direction of travel, and our awareness of choices along the way. By challenging gender inequalities in political power, economic resources and social status, a disadvantage framework imposes no fixed and final determinations of women's nature or women's interests. Rather, such an approach encourages us to confront that issue with greater sensitivity to social context and to the diversity of concerns at issue.

II

The limitations of difference as a policy framework have parallels in other more theoretical contexts. As previous discussion indicated, feminists have long differed over difference. During the last two decades, these controversies gained new dimensions. One branch of the feminist movement focused primary energy on challenging difference and exposing the cultural construction of ostensibly natural attributes.[29] By contrast, other theorists began emphasizing the centrality of sexual difference although disagreeing about its origins and consequences. Their discourse reflects a broad range of perspectives that do not easily fit under any single label. For present purposes, it is enough to summarize certain common themes which can be loosely grouped under the term 'relational feminism'.[30]

What unites these approaches is a focus on women's reproductive role and the nurturing relationships that it has encouraged. Some feminists, including those working within contemporary French traditions, attach overarching significance to biological difference.[31] Other theorists emphasize socialization and/or subordination; their frameworks underscore women's need to obtain status, control and approval through attachments to others.[32] A third approach draws most heavily on psychoanalytic theory. According to this last account, children develop closer attachments to a primary caretaker of the same sex. Individuals who form strong attachments in early life will be more likely later to define themselves in relation to others and to develop close nurturing bonds. Since most primary caretakers have been and continue to be female, girls grow up with a greater inclination towards, and capacity for, caretaking roles.[33]

One other relational feminist approach, which has been especially influential in the United States, focuses not on the origins of gender difference but on its normative significance. From this perspective, the problem for contemporary western women stems less from the exaggeration of difference than from its devaluation. This school of thought, popularized by Carol Gilligan, argues that conventional moral and legal theories have placed too great a priority on abstract rights, and too little on concrete relationships. Based on empirical and qualitative research, Gilligan claims that women tend to reason in 'a different voice', which is especially attentive to care, co-operation and context in the resolution of human problems.[34]

Relational feminism has made important contributions, but they come at a cost. Its strengths lie in its demand that the values traditionally associated with women be valued, and that public policy focus on restructuring social institutions, rather than just assimilating women within them. By affirming characteristics traditionally associated with women, such approaches can encourage greater political cohesiveness and collective self-esteem. As other commentary in this collection suggests, making values such as empathy and nurturance more central to political discourse has significant transformative possibilities. Relational feminism can also provide theoretical underpinnings for legal policies that are responsive to women's distinctive concerns.

Yet as was true during earlier feminist campaigns, this validation of difference raises its own set of problems at both strategic and substantive levels. As a strategic matter, affirmation of women's voice can deflect attention from the structural circumstances that construct and constrain it.[35] Emphasizing males' association with abstract rationality and females' concern for interpersonal relationships reinforces long-standing stereotypes that have restricted opportunities for both sexes. However feminist in inspiration, any dualistic world view is likely to be appropriated for nonfeminist objectives. As the previous discussion reflected, the perception that nurturance is women's responsibility has long served to justify women's under-representation in demanding positions and to reinforce roles that are more separate than equal.

Moreover, as a substantive matter, it is by no means clear how different women's 'different' voice is. Relational feminist work has generally failed to address variations across culture, class, race, ethnicity, age and sexual orientation.[36] For example, Gilligan's data drew on small unrepresentative samples, and most empirical studies of moral development do not disclose significant gender distinctions.[37] Nor does related research reveal the kind of strong sex-linked differences that relational feminism would suggest; there are few psychological attributes on which the sexes consistently vary.[38] For even these attributes, such as aggression, spatial ability and helping behaviour, gender typically accounts for only about 5 per cent of the variance; the similarities between men and women are far greater than the disparities, and small statistical distinctions do not support sweeping sex-based dichotomies.[39]

Gender differences fall along a continuum, and context matters greatly in eliciting traits traditionally associated with women.[40] When pressures for sex-typed behaviour are strong, individuals generally will behave in expected ways, which helps transform sex-based stereotypes into self-fulfilling prophesies.[41] It is misleading to discuss gender-related attributes as if they can be abstracted from the distinctive social expectations, opportunities and hierarchies that are also linked to gender.[42]

Such findings suggest reasons to qualify relational claims but not to deny all of their potential implications. Although psychological variations between the sexes are relatively minor and socially contingent, the variation in their roles and experience continues to be substantial. As relational feminists have noted, the fact that men and women give similar answers in most surveys of moral reasoning does not mean that they would choose similar ways of framing the question.[43] Nor is it clear that most women would structure workplace policy and governmental priorities in the same way as men if given greater decision-making opportunities.[44] To make sense of gender dynamics, we need frameworks that neither overstate nor undervalue gender difference.

Reformulating the problem in these terms builds on more contextual, less dualistic strains of contemporary feminist theory, those concerned with differences within, as well as between, the sexes. Post-modern theoretical accounts have drawn increasing attention to the multiple forces that constitute women's identity across race, ethnicity, class, age, religion, sexual orientation and so forth.[45] Yet this focus has also underscored a long-standing paradox in feminist theory and practice. What gives feminism its unique perspective is its claim to speak from women's experience. But that same experience counsels attention to the differences in women's backgrounds, perceptions and priorities. There is no 'generic woman', nor any monolithic 'woman's point of view'.[46] Feminism has increasingly become 'feminisms', which complicates the search for theoretical coherence and political cohesion.[47]

Yet the factors that divide us could also be a basis for enriching our analysis and broadening our coalitions. As Audre Lorde has noted, it is not 'our differences which separate [us as] women but our reluctance to recognize those differences and deal effectively with the distances that have resulted'.[48] The same values that underpin feminism's struggle against gender inequality demand its opposition to other forms of group-based disadvantage. We cannot empower all women without challenging the multiple sources of disempowerment that many women face. The problem is how to make such challenges a basis for psychological affinity and political activism.

To realize its full potential, the feminist movement must both expand its practical agenda and qualify its theoretical claims. No single categorical framework can adequately address the dynamics of difference. We remain caught between the need to affirm our gender identity and the need to transcend its constraints, to claim solidarity and to acknowledge diversity. The sameness/difference dilemma cannot be resolved; it can only be reformulated. Our focus needs to shift from difference to disadvantage and to the social conditions that perpetuate it.[49]

To challenge those conditions, our strategies must rest on feminist principles, not feminine stereotypes. The issues of greatest concern to women are not simply 'women's issues'. Although the feminist agenda incorporates values traditionally associated with women, the stakes in its realization are ones that both sexes share.

NOTES

1 For a fuller exploration of these themes see D. Rhode, *Justice and Gender*,

Cambridge, Mass. and London, Harvard University Press, 1989; D. Rhode, 'Theoretical perspectives on sexual difference', and 'Definitions of difference', in D. Rhode (ed.), *Theoretical Perspectives on Sexual Difference*, New Haven, Conn. and London, Yale University Press, 1990, pp. 1, 197; D. Rhode, 'The no problem problem: feminist challenges and cultural change', *Yale Law Journal*, 100, 1991.

2 See, generally, S. Okin, *Women in Western Political Thought*, Princeton, NJ, Princeton University Press, 1979; E. Flexner, *A Century of Struggle: The Women's Rights Movement in the United States*, revised edn, Cambridge, Mass., Harvard University Press, 1975; L. Newman (ed.), *Men's Ideas/Women's Realities*, New York, Pergamon Press, 1985.

3 S. Gould, *The Mismeasure of Man*, New York and London, Norton, 1981, pp. 103–22; H. Maudseley, 'Sex and mind in education', in J. Newman, *Men's Ideas/Women's Realities*, pp. 197–219; J. Hyde, 'Meta analysis and the psychology of gender differences', *Signs*, 16, 1990, pp. 54, 56–7; *In re Goodell*, 39 Wis. 232, 244–5 (1875).

4 B. Ehrenreich and D. English, *For Her Own Good: 150 Years of the Experts' Advice to Women*, Garden City, NY, Anchor, 1978, pp. 113–17; C. Smith-Rosenberg, *Disorderly Conduct*, New York, Knopf, 1984, pp. 259–60; E. Clarke, *Sex in Education*, New York, Houghton Mifflin, 1873.

5 *Bradwell* v. *State*, 83 US 130, 137 (1872) (upholding exclusion of women from bar).

6 W. Blackstone, *Commentaries on the Laws of England*, Oxford, Oxfordshire Professional Books, 15th edn, 1982; Rhode, *Justice and Gender*, pp. 9–10, 20–9; M. Salmon, 'The legal status of women in early America: a reappraisal', *Law and History Review*, 1, 1983, pp. 129–51.

7 *State* v. *Hussey*, 44 NC 60, 61 (1824); *State* v. *Black*, 60 NC (Winn.) 266 (1864); E. Pleck, 'Wife beating in nineteenth century America', *Victimology*, 4, 1979, p. 60; N. Oppenlander, 'The evolution of law and wife abuse', *Law and Policy Quarterly*, 3, 1981, pp. 382–405.

8 For sexual harassment see C. MacKinnon, *Sexual Harassment of Working Women: A Case of Sex Discrimination*, New Haven, Conn., and London, Yale University Press, 1979; M. Bularzik, 'Sexual harassment at the workplace: historical notes', *Radical America*, 12, July–August 1978, pp. 25–44. For welfare policies see M. Abramovitz, *Regulating the Lives of Women*, Boston, Mass., South End Press, 1988; M. Katz, *Poverty and Policy in American History: Social Welfare Policy from Colonial Times to the Present*, New York, Academic Press, 1983, and *In the Shadow of the Poorhouse: A Social History of Welfare in America*, New York, Basic Books, 1986.

9 E. Stanton, quoted in W. Leach, *True Love and Perfect Union*, New York, Basic Books, 1980, p. 147.

10 J. Addams, 'Why women should vote', in F. Bjorkman and A. Porritt, *Woman Suffrage: History, Arguments and Results*, New York, National Woman Suffrage Publishing Co., 1917, pp. 110–29; J. Addams, 'The modern city and the municipal franchise for women', in S. Anthony and I. Harper (eds), *History of Woman Suffrage*, Indianapolis, Ind., Hallenback Press, 1902, vol. IV, p. 178. For related arguments by European feminists see K. Offen, 'Defining feminism: a comparative historical approach', *Signs*, 14, 1988, p. 119.

11 Anthony and Harper, *History*, pp. 39, 308–9.

12 See P. Giddings, *When and Where I Enter: The Impact of Black Women on Race and Sex in America*, New York, Morrow, 1984, pp. 127–9; B. Hooks, *Ain't I a Woman? Black Women and Feminism*, Boston, Mass., South End Press, 1981,

pp. 130–1; R. Terborg-Penn, 'Discrimination against Afro-American women in the women's movement, 1830–1920', in S. Harley and R. Terborg-Penn (eds), *The Afro-American Woman: Struggles and Images*, Port Washington, NY, Kennikut Press, 1978, pp. 17–18.

13 *Lochner* v. *New York*, 198 US 45 (1905); *Mueller* v. *Oregon*, 208 US 412 (1908).

14 Women's Bureau, Bulletin 65, *The Effects of Labor Legislation on the Employment Opportunities of Women*, Washington, DC, US Government Printing Office, 1928; J. Baer, *The Chains of Protection*, Westport, Conn., Greenwood Press, 1978; E. Baker, *Protective Labor Legislation*, New York, AMS Press, 1979; N. Cott, *The Grounding of Modern Feminism*, New Haven, Conn., and London, Yale University Press, 1987.

15 J. Baer, *The Chains of Protection*, Westport, Conn., Greenwood Press, 1978; A. Kessler Harris, *Out to Work*, New York, Oxford University Press, 1980; E. Landes, 'The effect of state maximum hours laws on the employment of women', *Journal of Political Economy*, 88, 1980, p. 476.

16 J. Johnston and C. Knapp, 'Sex discrimination by law: a study in judicial perspective', *New York University Law Review*, 46, 1971, p. 675; W. Williams, 'Equality's riddle: pregnancy and the equal treatment–special treatment debate', *New York University Review of Law and Social Change*, 13, 1985, p. 325; F. Olsen, 'From false paternalism to false equality: assaults on feminist community: Illinois', *University of Michigan Law Journal*, 58, 1986, pp. 869–95; Rhode, 'Definitions of difference', pp. 200–11.

17 *Geduldig* v. *Aiello*, 417 US 484, n. 21 (1974); *General Electric Co.* v. *Gilbert*, 429 US 125 (1976).

18 *Geduldig* v. *Aiello*, 417 US 484, n. 21 (1974); *General Electric Co.* v. *Gilbert*, 429 US 125 (1976); K. Bartlett, 'Pregnancy and the constitution: the uniqueness trap', *California Law Review*, 62, 1974, p. 1532.

19 92 Stat. 2076 (Oct. 31, 1978).

20 S. Kammerman and A. Kahn, *The Responsive Workplace*, New York, Columbia University Press, 1987; Congressional Caucus for Women's Issues, fact sheet on parental leave legislation, Washington, DC, 1986; Rhode, 'The no-problem problem'.

21 L. Finley, 'Transcending equality theory: a way out of the maternity and workplace debate', *Columbia University Law Review*, 86, 1986, p. 1118; H. Kay 'Equality and difference: the case of pregnancy', *Berkeley Women's Law Journal*, 1, 1985, p. 1.

22 Williams, 'Equality's riddle'; National Organization for Women, Brief in *California Federal Savings* v. *Guerra*, 479 US 272 (1987).

23 J. Kingston, 'Women in the law say path is limited by mommy-track', *New York Times*, 8 August 1988, p. A1. See T. Lewin, 'Women say they still face obstacles as lawyers', *New York Times*, 4 December 1989, p. A15 (90 per cent of surveyed women lawyers believed their career would be slowed or blocked by accepting part-time or flexible-time schedules.)

24 N. Taub, 'From parental leaves to nurturing leaves', *New York University Review of Law and Social Change*, 13, 1985, p. 381; Williams, 'Equality's Riddle', p. 325.

25 R. Spalter-Roth, *Unnecessary Losses: Costs to Americans for the Lack of Family and Medical Leave*, Washington, DC, Institute for Women's Policy Research, 1988.

26 For assumptions about women's unsuitability for combat see W. Webb, 'Women can't fight', in N. Davidson (ed.), *Gender Sanity*, New York, Lanham, 1989, p. 208; M. Levin, *Feminism and Freedom*, New Brunswick, NJ, Transaction, 1987, p. 239; and sources cited in Rhode, *Justice and Gender*, pp. 98–100. See also *Rostker* v. *Goldberg*, 453 US 57 (1984) (upholding male-only registration system

for military service). For evidence concerning female performance see M. Binkin and S. Bach, *Women and the Military*, Washington, D.C. Brookings Institution, 1977, pp. 81–91; L. Laflin, *Women in Battles*, New York, Abelard Schuman, 1967, pp. 10, 22, 62–79; H. Rogan, *Mixed Company: Women in the Modern Army*, New York, Putnam's, 1981, p. 258; J. Steihm, *Bring Me Men and Women: Mandated Change at the US Air Force Academy*, Berkeley, Calif., University of California Press, 1981, pp. 129–30, 167, 199, 250; E. Gemmette, 'Armed combat, the woman's movement mobilizes troops in readiness for the inevitable constitutional attack on the combat exclusion for women in the military', *Woman's Rights Law Reporter*, 12, 1990, pp. 89–102; L. Kornblum, 'Woman warriors in a men's world: the combat exclusion', *Law and Inequality*, 2, 1984, pp. 351, 395–428.

27 For workplace safety see M. Becker, 'From *Muller v. Oregon* to fetal vulnerability policies', *University of Chicago Law Review*, 53, 1986, pp. 1219–45; W. Chavkin (ed.), *Double Exposure: Women's Health Hazards on the Job and at Home*, New York, Monthly Review Press, 1984. For work–family conflicts see Rhode, *Justice and Gender*, pp. 172–5, and 'The no problem problem'; S. Kamerman and A. Kahn, *The Responsive Workplace*, New York, Columbia University Press, 1987; N. Dowd, 'Work and family: restructuring the workplace', *Arizona Law Review*, 32, 1990, pp. 431–500.

28 J. Derrida, *Of Grammatology*, trans. G. Spivak, Baltimore, Md., Johns Hopkins University Press, 1977; K. Silverman, *The Subject of Semiotics*, New York, Oxford University Press, 1983.

29 See e.g. A. Fausto-Sterling, *Myths of Gender*, New York, Basic Books, 1987; R. Lowe and R. Hubbard (eds), *Woman's Nature: Rationalizations of Inequality*, New York, Pergamon Press, 1983; A. Eagley, *Sex Differences in Social Behavior: A Social Role Interpretation*, Hillsdale, NJ, Erlbaum, 1987; R. Hubbard, 'The political nature of human nature', in Rhode, *Theoretical Perspectives*, p. 63.

30 See Offen, 'Defining feminism', p. 134.

31 See C. Duchen, *Feminism in France*, London and Boston, Mass., Routledge & Kegan Paul, 1986; E. Marks and I. de Courtivron (eds), *New French Feminisms: An Anthology*, Amherst, Mass., University of Massachusetts Press, 1981; T. Moi, *Sexual/Textual Politics: Feminist Literary Theory*, London and New York, Methuen, 1985; R. West, 'Jurisprudence and gender', *University of Chicago Law Review*, 5, 1988, p. 1.

32 See C. MacKinnon, M. Dunlap, E. Dubois, C. Gilligan and C. Menkel-Meadow, 'Feminist discourse, moral values, and the law: a conversation', *Buffalo Law Review*, 34, 1985, pp. 11, 71–4 (comments of MacKinnon emphasizing subordination); E. Maccoby, 'Gender and relationships', *American Psychology*, 45, 1990, pp. 513, 516–19 (emphasizing peer socialization).

33 N. Chodorow, *The Reproduction of Mothering: Psychoanalytic Feminism and the Sociology of Gender*, Berkeley, Calif., University of California Press, 1978; D. Dinnerstein, *The Mermaid and the Minotaur: Sexual Arrangements and the Human Malaise*, New York, Harper & Row, 1976; N. Chodorow, 'Psychoanalytic feminism and the psychoanalytic in the psychology of women', in Rhode, *Theoretical Perspectives*, p. 114.

34 C. Gilligan, *In a Different Voice: Psychological Theory and Women's Development*, Cambridge, Mass., and London, Harvard University Press, 1982.

35 R. Hare-Martin and J. Maracek, 'Gender and the meaning of difference: postmodernism and psychology', in R. Hare-Mustin and J. Maracek (eds), *Making a Difference*, New Haven, Conn., and London, Yale University Press, 1990, pp. 22, 52. See also MacKinnan *et al.*, 'Feminist discourse', p. 74 (comments of MacKinnon, claiming that the voice Gilligan describes is the voice of the victim).

36 N. Fraser and L. Nicholson, 'Social criticism without philosophy: an encounter between feminism and postmodernism', in L. Nicholson (ed.), *Feminism/Postmodernism*, New York, Routledge, 1990, p. 19; J. Stacy and B. Thorne, 'The missing feminist revolution in sociology', *Social Problems*, 32, 1985, p. 301.

37 For critiques of Gilligan's methodology see C. Epstein, *Deceptive Distinctions: Sex, Gender, and the Social Order*, New Haven, Conn., and London, Yale University Press, 1988, pp. 76–94; S. Benhabib, 'The generalized and the concrete other: the Kohlberg–Gilligan controversy and feminist theory', in D. Cornell and S. Benhabib, *Feminism as Critique: Essays on the Politics of Gender in Late-Capitalist Societies*, Cambridge, Polity Press, 1987, pp. 77–9; A. Colby and W. Damon, 'Listening to a different voice: a review of Gilligan's *In a Different Voice*', in M. Walsh (ed.), *The Psychology of Women: Ongoing Debates*, New Haven, Conn., and London, Yale University Press, 1987, p. 321; C. Greeno and E. Maccoby, 'How different is the different voice?', *Signs*, 11, 1986, p. 310; see also Walsh, *Psychology*, pp. 275–7 (bibliography). For related criticisms of psychoanalytic theories such as those found in Chodorow and Dinnerstein's work see Fraser and Nicholson, 'Social criticism'.

38 Eagley, *Sex Differences*; E. Maccoby and C. Jacklin, *The Psychology of Sex Differences*, Stanford, Calif., Stanford University Press, 1974; Maccoby, 'Gender', pp. 513–15; K. Deaux and M. Kite, 'Thinking about gender', in B. Hess and M. Feree (eds), *Analyzing Gender*, Beverly Hills, Calif., Sage Publications, 1987, pp. 93–4; Hyde, 'Meta analysis', pp. 64–8.

39 Epstein, *Deceptive Distinctions*; K. Deaux, 'From individual difference to social categories: analysis of a decade's research on gender', *American Psychology*, 39, 1984, p. 105; K. Deaux and B. Major, 'A social-psychological model of gender', in Rhode, *Theoretical Perspectives*, p. 89; and sources cited in notes 38 and 40.

40 Eagley, *Sex Differences*, pp. 27–31, 125–32; Deaux and Kite, 'Thinking about gender'; Epstein, *Deceptive Distinctions*; B. Thorne, 'Children and gender: constructions of difference', in Rhode, *Theoretical Perspectives*, p. 100; R. Kanter, *Men and Women of the Corporation*, New York, Basic Books, 1977, pp. 206–10.

41 R. Unger, 'Imperfect reflections of reality', in Hare-Mustin and Maracek, *Making a Difference*, pp. 102–6.

42 B. Lott, 'Dual natures or learned behavior', in Hare-Mustin and Maracek, *Making a Difference*, p. 70 (noting that if average differences between women and men are attributed to gender rather than to different experiences correlated with gender, description is confused with explanation).

43 C. Gilligan, 'Reply', *Signs*, 11, 1986, pp. 324, 328–31.

44 See e.g. J. Roesner, 'Ways women lead', *Harvard Business Review*, November–December 1990, pp. 119, 120 (finding that in certain medium-size organizational settings, women leaders are more likely than men to practise interactive leadership, i.e. to share knowledge and power, to encourage participation and to enhance subordinates' self-worth).

45 C. Di Stefano, 'Dilemmas of difference: feminism, modernity and postmodernism', in Nicholson, *Feminism/Postmodernism*, p. 73; J. Flax, 'Postmodernism and gender relations in feminist theory', *Signs*, 12, 1987, pp. 621, 634–9; R. Gagnier, 'Feminist postmodernism: the end of feminism or the ends of theory?', in Rhode, *Theoretical Perspectives*, p. 26.

46 E. Spellman, *Inessential Woman: The Problems of Exclusion in Feminist Thought*, Boston, Mass., Beacon Press, 1988, pp. 114, 167; D. Rhode, 'The woman's point of view', *Journal of Legal Education*, 38, 1988, pp. 39, 41, 44. For the failure of much feminist jurisprudence to take adequate account of diversity

see A. Harris, 'Race and essentialism in feminist legal theory', *Stanford Law Review*, 42, 1990, pp. 581, 585–608.

47 L. Alcoff, 'Cultural feminism versus post-structuralism: the identity crisis in feminist theory', *Signs*, 13, 1988, p. 405; S. Bordo, 'Feminist postmodernism and gender skepticism', in Nicholson, *Feminism/Postmodernism*, pp. 133, 134–42; S. Harding, 'The instability of the analytic categories of feminist theory', *Signs*, 11, 1986, pp. 645, 647–64; E. Keller, 'Holding the center of feminist theory', *Women's Studies International Forum*, 12, 1989, pp. 313, 314; A. Rich, 'Disloyal to civilization: feminism, racism, cynephobia', in *On Lies, Secrets and Silence*, New York, Norton, 1975, pp. 275, 299.

48 A. Lorde, *Sister Outsider*, Trumansberg, NY, Crossing Press, 1984, p. 116.

49 C. MacKinnon, *Towards a Feminist Theory of the State*, Cambridge, Mass., and London, Harvard University Press, 1989, pp. 117–25, 180–8, 306–13; Rhode, *Justice and Gender*, and *Theoretical Perspectives*. For an account of relational frameworks that focus on the construction and consequences of difference see M. Minow, *Making All the Difference*, Ithaca, NY, Cornell University Press, 1990, pp. 18, 19–23, 41–2, 56–60, 217–19, 375–7.

Chapter 9

Gender, subjectivity and language

Patrizia Violi

The binary opposition 'equality and difference' has recently been widely discussed, and its character as an absolute dichotomy called into question in a number of ways. Among the challenges to its over-arching status is the view that there are many kinds of difference; gender difference is only one of many components that structure subjectivity, others being race, sexuality and class. The shift of emphasis implicit in this claim, from difference to differences, is of central importance within the Anglo-American feminist tradition. Italian radical feminism, however, has approached the issue from quite another angle, which needs to be understood in its own historical context. Inspired by Carla Lonzi's first seminal work in the 1970s, Italian feminists have perceived 'difference' as a fundamental value opposed to, and to be defended against, 'equality'. 'Equality', as Lonzi writes,

> is a juridical principle ... Difference is an existential principle which concerns the modes of being human, the peculiarity of one's sense of existence in a given situation and in potential situations. The difference between women and men is the basic difference of humankind.[1]

Difference is here made the very foundation of subjectivity, and a neutral subject is unthinkable; human beings are either women or men, and their belonging to one gender is a basic feature of their experience. Indeed, subjectivity cannot but be engendered; the way we feel, the way we think, the way we experience reality is affected by our being women or men. This fundamental assumption of what has come to be known as *pensiero della differenza sessuale* (the theory of sexual difference) has been the focus of discussion in the Italian feminist movement during the last few years. It is forcefully stated by Adriana Cavarero:

> By sexual difference I mean that, for women, being engendered differently is not negotiable; for each one who is born female, it is always so and not otherwise, rooted in her being not as something superfluous or something more, but as that which she necessarily is: female.[2]

Italian feminism has therefore been more willing than its Anglo-

American counterpart to risk taking an essentialist position and to argue that sexual difference is the most basic of all differences. And although this view has been hotly debated, it is by now rooted in a shared language and a common culture. Central to the latter is a move away from the emphasis on emancipation and equality which dominated feminism during the 1960s to the conviction that female subjectivity must be understood in terms of difference.

In this chapter I shall try to show how this shift has affected recent debates in Italy about language. In particular I shall discuss three points; the way in which the issue of equality and difference is raised in discussions of women's language; how language, as just one cultural and semiotic mechanism, affects the construction of male and female subjectivity; and the role of social and private representations in the construction of female subjectivity, along with the related issue of the 'visibility' of sexual difference.

I

In order to relate the theme of difference and equality to the question of women's language, it is helpful to place this issue against the background of a series of studies on sex and language carried out since the mid-1970s. The earliest of these pieces of work aimed principally to characterize so-called 'women's language', the specific linguistic forms (phonological, syntactic, semantic and pragmatic) used by women speakers. As time went by, however, research tended to focus on the interactional aspects of linguistic activity, on the analysis of conversations between men and women, and among women themselves. In these latter studies, more attention was paid to the context of conversations, and the use of language came increasingly to be seen as a dynamic process.

Despite the differences between them, these two approaches nevertheless possessed a number of common features. In particular, all the studies in question took for granted two basic and interdependent hypotheses; the primacy of social over linguistic facts, and an implicit evaluation of men's language. Men's language was consistently seen as more precise and consequently superior to that of women. Thus, when women were invited to be 'like men', they were invited to undergo a form of linguistic adaptation.

As far as the first hypothesis is concerned, the studies in question tend to interpret linguistic facts as a mere reflex of the social order. Language is seen as simply replicating mechanisms of exclusion and domination which originate elsewhere. Such an approach could be defined as 'sociologizing': the biological datum is replaced by social structure. Rather similarly, behaviouristic models treat social structure as an extra-linguistic antecedent which determines linguistic production. Thus, language only *reflects* the world, reproducing an independent external reality.

Language, however, is more than these accounts allow: it is a semiotic system that not only reproduces external reality, but also produces a reality of its own by manipulating powers and competencies. Language does not merely reflect social dynamics; it creates collective images and representations, including sex roles. Once this is recognized, it becomes crucial to distinguish between sex and gender, between an extra-linguistic reality (sex) and the way it is linguistically and semiotically interpreted (gender). Our attention should be focused on the processes through which language structures social representations of what a 'woman' is, and affects the way in which female individuals become 'women'. Important as it is, however, the distinction between sex and gender nevertheless needs to be handled cautiously. When, in conformity with a usage now firmly established within the Italian feminist movement, I speak of 'sexual difference', this is not to be understood as referring to some form of biological essentialism. Current *pensiero della differenza sessuale* holds that subjectivity cannot but be engendered, and that any expression of our subjectivity will exhibit traces of our membership of one gender. Moreover, the result of overlooking the distinction between sex and gender is to breed obfuscation and confusion.

Turning now to the second hypothesis – that men's language is superior to that of women – we know that, in a society dominated by a patriarchal order, men and women do not have the same power. Considered from an egalitarian standpoint, this unbalanced state of affairs cries out for emancipation, for the achievement by women of all that men have already gained. Moreover, if language simply reproduces social dynamics, part of this emancipation will consist in women adapting themselves and learning to conform to male linguistic norms. Men's language will be seen as 'correct', and as constituting an ideal world. This assumption can be clearly seen in many works on sex and language, at the point where they move from phenomenological description to practical suggestions. Given that their authors have no theory of how sexual difference as a set of representations is semiotically produced, they can only read their data as the linguistic effect of a social state of domination. Such a reading in turn gives rise to the suggestion that women should eradicate all traces of difference, since these can only be an external mark of their inferiority: they should 'talk like men', and not like women.

This conclusion, then, is already implicit in the premises of the studies with which we are concerned. If the difference between women's and men's language is only the deterministic effect of a difference in social roles, it cannot be anything but a deficiency, the linguistic expression of social subordination. Hence the attempt to 'desexualize' language and create an androgynous discourse.

Within the Italian women's movement, we are now able to subject positions of this type to a series of cogent criticisms. This is mainly because we have overcome the idea of equality implicit in the studies I have outlined, by rethinking the concept of difference. Our *pensiero della differenza sessuale* has enabled women to make a theoretical shift and to focus on the issue of gendered subjectivity, which was previously almost universally neglected.

The absence of any discussion of this issue is a general deficiency of the socio-linguistic approach to the study of language. While other contemporary linguistic theories, such as generative grammar, have developed an articulated theory of the subject, this is not true of socio-linguistics. So much so that the only subject to which socio-linguists can refer is an empirical one constituted by a set of empirical features, an *a posteriori* reconstruction inferred from the analysis. Because of the way in which data are collected and constructed in socio-linguistic work, complex individual behaviour is broken down into a sequence of single variables. The subject consequently emerges as a combination of social, economic, cultural or biographical traits, such as race, age, class and occupation. Each variable contributes to a classificatory scheme which is then used to categorize individuals. Subjectivity can therefore only be defined as a set of such variables. Within this approach, sexual difference is seen as just one more variable, an external feature of an individual's life on a par with other variables such as education or social class. Socio-linguistics therefore cannot yield any insight into different forms of subjectivity.

This lack of a theory of subjectivity in general, and of female subjectivity in particular, was a consequence not only of the status of socio-linguistics as a discipline, but also of the state of feminist theory at that time. Sexual difference was seen as a purely biological, pre-linguistic datum, and/or as an effect of social subordination. In these circumstances, it was impossible to develop a more satisfactory account of female subjectivity than the one incorporated in the linear sequence of empirical features, of the form $1 + 1 + 1 + \ldots$

The issues I have raised so far are closely linked to other aspects of the current discussion surrounding equality and difference. Alongside a broad spectrum of divergent views, there are today in the Italian feminist movement several points of general agreement. The first concerns the meaning and value of difference. There exists a strong consensus in favour of the view that the most innovative and thought-provoking ideas and projects have developed in the past ten years around this central core, ranging from the earliest writings of Carla Lonzi to the establishment of numerous women's centres – to quote just two quite different experiences. It was, however, only possible for difference to emerge as a theme once another line of thought prominent during the 1970s had been brought to a conclusion – namely the critique of male culture and subjectivity. There is now a widespread critical understanding of the character of male forms of discourse. In particular, the process whereby male subjectivity has hidden its own partiality in order to present itself as universal – as the Himself, to use Luce Irigaray's words – has been analysed and deconstructed in many different ways. Since the appearance of Irigaray's *Speculum*[3] (still a mandatory point of reference for critical feminist theory, whether philosophical or psychoanalytic), a great deal of critical and analytical work has been done.

Even more interesting is the way that women's critical thinking has developed in many different disciplines, including the most objectivist and apparently gender-neutral ones, such as the natural sciences. In consequence, feminist women engaged in intellectual work have had to confront their own research with the basic issues of feminist thought, calling into question the idea of neutral skill and searching for an engendered way of thinking. This aspect of contemporary feminism in Italy contrasts sharply with that of the early 1970s, which was concerned almost exclusively with the themes of sexuality and the private sphere.

II

From a theoretical point of view, the 'critical phase' of women's thinking has already been accomplished, not because critical discourse is exhausted, but because its basic contours have now been sketched out. Women have developed precise reference points and know how to move forward. Now, however, we face a still more crucial and certainly more difficult problem, which could not have been tackled before the phase of critical analysis had reached a conclusion. This problem, which lies at the heart of *pensiero della differenza sessuale*, concerns female subjectivity. The most advanced work being done today within the Italian feminist movement – and to some extent in other European countries too – amounts to an attempt to articulate it.

To address the issue of the female subject is to ask what role is played by the symbolic in the structuring of subjectivity. The symbolic is what mediates between private experience and the general forms in which individual experience is inscribed. For the male subject, a means of mediating between personal experience and the universal symbolic order is already given. Patriarchal culture mediates, for men, between the individual experience of one's subjectivity and the general forms in which it is set.

We already know a great deal about the forms this mediation takes in male culture. We know, for example, that the 'neutral' concept of 'human', taken as universal, is nothing but a generalization of male subjectivity, and we also know how such a generalization enables individuals who happen to be male to be inscribed into the symbolic category of Man. Here I would like to concentrate on one aspect of this process that does not generally receive the attention it deserves. For men, the levels of individual experience and of cultural and symbolic order are perceived as contiguous, since there are accessible mediations that relate one to the other. Such mediations do not only exist at the level of high culture, as we are sometimes inclined to believe. Although philosophical, psychoanalytic and theoretical discourses are crucial to the male symbolic order, there are also other, more pervasive and perhaps more powerful forms of masculine mediation. The symbolic image of Man is constructed through a complex system of collective representations which are expressed above all in narrative, in the stories that men tell and have always told each other about themselves and about the world. Narrative is crucial to the construction of male subjectivity because it enables men to objectivize themselves and their own experience in the stories that represent it. Representation, narrative and subjectivity are joint aspects of one and the same process. In the unusually broad sense of the term that concerns us here, narrative includes both 'high' literary genres and, perhaps more crucially, what are generally considered 'low' genres. In the most trivial comic strip, as in the most stereotyped western movie, the very same story is always told, the story of male subjectivity.

The structure of subjectivity is inscribed in the deep structure of narrative itself. As Teresa de Lauretis has shown: 'Subjectivity is engaged in the cogs of narrative and indeed constituted in the relation of narrative, meaning and desire, so that the very work of narrative is to engage the subject with certain positions of meaning and desire.'[4]

Greimas, in his work on narrative structures,[5] and Lévi-Strauss, in his structural anthropology,[6] have shown the existence of a deep level of meaning underlying the various superficial forms of myths and narratives. At that deep level we can find universal elements and invariant structures that are responsible for the generation of meaning and narration, such as the basic semantic oppositions between life and death or nature and culture. This connection between the generation of meaning and narrative structure is, of course, no coincidence, since it is only within a narrative structure that meaning can occur.

Now, the basic semantic structure of any narrative form is given by the relationship set up between an acting subject and an acting object, a relationship which takes the form of a twofold movement of conjunction and disjunction, depending on whether the object is positively or negatively valued. In other words, any story is always the story of a subject in search of an object. Moreover, if narrative is constituted in the subject/object relation, the very same movement characterizes the structure of desire; for according to Freud, the dialectic of attraction and repulsion is the basic double movement of the drives. This parallel between the structure of desire and the work of narrative is closely represented in what can be seen as the paradigm of all narrations, the story of Oedipus. We know from anthropology that Oedipus' story is universal, and appears in different forms in almost all myths. Lévi-Strauss, for instance, analysed more than eight hundred myths from North and South America, and found that the basic form of the Bororo myth is nothing but an autochthonous variant of the Oedipus myth. Oedipus can thus be seen both as the paradigmatic form of narrative and as emblematic of the structure of desire.

It remains to ask, however, what desire (and hence what subjectivity) we are dealing with here. Oedipus's search is the structuring of a male subjectivity. The desire described in this archetypal narrative is the desire of a male subject whose object is woman.

> The desire is Oedipus's, and though its object may be woman (or Truth, or knowledge, or power), its term of reference and address is man: man as social being and mythical subject, founder of the social order, and source of mimetic violence; hence the institution of the incest prohibition, its maintenance in Sophocles' Oedipus as in Hamlet's revenge of his father, its costs and benefits, again, for man.[7]

In her analysis of 'Desire in narrative',[8] Teresa de Lauretis refers particularly to two pertinent and illuminating texts, an essay by Propp[9] and a more recent article by Lotman.[10] It is worth briefly outlining her interpretation of these works, since it may help to show how the mythical structure which is the foundation of both narrative and male subjectivity was shaped.

Propp combines a synchronic analysis of motives with a diachronic analysis of transformations. Transformations in the structure of the plot do not, in his view, derive directly from social structure but emerge instead from conflicts between different social orders at times of transition from one system to another. In particular, the Oedipus myth is supposed to have emerged at the point of transition from matriarchy to patriarchy. In an initial phase (corresponding to matriarchy), power was transferred from the king to his son-in-law through the mediation of marriage with the princess, the king's daughter. At a second stage, however, power passed directly from the king to his male child without the mediation of a female figure. This latter stage corresponds to the setting up of the patriarchal order. Moreover, since the passage of power from father to son implies the death of the old king, it gives rise to the theme of parricide (and to the related theme of prophecy).

Propp analyses the development of this narrative in myths and legends from Europe, Asia and Africa. In all its versions, it is structured at a point of transition from one social form to another. Indeed, in its most ancient forms, it is the princess, the daughter of the king, who sets her suitor a series of tests which he must pass before she will accept him as her husband. The man thereby becomes a member of her genealogy through a matriarchal marriage. In these stories the princess does not have brothers; they only appear later on, to become the heirs of the king in accordance with a patriarchal mode of succession.

In the Oedipus myth itself, which marks the transition to patriarchy, the princess's role is much less prominent, though according to Propp it is retained in the figure of the Sphinx. Gradually, however, she loses power as patriarchal systems get established, until she disappears completely.

Lotman's article casts light from the inside on an ideological aspect of the representation of women and supplies a good example of the ideology implicit in theoretical discourse. He reduces the number of principal actors in the myth to two: the hero, and the antagonist who is defined as an obstacle. In addition, the narrative chain is made up of only two links: entry into a closed space, and emergence from it.

> Inasmuch as closed space can be interpreted as 'a cave', 'the grave', 'a house', 'woman' (and, correspondingly, be allotted the features of darkness, warmth, dampness), entry into it is interpreted on various levels as 'death', 'conception', 'return home', and so on; moreover all these acts are thought of as mutually identical.[11]

According to this reading, the hero of the myth must be male, because the obstacle, whatever form it takes, is morphologically female – a womb. Such an interpretation has important consequences; for if the function of the mythic structure is to establish distinctions, the primary distinction on which all others depend is in this case sexual difference, which is even prior to the distinction between life and death. Opposing pairs such as inside/outside, death/life or raw/cooked derive from the basic opposition between edge and passage. Thus the hero is characterized as he who goes over the edge and penetrates the closed space. In this movement, as de Lauretis points out,

> the hero, the mythical subject, is constructed as human being and as male; he is the active principle of culture, the establisher of distinction, the creator of differences. Female is what is not susceptible to transformation, to life or death, she (it) is an element of plot-space, a topos, a resistance, matrix and matter.[12]

The studies I have discussed focus on the deep structure of narrative and show how the positions of subject and object are constructed from the very beginning as respectively male and female. Yet, at a less 'deep' level, the analysis of narrative can also tell us something else. In narrative it is not only the positions of subject and object – and therefore the relation of man to woman – that are symbolized, but also the relation of man to his own gender, in the twofold articulation of hierarchical relationships (master/pupil) and relationships among peers (group relationships and male solidarity).

These two aspects constitute key sequences in the process of constructing male subjectivity, and we can find them represented in an infinity of narrative variants in our culture. Consider, for example, the relationship of initiation between master and pupil and the role it plays in western culture, from Dante and Virgil to Guglielmo and Adso in *The Name of the Rose*.[13] Or take the representation of male solidarity relationships in a group. Male groups almost always unite individuals by engaging them in a joint project (be it war, conquest or founding a city), directed to a common goal which transcends their particular individuality. Some narrative genres – the western, for instance – may be regarded as infinite variations on this single theme.

The symbolic representation of these male relationships also allows the temporal dimension to be symbolized, since it offers a means of generalizing individual subjective experience. It creates a trans-individual space in which it is possible for men to identify with the collective and to inscribe their individual subjectivity into forms of collective subjectivity, such as that of groups, political parties and institutions. This process brings with it a different perception of time, which is no longer the time of a single individual life but the historical time of a society.

For women, there exist no forms of symbolic mediation between individual and social experience which are not partial and contradictory, so that the generalization of individual subjectivity does not take place – it is missing, cut off. In the next section of this chapter I shall analyse this lack, the lack of a visible means of self-representation.

III

Literary genres have, of course, provided women with forms of self-representation. In them, women have represented themselves through biographical and autobiographical narrative as the subjects of their own lives, so that literary production has always had an important subjectivizing function, akin to psychoanalysis. As Vegetti Finzi observes: 'Writing by women has always been born out of a pre-psychoanalytic desire to represent themselves through writing, to make themselves the subjects of their own lives through biographical narration.'[14] However, a subject which establishes its identity through autobiography is not the 'universal' subject represented in the Oedipus myth. It is a particular rather than a general subject, what one might call an 'exclusive' subject, deeply rooted in the particularity of its own story and in its own unique life experience. This exclusivity of female subjectivity is complex and endowed with various valencies. On the one hand, it carries within it the positive value of loyalty to oneself and one's own experience, which cannot be reduced to the values of male culture. This is crucially important for female subjectivity. On the other hand, it may also convey a constriction within rather narrow limits, the loss of a broader sense of belonging, whether in time or in gender.

The sense of belonging to a gender and the sense of belonging to a time are thus two vital factors that distinguish male from female experience and identity. For men, the sense of belonging to a collectivity is inscribed in the symbolic order, in initiation by the master and in solidarity among a group of peers. Moreover, the symbolically represented consciousness of belonging to a collectivity gives rise to a particular positioning of the male subject in relation to time, to a position which transcends individual experience. One's own individual life becomes part of a more general becoming, and individual time is inscribed into historical time. Man enters into History; indeed, Man creates his own History. However much the crisis of modernity may have undermined and changed the face of this optimistic illusion, it is nevertheless still present in the symbolization of male subjectivity.

Women, by contrast, face a different situation. First of all, their relationships with other women are both more complex and more contradictory than are the relations between men. Historically, women have devised mutual (and often mute) ways of helping one another, but at the same time their relationships have been characterized by a diffuse diffidence and secret rivalries. In the first place, the bonds between women are almost always sacrificed when a man comes on the scene; they lose out in the face of the patriarchal order, which in this case takes the form of love between a woman and a man. But another fact is even more important. The relationships between women have never been symbolized in male culture, as men's relationships have, and therefore cannot be internalized by women. They have remained (even where they existed) tragically confined to the private sphere, to the unspoken and unspeakable aspects of women's experience. Consequently, it is hard to find exemplary stories of solidarity and initiation among women, while for men such stories are legion. The same holds, moreover, for the temporal dimension, which is generally presented by women as the limited span of their own lives, and is rarely projected into a supra-individual becoming.

Because these representations are missing, sexual difference remains invisible. Women do not have social and collective forms of self-representation which they have produced themselves, as subjects. Instead, the only representations of their gender available to them are those established by patriarchal culture. Since subjectivity requires a level of social generalization, some social and collective representations of gender are necessary, to mediate between individual experience and more general forms of subjectivity. These representations would have to be socially visible in narratives, in stories or in myths, as they are at present for men.

Collective representations are the structures that, in a given society at a given time, give shape to the culture of that moment. They do not necessarily represent a rigid, homogeneous whole, but they do possess an internal structure. Recently, cultural anthropology and cultural theory have begun to develop models of the ways in which these collective representations spread and are diachronically transformed. Sperber, for example, discusses an epidemiological model in which collective representations are presented as epidemics which spread by infecting single individuals.[15] A particularly interesting feature of this model is the manner in which it links collective and individual representations, a link which may be defined in various ways: between ideology and individual psychology, or as a relation between self-representations and collective representations.

For our purposes, this connection is of fundamental importance. The way we become women, the way we establish an identity as women which is at the same time individual and social, internal and collective, depends precisely on how we work out the images of what it means to be a woman that are bequeathed to us by a particular culture at a given time. These images may be used in very different ways: women may adjust completely to existing social representations of the female image, or they may reject them altogether (though perhaps absolutely total rejection is impossible); or they may hold them at arm's length and try to modify them, as the women's movement has always sought to do.

It is especially important to emphasize the twofold nature of the process of self-representation, which involves on the one hand our internal image or individual representation and, on the other, the collective images constructed upon us, with which we are compelled to deal in one way or another. Subjectivity is like a sort of hinge between these two realities; it is the way we inscribe our internal self-representations into existing forms of social and hence visible representations. Without this inscription and mediation, subjectivity cannot develop fully, but is forced into a partiality which for women is the partiality of the 'vestals' of feeling and of the private sphere, or, at a different level, the partiality of woman as Nature, Mother, Original Matrix and so on.

Sexual difference, and hence gendered subjectivity, is constituted on the basis of two realities. It is rooted in the biological, pre-semiotic realm, and in this sense precedes the universe of representations, always bearing traces of its 'biological destiny'. At the same time, it is the elaboration and cultural transformation of this 'natural' reality, and therefore coincides with the whole set of representations that define what a woman is, what it is to 'be a woman'. It is worth noting that the 'value' of women – for example, their value as exchange objects, in Lévi-Strauss's terms – depends not on the first factor but on the second; not on any biological datum but on its symbolization. In other words, if women have a value as objects of exchange, it is because sexual difference has already been symbolized within the system of representations of a given society and has already become a part of culture.

The 'enigma of the feminine' consists in the way in which the female sex is transformed into 'woman', or, to put the point differently, in the way in which sex becomes gender. A biological datum is elaborated in a system of representations which in turn feeds back into the biological sphere (as, for example, with our conception of maternity, a locus *par excellence* of a cultural elaboration of a biological datum).

Collective representations of women are significant because they define our gender identity and because the construction of our gendered subjectivity is affected by them. Accordingly, it is vital that women should transform and modify the dominant patriarchal system of representations and make a different system visible. For existing representations convey only an image of sexual difference as subordination, a twisted difference that is nothing but a caricature of itself.

In addition, collective representations of sexual difference which are not themselves inscribed within the patriarchal order are a necessary condition of the very possibility of putting our own experience into narrative, not merely as biography but as history. This aspect of recounting one's own experience is fundamental for the constitution of subjectivity, since it allows us to objectivize our individual experience in a narrative form which is at the same time visible and general. The 'objectivizing' function of narrative should not be regarded as the negation or cancellation of one's own subjectivity. On the contrary, it should be understood as the foundation of subjectivity itself, since it gives subjectivity access to generality and to the temporal dimension in a way that merely autobiographical accounts, confined within the sphere of private feeling, can never do.

IV

Language clearly plays a central role in making a different order of representations visible and recognizable, for such social representations, be they discourses or images, are systems of signs, and are hence intrinsically semiotic and linguistic. Even if women have always talked among themselves, and have almost always had a network of distinctively female relationships, these relationships have never become visible, have never been fully symbolized. This absence may in turn explain some of the contradictions that have always characterized the position of women within patriarchy.

Even if women have a subordinate position in the patriarchal order, they nevertheless take part in it and often actively transmit it; for example, mothers frequently assume the primary responsibility for the castration and submission of their daughters. Contradictions of this sort are possible because relations between women are not incorporated into culture, and cannot create conditions in which they would be visible. And without visible, non-patriarchal representations of women, a different form of subjectivity cannot be internalized.

In recent years there has been in Italy a lively debate about language, sparked off by the publication of Alma Sabatini's manual for a non-sexist language.[16] The central issue here concerns the problem of change. Ought language to be changed? If so how, and through what kinds of linguistic innovation? Many people, especially men, have been profoundly critical of the very idea of such a transformation, and even within the women's movement linguistic change was often regarded as a marginal problem. This was, however, a mistake. While it may appear a trivial issue, linguistic change is part of the more general project of transforming social representations. Anything that contributes to making sexual difference visible is important in so far as it helps to create the conditions for a culture in which non-patriarchal, gendered subjectivity has a place.

Today, women are represented in numerical terms in many fields and this is a necessary condition of changing the patriarchal order. But it is not sufficient. For unless female subjectivity can be symbolized and thereby become visible, it will remain confined within the closed space of individual experience, in the secret place of individual consciousness, unsaid and unsayable.

Many requirements must be met before gendered subjectivity can gain a footing, and the women's movement obviously has a central role to play in making sexual difference representable and symbolizable, and in giving sexual difference its true value. We must give women both an individual and a collective value, and, even more important, learn to recognize and reveal the intrinsic value that sexual difference can express for women – and for men too – as long as it is not humiliated and crushed by patriarchal culture.

NOTES

1 C. Lonzi, *Sputiamo su Hegel*, Milan, Rivolta Femminile, 1974, p. 20. The best account of the Italian feminist movement compared to the Anglo-American is, to my knowledge, Teresa de Lauretis, 'Taking the risk of essentialism seriously: feminist theory in Italy, the US, and Britain', *Differences*, 1(2), 1988, pp. 3–37.
2 A. Cavarero, 'L'elaborazione filosofica della differenza sessuale', in M. C. Marcuzzo and A. Rossi Doria (eds), *La ricerca delle donne: studi femministi in Italia*, Turin, Rosenberg & Sellier, 1987, pp. 173–87, p. 180 (quote).
3 L. Irigaray, *Speculum: de l'autre femme*, Paris, Editions de Minuit, 1974.
4 T. de Lauretis, *Alice Doesn't: Feminism, Semiotics, Cinema*, Bloomington, Ind., Indiana University Press, 1984, p. 106.
5 A. J. Greimas, *Sémantique structurale: recherche de méthode*, Paris, Larousse, 1969, and *Introduction à l'analyse du discours en sciences sociales*, Paris, Hachette, 1979.
6 C. Lévi-Strauss, *Anthropologie structurale*, 2 vols, Paris, Plon, 1973–4.
7 De Lauretis, *Alice Doesn't*, p. 112.
8 ibid., pp. 103–57.
9 V. Propp, 'Edip v svete fol'klora', 1944; Italian trans. *Edipo alla luce del folklore*, Turin, Einaudi, 1975.
10 J. M. Lotman, 'The origin of plot in the light of typology', *Poetics Today*, 1(1–2), 1979, pp. 161–84.
11 ibid., p. 168.
12 De Lauretis, *Alice Doesn't*, p. 119.
13 U. Eco, *The Name of the Rose*, trans. from Italian, San Diego, Calif., Harcourt Brace Jovanovich, 1983.
14 S. Vegetti Finzi, 'Alla ricerca di una soggettività femminile', in Marcuzzo and Rossi Doria, *La ricerca delle donne*, pp. 228–48, 235 (quote).
15 D. Sperber, 'Anthropology and psychology: toward an epidemiology of representations', *Man*, 20, pp. 73–89.
16 A. Sabatini, *Il sessismo nella lingua italiana*, Rome, Presidenza del Consiglio dei Ministri, 1987.

Chapter 10

On the female feminist subject, or: from 'she-self' to 'she-other'

Rosi Braidotti   For A.S.

Qui a connu la dépersonnalisation reconnaîtra
l'autre sous n'importe quel déguisement: le
premier pas vers l'autre est de trouver en soi
l'homme de tous les hommes. *Toute femme est la*
femme de toutes les femmes, tout homme est
l'homme de tous les hommes et chacun d'eux
pourrait se présenter ou que l'on juge l'homme.

Clarice Lispector[1]

So far, everything that has befallen me has struck an answering chord.
This is the secret that encircles and holds me together. Only here, at the
uttermost rim of my life, can I name it to myself: *there is something of*
everyone in me, so I have belonged completely to no one, and I have even
understood their hatred for me.

Christa Wolf[2]

APPROACHING LISPECTOR

The story takes place at the top of a top building in one of the many
metropolises that pollute our planet. The event itself occurs in the further-
most room of this spacious apartment, which is also the humblest, being the
maid's quarters. The spatial metaphor is all-pervading in the text; as Jessica
Benjamin suggests, it can be seen as the representation of the woman's
desire. The character sees her dwelling as her bodily self, defining the maid's
room as 'le ventre de mon immeuble'.[3] This space is compared to the top of a
mountain, or the tip of a minaret: it is a microcosm endowed with a
heightened level of intensity, of depth.

The experience that G.H. undergoes at the top of that building is her
encounter with dimensions of experience and levels of being that are other
than herself and other than human. The otherness begins in her interaction
with the absent maid: by entering her quarters, G.H. crosses the boundaries

of both class and ethnicity, the maid being of a different ethnic origin from the comfortable urban, middle-class G.H. There is also a dislocation of both space and time. The shape of the room seems to defy description according to Euclidean geometry; it has the dry hostile appeal of the desert: it is more akin to raw matter than to urban dwellings. It is an empty, anorexic space of suspension.

In this environment, G.H. will experience total depersonalization, or the failure of her socialized identity: this process of dissolution of the boundaries of the self ('dépouillement') is an experience both of expansion and of limitation of her subjectivity. It is described with great intensity and precision. The event that triggers off the most intense sense of desubjectification is her relationship to a hideous insect, a cockroach, that inhabits the undescribable space of this room. The insect as non-human is totally other; it is also a borderline being, between the animal and the mineral. As ancient as the crust of the earth and gifted with astonishing powers of survival, it is a configuration of eternity. It is also, by definition, an abject being, object of disgust and rejection.

G.H.'s experience will consist of realizing first the proximity and then the commonality of being between herself and the living matter, half-animal, half-stone, the matter that lives independently of the gaze of the human beholder. Through the other and the abject, G.H. encounters primordial being in its incomprehensibly and blindly living form. The realization of the non-centrality of the human to life and to living matter leads G.H. to undertake the dehumanization of herself. This experience puts her in touch with the most remote and yet existentially most alive parts of her being: it triggers off her being-animal and being-insect, as the French philosopher Gilles Deleuze would phrase it. This process becomes for her a form of admiration and, finally, adoration of the life that, in her, does not carry her name; of the forces that, in her, do not belong to her own self. She enters the perfectly alive, that is to say, the inexpressive, the pre-discursive, the pre-symbolic layers of the being. Almost like a zombie, seduced by a force that she cannot name because it inhabits her so deeply, she consummates the intercourse with the other by the totemic assimilation of the cockroach: a gesture which transgresses a number of boundaries and taboos (human/non-human, fit to eat/unfit to eat, cooked/raw, etc.).

The ecstasy that follows from this encounter is one of utter dissolution of her own boundaries. And it is at that moment, when she is both pre-human and all too human, that she discovers the femaleness of her being: that, in her, which is prior to socialization is already sexed female. The woman in her, like the woman in all women, is the being whose relation to living matter is one of concomitance and adoration. It is in a pose of careful and receptive 'being one' with 'the world' that the story is concluded, though there is no ending as such.

It is tempting to have a mystical reading of this story, such as is proposed, for instance, by the Italian philosopher Luisa Muraro.[4] She sees a religious significance in the topography of the room and in the 'verticality' of the entire building. Resting on Luce Irigaray's notion of the 'divinity of woman',[5] she compares the location of the story to the Cross on Golgotha and reads the events as a moment of intense *passio*, resulting in transcendence towards the superhuman. In Muraro's understanding, the passion of G.H. is of the religious kind; the religion in question, however, is not patriarchal. What G.H. celebrates on the top of her sacred mountain is the divinity of her gender, the mystery and grace of sexual difference meant as a specifically female experience of transcending the boundaries of the human.

Luisa Muraro is careful to separate the transcendence in question and the sense of being that G.H. perceives from the dominion of the phallus, that is to say, of phallo-logocentric language. In other words, in order to gain access to the universal, Lispector knows she has to abandon human subjectivity altogether, but in that moment of ascesis what she does find is the universality of her gender, of her being the woman of all women. Her 'being sexed' is part of her innermost essence.

In a more laic and less mystical reading, Adriana Cavarero[6] sees instead in the passion of G.H. the affirmation of a feminist materialism. The life which, in one, does not bear one's own name, is a force that connects one to all other living matter. Cavarero reads this insight as the woman's attempt to disconnect her sense of being from the patriarchal Logos; in so doing she proposes the dislocation of one of the central premises of western thinking: that being and language are one.

Following the insight of Irigaray, Cavarero criticizes the assimilation of the universal to the masculine and defends the idea of a female-specific notion of being. That the living matter may not require the thinking 'I' in order to exist results in more emphasis being placed on the centrality of the sexed nature of the 'she-I'. Her 'being sexed' is primordial and inextricable from her being, in a way that is unrepresented by the grammatical structure of language, that is to say, by her 'I'. Sexual difference is definitional of the woman and not contingent; it is always already there.

In a very different reading of the same text, the French writer Helen Cixous[7] reads the event as a parable for women's writing, 'écriture féminine', meant as a process of constitution of an alternative female symbolic system. G.H.'s passion is for life without mastery, power or domination; her sense of adoration is compared to a capacity for a giving kind of receptivity, not for Christian martyrdom. Cixous connects this faculty to the ability both to give and to receive the gift, that is to say, to receive the other in all of his/her astounding difference.

In her ethical defence of the politics of subjectivity, Cixous speaks of the ability to receive otherness as a new science, a new discourse based on the idea of respectful affinity between self and other. The passion is about belonging to a common matter: life, in its total depersonalized manner. The term 'approach' defines for Cixous the basis of her ethical system; it is the way in which self and other can be connected in her new world view where all living matter is a sensitive web of mutually receptive entities. The other-than-human at stake here is that which, by definition, escapes the domination of the anthropocentric subject and requires that he/she accept his/her limitations. More specifically, the divine in all humans is the capacity to see interconnectedness as the way of being. For Cixous this heightened sense of being is the feminine, it is the woman as creative force; poet and writer. The divine is the feminine as creativity.

FEMINISM AND MODERNITY

The first and foremost element for women's becoming, in both a political and an existential sense, is time. The Brazilian writer Clarice Lispector in her book *The Passion according to G.H.* tells us about the time, the rituals, the repetition, the symbolic transactions and blank spaces of that continuum that is commonly called time. In the choice of language and situations, Lispector echoes the centuries-old tradition of mystical ascesis, but also moves clearly out of it. As Cavarero suggests, G.H. symbolizes a new post-modern kind of materialism: one that stresses the materiality of all living matter in a common plane of coexistence, without postulating a central point of reference or of organization for it. Lispector's point is not only that all that lives is holy; or rather, it is not even that. She strikes me rather as saying that on the scale of being there are forces at work that bypass principles of form and organization; there is raw living matter, as there is pure time, regardless of the form they may actually take. The emphasis is on the forces, the passions, and not on specific forms of life. In other words, I think Lispector is better read with Spinoza and Nietzsche than as a Christian mystic.[8]

Lispector's text seems to me an excellent exemplification of one of the central issues in the debate between feminism and post-modern discourse.[9] What is at stake in this debate is the 'deconstruction of meta-discourses', as Jean-François Lyotard argues,[10] and therefore also the assessment of the vision of subjectivity embedded in the tradition of the Enlightenment, that is to say, the question of modernity as a whole. Several analysts of feminist theory[11] have pointed out the shift away from the mere critique of sexist or androcentric biases and the construction of alternative theories based on the experience of women, towards the elaboration of more general epistemological frameworks. These concern both the pursuit of scientific knowledge, as Sandra Harding puts it,[12] and the revision of the very foundations of abstract scientific reasoning, as both Evelyn Fox-Keller[13] and Genevieve Lloyd[14] have argued.

The specific angle of debate that interests me here is the extent to which the feminist critiques of theoretical reason as a regulative principle, by paving the way for the deconstruction of the dualistic oppositions on which the classical notion of the subject is founded, have resulted in approaching the notion of sexual difference as laying the foundations for an alternative model of female subjectivity. In other words, I think that the specific feminist approach to the question of modernity consists in the evaluation of the links or complicity between knowledge and power, reason and domination, rationality and oppression, and of them all with masculinity.

Thus defined, the problem of feminist theory also implies the questioning of the notion of equality, one of the pillars of Enlightenment thinking. The central question here seems to me: are today's feminists closet humanists, wanting to rescue the shaken edifice of reason, resting on some realist theory of truth? Or are they radical epistemologists, having given up the idea of gaining access to a real, fixed truth? In other words, what is the image of theoretical reason at work in feminist thought? What images and representations do feminists propose for their specific approach to theoretical practice?

As Jane Flax argues,[15] this is clearly a meta-discursive approach, related to the simultaneous occurrence of the crisis of western values[16] and the emergence of a variety of 'minority' discourses, as Gayatri Spivak,[17] Chandra Mohanty[18] and Trinh T. Minh-ha[19] have pointed out. This historical circumstance makes it urgent to think through the status of thinking in general and of the specific activity of theory in particular. For feminists, it is especially urgent to work towards a balanced and constructive assessment of the mutual interdependence of equality and the practice of differences.

In one of her most outspoken statements on this issue, significantly called 'Equal to whom?', Luce Irigaray[20] shows the intrinsic reliance of the notion of equality on masculine parameters and argues for the political necessity of setting the notion of difference at the centre of our political activity and thought. The revindication of difference implies releasing it from the dualistic logic in which it has traditionally been inscribed as a mark of pejoration, so as to make it expressive of the positive value of being 'other than' the masculine, white, middle-class norm.

All this is linked to the lesson of G.H. By raising the question of whether the links between reason and exclusion/domination are implicit and therefore inevitable, feminists have put forward the idea that rationality is not the whole of reason and that reason does not sum up the totality of, or even what is best in, the human capacity for thinking. They have therefore challenged the equation between being and logocentric language. In other words, feminist theory is the critique of the power in/as discourse and the active endeavour to create other ways of thinking: it is the engagement in the process of learning to think differently. In my understanding, the feminist is a critical thinker, unveiling and criticizing the modalities of power and domination implicit in all theoretical discourse, including her own. She is also, however, a creative thinker in so far as she has to bring about new forms of representation and definition of the female subject. Feminism as critical thought is therefore a self-reflexive mode of analysis, aimed at articulating the critique of power in discourse with the affirmation of what Teresa de Lauretis defines as the female feminist subject.[21]

I would then ask: what does it mean to think as a female feminist? What sort of a subject is the subject defined by the political and theoretical project of 'sexual difference'? By adopting this standpoint, I mean to distance myself from the standard Anglo-Saxon feminist distinction between 'sex' on the one hand and 'gender' on the other and follow the continental tradition of approaching sexuality as a simultaneously material and symbolic institution.[22]

Consequently, I see as the central aim of the practice of sexual difference the articulation of questions of individual gendered identity with issues related to political subjectivity. The interaction of identity with subjectivity also spells out the categorical distinction between dimensions of experience that are marked by desire and therefore the unconscious and others that are rather subjected to willed self-regulation. I will argue that, although both levels are the site of political consciousness, there is not one dominant form of political action that can encompass them both: the locality and specificity of political activity are central to the vision of the politics of subjectivity which is implied in the practice of sexual difference.

ANOTHER IMAGE OF THOUGHT

In other words, feminist theory, far from being a reactive kind of thought, expresses women's ontological desire, women's structural need to posit themselves as female subjects, that is to say, not as disembodied entities but rather as corporeal and consequently sexed beings. Following Adrienne Rich, in fact,[23] I believe that the redefinition of the female feminist subject starts with the revaluation of the bodily roots of subjectivity, rejecting the traditional vision of the knowing subject as universal, neutral and consequently gender free. This 'positional' or situated way of seeing the subject states that the most important location or situation is the rooting of the subject into the spatial frame of the body. The first and foremost of locations in reality is one's own embodiment. Rethinking the body as our primary situation is the starting point for the epistemological side of the 'politics of location', which aims at elucidating the discourse produced by female feminists.

In other words, identity and subjectivity are different moments in the process of defining a subject position. This idea of the subject as process means that he/she can no longer be seen to coincide with his/her consciousness, but must be thought of as a complex and multiple identity, as the site of the dynamic interaction of desire with the will, of subjectivity with the unconscious: not just libidinal desire, but rather ontological desire, the desire to be, the tendency of the subject to be, the predisposition of the subject towards being. Jean-François Lyotard describes this notion of the subject as a clear break from the modernist project; the latter is understood not only in terms of the Enlightenment legacy of the complicity of reason, truth and progress with domination, but also as the marriage of the individual will with the general will of capital. According to Lyotard, modernism marked the triumph of the will-to-have, to own, to possess, within each individual; this in turn entailed the correlative objectification of many minority subjects.

By contrast, post-modernism marks the emergence of the desire to be at the very heart of the question of subjectivity. It is the triumph of the ethical vision of the subject as a discontinuous and yet unified bodily entity. The distinction between will and desire is useful in that it separates different qualitative levels of experience. It can also help us rescue post-modern thought from the charges that are often made against it: of being merely nihilistic. That post-modern thought, including the feminist strand, is a reaction to a state of crisis does not make it necessarily negative; on the contrary, I see it as offering many positive openings.

The crisis of modernity is marked, as Foucault points out,[24] by the emphasis placed both on the unconscious and on desire by psychoanalysis, taken as the exemplary modern discourse. The hypothesis of the unconscious can be seen as inflicting a terrible wound on the transcendental narcissism of the classical vision of the subject. The unconscious as an epistemological assumption marks the non-coincidence of the subject with his/her consciousness; it is the grain of sand in the machine that prevents the enunciation of yet another monolithic, self-present subject.

The fundamental epistemological insight of psychoanalysis is that the thinking process as a whole plunges its roots in pre-rational matter; thinking is just a form of sensibilization of matter, it is the specific form of intelligence of embodied entities. Thinking is a bodily, not a mental process. Thinking precedes rational thought.

The crisis of rational thought is nothing more than the forced realization, brought about by historical circumstances, that this highly phallocentric mode of thought rests on a set of unspoken premises about thinking which are themselves non-rational. In other words, the logocentric posture, the enunciation of a philosophical stance, rests on a pre-philosophical moment, namely the human being's capacity for disposition, receptivity and desire for thinking. The disposition of the subject towards thinking, i.e. representing him-/herself in language, is the non-philosophical basis of philosophy; it is a pre-discursive element, as Patrizia Violi points out,[25] which is in excess of and nevertheless indispensable to the act of thinking as such. It is an ontological tendency, a predisposition that is neither thinking nor conscious and which inscribes the subject into the web of discursiveness, language and power.

This predisposition or receptivity of the subject towards 'making sense' frees our vision of subjectivity from what Gilles Deleuze[26] aptly calls the imperialism of rational thought, which appears in this perspective inadequate as a tool of analysis. Thinking thus becomes the attempt to create other ways of thinking, other forms of thought: thinking is about how to think differently.

The vision of the subject as an interface of will with desire is therefore the first step in the process of rethinking the foundations of subjectivity. It amounts to saying that what sustains the entire process of 'becoming subject' is the will to know, the desire to say, the desire to speak, to think and to represent. In the beginning there is only the desire to: the desire to know, that is to say, the knowledge about desire.

This founding, primary, vital, necessary and therefore original desire to know is what remains unthought at the very heart of thought in so far as it is the very condition of possibility for thought to occur at all. Desire is that which, being the *a priori* condition for thinking, is in excess of the thinking process itself.

This is why I want to argue here that the task of thinking about new forms of female subjectivity, through the project of sexual difference meant as the expression of women's ontological desire, implies the transformation of the very structures and images of thought, not just the propositional content of the thoughts. Thinking through the question of sexual difference implies the reformulation of the relation of thought to life and also of thought to philosophy. In other words, sexual difference opens out towards the redefinition of general structures of thought, not only female-specific ones.

EMBODIMENT AND DIFFERENCE

The body, or the embodiment of the subject, is a key term in the feminist struggle for the redefinition of subjectivity. It is to be understood neither as a biological nor as a sociological category, but, as Patrizia Violi argues in this volume, rather as a point of overlapping between the physical, the symbolic[27] and the sociological.[28]

The concept of the body in the specific inception given to it by the philosophy of modernity and the theories of sexual difference refers to the multifunctional and complex structure of subjectivity, the specifically human capacity for transcending any given variable – class, race, sex, nationality, culture, etc. – while remaining situated within them. The body in question is best understood as a surface of signification, situated at the intersection of the alleged facticity of anatomy[29] with the symbolic dimension of language. As such, the body is a multifaceted sort of notion, covering a broad spectrum of levels of experience and frames of enunciation. In other words, the subject is defined by many different variables: class, race, sex, age, nationality and culture overlap in defining and coding the levels of our experience.

In a move which characterizes it among all others, however, western culture has set very high priority on the production of the sexed body, situating the variable sexuality on top of the list. The embodied sexed subject thus defined is situated in a web of complex power relations which, as Foucault pointed out,[30] inscribe the subject in a discursive and material structure of normativity. Sexuality is the dominant discourse of power in the west. In this respect the feminist redefinition of the subject as equally though discontinually subjected to the normative effect of many complex and overlapping variables (sex, race, class, age, etc.) both perpetuates the western habit of giving sexuality a high priority and also challenges it as one of the dominant traits of western discursive power.

Sexuality as power, that is, as institution, is also a semiotic code that organizes our perception of morphological differences between the sexes. It is obviously the inscription into language that makes the embodied subject into a speaking 'I', that is to say, a functional, socialized gendered entity. In my understanding, there can be no subjectivity outside sexuation, or language, that is to say, the subject is always gendered: it is a 'she-I' or a 'he-I'. That the 'I' thus engendered is not a nominal essence, but merely a convenient fiction, a grammatical necessity holding together a multiplicity of levels of experience that structure the embodied subject, as post-structuralist thought convincingly argues,[31] does not alter the fact that it is genderized, that is to say, sexually differentiated.

The view I am putting forward is that the starting ground for feminist redefinitions of female subjectivity is a new form of materialism that inherits the corporeal materiality of the post-structuralists and thus places emphasis on the embodied and therefore sexually differentiated structure of the speaking subject. The variable of sexuality has high priority in the bodily materialism thus advocated. In feminist theory one *speaks as* a woman, although the subject 'woman' is not a monolithic essence defined once and for all, but rather the site of multiple, complex and potentially contradictory sets of experience, defined by overlapping variables. 'Speaking as' refers to Adrienne Rich's 'politics of location', that is to say, to embodiment as positionality, the aim of which is to set the boundaries and the epistemological parameters of a community of female feminist knowing subjects. As a consequence, the female feminist subject, to whom I will refer to as 'she-self' and 'I, woman', is to be redefined through the collective quest for a political re-examination of sexuality as a social and symbolic system.

One of the points of tension of this project is how to reconcile the feminist critiques of the priority traditionally granted to the variable 'sexuality' in western discourse about the subject, with the feminist proposition of redefining the embodied subject in a network of interrelated variables of which 'sexuality' is one but is set alongside other powerful axes of subjectification, such as race, culture, nationality, class and life-choice preferences. This double-edged project of relying both on genderized or sex-specific notions in order to redefine the female feminist subject, and on deconstructing them at the same time, has led to some strong feminist rejections of sexed female identity, and to the critique of the signifier 'woman' as a meaningful political term.

For my part, however, I do not experience this tension as anything more than historical contradiction. That the signifier 'woman' is both the concept around which feminists have gathered, in a movement where the politics of identity are central, and also the very concept that needs to be analysed critically, is a perfect description of our historical situation in post-modern late capitalism. I think that the best way out of the dichotomous logic in which western culture has captured sexed identities is to *work them through*. In this respect, I find Luce Irigaray's notion of 'mimesis'[32] highly effective, in that it allows women to revisit and repossess the discursive and material sites where 'woman' was essentialized, disqualified or quite simply excluded. *Working through* is a deconstructive notion which has already given proof of both its strengths and its limitations.[33] Working through the networks of discursive definitions of 'woman' is useful not only in what it produces as a process of deconstruction of female subjectivity, but also *as process*, which allows for the constitution and the legitimation of a gendered female feminist community.

In other words, the 'she-self' fastens upon the presence of the female embodied self, the woman, but it does so only as long as other women sustain, *hic et nunc*, the project of redefining female subjectivity. It is a sort of ontological leap forward by which a politically enforced collective subject, the 'we women' of the women's movement, can empower the subjective becoming of each one of us 'I, woman'. This leap is forward, not backwards towards the glorification of an authentic archaic feminine power or of a well-hidden 'true' essence. It does not aim at recovering a lost origin or a forgotten land, but rather to bring about here and now a mode of representation that would take the fact of being a woman as a positive, self-affirming political force. It is an act of self-legitimation whereby the 'she-self' blends her ontological desire to be with the conscious willed becoming of a collective political movement. This distinction between the will and desire marks a separation of registers, of levels of experience, which must be underlined and never confused. As I said earlier, the distinction between identity and subjectivity is to be related to that between will and desire.

That is to say, between 'she-self' and 'she-other' there is a bond that Adrienne Rich describes as the 'continuum' of women's experience. This continuum draws the boundaries within which the conditions of possibility of a redefinition of the female subjects can be made operative. The notion of the community is therefore central; what is at play among us today, in the here and now of the game of enunciation we are playing together, in the interaction between the writer and her readers, is our common engagement in the recognition of the political implications of a theoretical project: the redefinition of female subjectivity.

Several attempts have been made by feminists to theorize the community of women, some in pedagogical terms.[34] Evelyn Fox-Keller takes Kuhn's notion of scientific community; Teresa de Lauretis uses the Foucauldian model of a micro-politics of resistance; several others such as Jane Flax and Jessica Benjamin[35] turn to Winnicott's object-relation theory as a model. Jessica Benjamin argues that self and other are inextricably linked and that it is in being with the other that I experience the most profound sense of self; Jane Flax argues along similar lines that it is the capacity for mutual, reciprocal intersubjective connections that allows for the constitution of subjectivity.

Feminist theoretician Jessica Benjamin takes this even further, arguing that female desire must be conceptualized as the in-between space, connecting inside to outside, in a constant flow of self into other that cannot and should not be disrupted by falsely dichotomous distinctions. Emphasizing the genderedness of embodiment, Benjamin collapses the inside/outside distinction of the body, stressing the in-between spaces. She thus attempts to replace the mediation by the phallus with the capacity for interconnectedness and agency, so that desire need not be conceptualized according to the murderous logic of dialectical oppositions.

The 'transitional space' that Benjamin defends must be understood as an interface, marking both the distance and the proximity between the spatial surface of bodies. 'Something that both forms a boundary and opens up into endless possibility',[36] it is a space not only of reception of the other but also of receptivity as the very condition for otherness to be perceived as such. I would relate it to the Spinozist emphasis on the subject's structural capacity to be affected, to be in contact with others. Something in the ontological structure of the subject is related to the presence of the other.

It would be interesting to compare this vision of the Winnicottian transitional space as a model for female desire to Habermas's idea of the communicative bond, but I cannot expand on this here. Let me instead come back to my question of the community: what sort of discursive space is being constructed here and now? The levels of complex and layered interconnection that form subjectivity are operational in the act of our enunciation of feminist, as all other, statements.

Consequently, it is in language, not in anatomy, that my gendered subjectivity finds a voice, becomes a corpus, is engendered. It is in language as power, that is to say, in the politics of location, that I as 'she-self' make myself accountable to my speaking partners, you, the 'she-other' fellow feminists who are caught in the web of discursive enunciation that I am spinning as I speak. You, the 'she-you', like me, the 'she-I', are politically engaged in the project of redefining the gender that we are. The language cracks under the strain of this excessive genderization; the personal pronouns cannot sustain the interpersonal charge required by the feminist project. Something in the structure of the language resists; how can you express adequately what is lacking from or in excess of existing parameters? How does one invent new ways of thinking?

Accountability makes the feminist project into a critical theory and at the same time an ethical one in so far as it stresses the primacy of the bond, the presence of the other, of the community as a vital step in the redefinition of the self. In *Technologies of Gender*, Teresa de Lauretis argues that this is, however, fundamentally an epistemological project. In her understanding of the term, epistemology is the process of comprehending and of formalizing subjectivity as a process, as a network of complex interplay between different axes of subjectification.[37]

The female feminist subject thus defined is one of the terms in a process that cannot and should not be streamlined into a linear, teleological form of subjectivity. The female feminist subject is the site of intersection of subjective desire with willed social transformation. The assertion that women should be something more and other than non-men, which Adriana Cavarero makes very strongly in this volume, is the first step in this process.

What I want to emphasize is that desire is what is at stake in the feminist pursuit of alternative definitions of female subjectivity. The attempt to activate a discursive ethics based on sexual difference as the site of empowerment of the feminine is both an epistemological and a political move. The question is how to determine the angle through which we can gain access to a non-logocentric mode of representation of the female subject. To determine that, we need to think anew about power: not power only as a site of visible forces, where it is the most identifiable because that is where it displays itself (parliament, churches, universities, etc.), but power also as an invisible web of interrelated effects, a persistent and all-pervading circulation of effects.

The importance of this point is not only epistemological and methodological, but also political. It will in fact determine the kind of alliance or social pact that we women are likely to undertake with each other. The notion of desire in this configuration is not a prescriptive one. The desire to become and to speak as women does not entail the imposition of a specific propositional content of women's speech. What is being empowered is women's entitlement to speak, not the propositional content of their utterances. What I want to emphasize is women's desire to become, not a specific model for their becoming.

TOWARDS A GENDERIZED UNIVERSAL

Thinking about thinking, in the meta-discursive mode I have been defending, is not just thinking for its own sake; it rather marks the feminist intellectual's responsibility for and towards the act of thinking, lingering in the conceptual complexities that we have ourselves created. Give ourselves the time to think through and work through these complexities so as not to short-circuit the process of our own becoming. As Lispector pointed out, we are nurturing the beginning of the new; the depersonalized female subject lays the foundations for the symbolization of women's ontological desire.

This implies the redefinition of the relationship of power to knowledge within feminism. As women of ideas devoted to the elaboration of the theory and practice of sexual difference, we are responsible for the very notions that we enact and empower. Thinking justly – of justness and not only of justice – is a top item on our agenda. This ethical dimension is for me as important as the political imperative. Feminist thinking cannot be purely strategic, that is, be the expression of a political will; it must rather attempt to be adequate as a representation of experience. Feminist theorizing must be adequate conceptually, as well as being suitable politically; one's relationship to thinking is the prototype of a different relationship to alterity altogether. If we lose sight of this ethical, relational foundation of thinking, that is to say, the bond that certain discourses create among us, we are indeed in danger of homologation and therefore of purely strategic or instrumental kinds of thought. There can be no justice without justness, no political truth without adequation of our words, our ideas and consequently our thought to the project of redefining female subjectivity in a non-logocentric mode.

As a consequence, the first priority for me today is to redefine the subject as a gendered unity inextricably connected to the other. For feminism, in the beginning there is alterity, the non-one, a multiplicity. The founding agent is the common corpus of female subjects who posit themselves theoretically and politically as a collective subject. This communal bond comes first; then and only then there arises the question of what political line to enforce. It is the ethical that defines the political and not vice versa: hence the importance of positing the feminist audience as the receptive, active participant in a discursive exchange that aims at changing the very rules of the game. This is the feminist community to which the 'she-I' makes herself accountable.

The paradox of the ontological basis of desire is that not only is it intersubjective, but also it transcends the subject. Desire also functions as the threshold for a redefinition of a new universal, a new common plane of being: 'each woman is the woman of all women', a genderized universal. If we take as our starting point sexual difference as the positive affirmation of my facticity as a woman, that is to say, if we push to the extreme the recognition of sexual difference, *working through* the layers of complexity of the signifier 'I, woman', we end up opening a window onto a new genderized universal.

It sounds like a contradiction in terms, given all we have learnt about the universal as the inflation of masculinity into cosmic transcendental narcissism. By genderized universality I mean a symbolic dimension proper to each sex, that is, the non-reducibility of the feminine to the masculine, and yet, at the same time, the indestructible unity of the human as an embodied self structurally linked to the other: gendered universality as the complex intersecting of never-ending levels of differing of self from other and self from self. As Adriana Cavarero[38] put it, what is at stake in this is the thinkability or representability of a feminine subject as a self-representing entity. It is less a question of founding the subject than of elucidating the categories by which the female feminist subject can be adequately represented.

This is an important political gesture, because thinking through the fullness of one's complexity, in the force of one's transcendence, is something women have never historically been able to afford. What seems to be at stake in the project of sexual difference is, through the extreme sexualization of the subject, a Nietzschean transmutation of the very value we give to the human and to a universal notion of commonness, of common belonging.

I will want to argue that the aim of this transmutation of values is to be able to bring to the fore the multi-layered structure of the subject. As Lispector points out, 'the life in me does not have my name'; 'I' is not the owner of the portion of being that constitutes his/her being. To the extent that 'she-I' accepts this, can 'she-I' become the woman of all women and be accountable for her humanness? Only this highly defined notion of singularity can allow us to posit a new general sense of being.

NOTES

1 C. Lispector: *La passion selon G.H.*, Paris, Editions des Femmes, 1978, pp. 192–3.
2 C. Wolf, *Cassandra*, London, Virago, 1984, p. 4.
3 'The womb of my building', Lispector, *La passion*, p. 45. See J. Benjamin, 'A desire of one's own: psychoanalytic feminism and intersubjective space', in T. de Lauretis (ed.), *Feminist Studies/Critical Studies*, Bloomington, Ind., Indiana University Press, 1986, pp. 78–99.
4 L. Muraro, 'Commento alla: *Passione secondo G.H.*', *Donna woman femme*, 5–6, 1986, pp. 65–78.
5 L. Irigaray, 'Femmes divines', *Critique*, 454, 1985.
6 A. Cavarero, *Nonostante Platone*, Rome, Editori Riuniti, 1990.
7 H. Cixous, 'L'approche de Clarice Lispector', in *Entre l'écriture*, Paris, Editions des Femmes, 1986, pp. 115–99.
8 I cannot expand on this point here; for a fuller analysis see my forthcoming study *Organs without Bodies*, London, Routledge.
9 A. Jardine, *Gynesis: Configurations of Woman and Modernity*, Ithaca, NY, Cornell University Press, 1984; L. Nicholson (ed.), *Feminism/Postmodernism*, New York and London, Routledge, 1990; L. Hutcheon, *A Poetics of Post-*

modernism, London, Routledge, 1988, and *The Politics of Postmodernism*, London, Routledge, 1989; J. Scott, 'Deconstructing equality vs difference', *Feminist Studies*, 14(1), 1988, pp. 35–50; N. Fraser and L. Nicholson, 'Social criticism without philosophy: an encounter between feminism and post-modernism', *Theory, Culture and Society*, 5, 1988, pp. 373–94.

10 J.-F. Lyotard, 'Some of the things at stake in women's struggles', *Wedge*, 1984, 6. He is also credited with providing the clearest definition of post-modernism, in J.-F. Lyotard, *La condition post-moderne*, Paris, Editions de Minuit, 1979. For a feminist reply to Lyotard see S. Benhabib, 'Epistemologies of postmodernism, a rejoinder to Jean-François Lyotard', in Nicholson, *Feminism/Postmodernism*, pp. 107–32. See also R. Braidotti, *Patterns of Dissonance*, Cambridge, Polity Press, 1991.

11 H. Eisenstein, *Contemporary Feminist Thought*, Sydney, Allen & Unwin, 1983; C. Stimpson, *Where the Meanings Are*, New York, Routledge, 1989.

12 S. Harding, *The Science Question in Feminism*, London, Open University Press, 1986, and *Feminism and Methodology*, London, Open University Press, 1987; S. Harding and M. B. Hintikka (eds), *Discovering Reality*, Boston, Reidel, 1983.

13 E. Fox-Keller, *Reflexions on Gender and Science*, New Haven, Conn., Yale University Press, 1983, and *A Feeling for the Organism*, New York, Freeman, 1985.

14 G. Lloyd, *The Man of Reason*, London, Methuen, 1985.

15 J. Flax, 'Postmodernism and gender relations in feminist theory', *Signs*, 12(4), 1987, pp. 621–43. See also J. Flax, *Thinking Fragments*, Berkeley, Calif., University of California Press, 1990.

16 J. Kristeva, 'Women's time', *Signs*, 7(1), 1981, pp. 13–35, also reprinted in N. O. Keohane, M. Z. Rosaldo and B. C. Gelpi (eds), *Feminist Theory: A Critique of Ideology*, Chicago, University of Chicago Press, 1982.

17 G. C. Spivak, *In Other Worlds*, New York, Routledge, 1987.

18 C. Mohanty, 'Under western eyes: feminist scholarship and colonial discourse', *Boundary*, 2(3), 1984, pp. 333–58.

19 Trinh T. Minh-ha, *Woman, Native, Other*, Bloomington, Ind., Indiana University Press, 1989.

20 L. Irigaray, 'Egales à qui?', *Critique*, 480, 1987, pp. 420–37; English trans. 'Equal to whom?' *Differences*, 1(2), 1988, pp. 59–76.

21 De Lauretis, *Feminist Studies/Critical Studies* and *Technologies of Gender*, Bloomington, Ind., Indiana University Press, 1987.

22 For an enlightening comparative discussion of these two traditions and of their implications for feminist theory see T. de Lauretis, 'The essence of the triangle, or taking the risk of essentialism seriously', *Differences*, 1(2), 1988, pp. 3–37.

23 A. Rich, *Of Woman Born*, New York, Norton, 1976; *On Lies, Secrets and Silence*, New York, Norton, 1979; *Blood, Bread and Poetry*, New York, Norton, 1985.

24 M. Foucault, *Les mots et les choses*, Paris, Gallimard, 1966, and *Histoire de la folie*, Paris, Gallimard, 1972.

25 P. Violi, *L'infinito singolare*, Verona, Essedue, 1987.

26 G. Deleuze, *Logique du sens*, Paris, Editions de Minuit, 1969; *Différence et répétition*, Paris, PUF, 1968; *Nietzsche et la philosophie*, Paris, PUF, 1962.

27 The term 'symbolic' is complex; I am using it here in a post-Lacanian sense, as referring to the cumulated and multi-layered structure of signification of language, where language encapsulates the fundamental structures of a given culture. The literature on Lacanian feminism is so vast that I shall not even attempt to discuss it here; for an excellent summary see T. Brennan, 'Introduc-

tion' to T. Brennan (ed.), *Between Feminism and Psychoanalysis*, London, Routledge, 1989, pp. 1–23.

28 For a fuller analysis of this vision of the body see my article 'Organs without bodies', *Differences*, 1(1), 1989, pp. 14–61. See also E. Grosz, 'Notes towards a corporeal feminism', *Australian Feminist Studies*, 5, 1987, pp. 1–16.

29 The terminology is reminiscent of the existentialist legacy: the 'facticity' of the body as opposed to the 'transcendence' of the thinking consciousness. I am aware of the dualism implicit in the existentialist position, while I appreciate the effort at actually thinking the body. For a pertinent critique of existentialism in relation to feminism see M. le Doeff, *L'étude et le rouet*, Paris, Seuil, 1989. For a lucid critique of the category 'sex' meant as an anatomical reality, allegedly opposed to the 'gender' system by which in fact it is constructed, see J. Butler, *Gender Trouble*, New York, Routledge, 1990.

30 M. Foucault, *Surveiller et punir*, Paris, Gallimard, 1975; *Histoire de la sexualité vol. I, La volonté de savoir*, Paris, Gallimard, 1976; vol. II, *L'usage des plaisirs*, Paris, Gallimard, 1984; vol. III, *Le souci de soi*, Paris, Gallimard, 1984. For a feminist analysis see J. Diamond and L. Quinby (eds), *Foucault and Feminism*, Boston, Mass., Northeastern University Press, 1988.

31 Much has been written about the 'death of the subject' as leitmotiv in the poststructuralist crusade against classical visions of the subject as coinciding with *his* consciousness. The double move that comes under criticism is the simultaneous identification of subjectivity with consciousness and both of them with masculinity. For a summary of the feminist reactions to this, see my *Patterns of Dissonance*.

32 L. Irigaray, *Speculum*, Paris, Editions de Minuit, 1974; *Ce sexe qui n'en est pas un*, Paris, Editions de Minuit, 1977; *L'éthique de la différence sexuelle*, Paris, Editions de Minuit, 1984.

33 For evidence of its limitations see G. C. Spivak, 'Displacement and the discourse of woman', in M. Krupnick (ed.), *Displacement, Derrida and After*, Bloomington, Ind., Indiana University Press, 1983, pp. 169–95, and 'Feminism and deconstruction again: negotiating with unacknowledged masculinism', in T. Brennan (ed.), *Between Feminism and Psychoanalysis*, London, Routledge, 1989, pp. 206–24.

34 M. Culley and C. Portuges, *Gendered Subjects: The Dynamics of Feminist Teaching*, Boston, Mass., Routledge & Kegan Paul, 1985; see also G. Bowles and R. Duelli-Klein (eds), *Theories of Women's Studies*, London, Routledge & Kegan Paul, 1983.

35 J. Benjamin, *The Bonds of Love*, New York, Pantheon, 1988, and 'A desire of one's own', pp. 78–99.

36 Benjamin, 'A desire of one's own', p. 94.

37 The term is better rendered in French, where 'assujettissement' covers the multi-layered nature of subjectivity, as the process of interaction of self and other, in a multiplicity of relations of difference.

38 Cavarero, *Nonostante Platone*.

Chapter 11

Beyond equality: gender, justice and difference

Jane Flax

GENDER, DIFFERENCE AND JUSTICE

A central tenet of feminist theory is that gender has been and remains a historically variable and internally differentiated relation of domination. Gender connotes and reflects the persistence of asymmetric power relations rather than 'natural' (biological/anatomical) differences. In the modern (post-seventeenth-century) west, gender has been constituted through a vicious, circular logic. A range of 'differences' (e.g. mind/body, reason/emotion, public/private) is identified *as* differences and as salient to and constituent of gender. These differences are also conceived as oppositional, asymmetric dualisms on a hierarchial, binary and absolute scale rather than as pluralisms in an indefinite and open-ended universe. 'Woman' is defined as and by the cohering of certain elements, always the lesser side of the dualistic pairs. Man, her superior opposite, 'naturally' incorporates and is constituted by the greater. Thus in the contemporary west, the recognition of differences seems inseparable from asymmetric dualisms and relations of domination. Within contemporary western culture, differences appear to generate and are certainly used to justify hierarchies and relations of domination including gender-based (or gender-ascribed) ones.

Hence, we can understand the appeal of the concept of equality. In modern western political thought it has functioned as the (apparently) dualistic opposite of difference and domination. Feminists have hoped that extending equality to women will provide a cure for gender-based relations of domination. None the less, I will argue that precisely because equality as currently understood and practised is constituted in part in and by a denial and ranking of differences, it is less useful as an antidote to relations of domination than is justice.

Domination arises out of an inability to recognize, appreciate and nurture differences, not out of a failure to see everyone as the same. Indeed, the need to see everyone the same in order to accord them dignity and respect is an expression of the problem, not a cure for it. Since the fundamental problem with gender is that, as currently constituted, it is a relation of domination, feminists should seek to end domination – not gender, not differences and certainly not the feminine. The issue as I understand it is not equality and/or differences but rather how and why gender is a relation of domination – and how to end such domination.

Modern liberal political theory arose as a response to and rejection of a way of life built on the recognition and enforcement of unequal statuses, powers and qualities (domination based on differences). The claim of equality which is so central in modern liberal political thought is grounded in a rejection of 'natural' authority based on difference and on the assertion of the existence of a fundamental human sameness – for example, possession of the same bundle of natural rights or of reason. Hence, ironically, liberal theorists accepted or incorporated a fundamental tenet of their medieval forefathers (differences, inequalities and domination are inseparable) but insisted that an essential sameness existed which overrode, at least in the public sphere, these natural differences.

In contrast, the necessity for justice in classical political theory arises out of the recognition of differences. The problem of justice arises because persons have different skills, qualities, claims and ideas about the good. Yet because none of us is self-sufficient, these differences must somehow be harmonized within a whole which strives to achieve the good for all and in which relations of domination are minimized. However, in classical political theory differences are also arranged on a scale of intrinsic goodness and even the best woman is less excellent than the best man. But because justice at least leaves space for a consideration of differences, it seems to me to be a more potentially useful concept than equality. I cannot imagine equality apart from some measure of sameness. Equality seems to require some uniform way to answer the question, equal in regard to what? None of the measures offered so far have been gender neutral in nature or implications.[1]

When modern western feminism arose in the eighteenth century it naturally inherited the political vocabulary as well as the problems of its cultural contexts. As western feminists confronted gender-based and gender-constituting relations of domination, the issues of difference and equality were inescapable. If differences are the generative ground of domination, can domination be eliminated without the annihilation of differences – including gender? Yet if equality requires and reflects sameness, the nature of this sameness itself must be questioned. For it did not escape attention that the concepts different/same were also constituted dualistically and were gendered. The feminine is the 'different' to the masculine 'same'. Hence to attain equality it would appear necessary for women to cease being feminine, at least in the public sphere. Since one of the defining and unique purposes of the public sphere is to eliminate domination and to ensure and secure its opposite – freedom – without access to and power in the public world how could gender-based domination be abolished? Yet if women must cease being feminine to be citizens, to speak of *women's* political emancipation would be an oxymoron since we must eliminate our 'difference' before entering the public world.[2]

FEMINISM AND POST-MODERNISM

Such are the paradoxes feminists inherit as persons (if not full citizens) within modern western liberal democracies. While the necessity of the feminist project of ending gender-based relations of domination remains, the appropriate means to do so seem ever more elusive and uncertain. As the gender-biased aspects of western liberal thought are elucidated by contemporary feminist theorists, its utility and relevance to feminist projects become more and more controversial. In recognizing that western liberal thought itself is partially constituted by 'homosexual' tendencies in which differences are reduced to either confirmation of the superiority of the (masculine) same or deviations from it, feminist theorists however reluctantly find ourselves occupying and mapping terrain that overlaps with that of many post-modernist philosophers.[3]

The relations of feminist theorizing to the post-modernist projects of deconstructing the self-same and freeing differences from their status as the (lesser) other of the same are often pervaded by ambivalence. In many ways women never fully experienced the benefits of bourgeois-liberal emancipation. Liberal-Enlightenment discourses such as that of Locke or Kant were not meant to include women, and their coherence depends partially on our continuing exclusion. Concepts such as the autonomy of reason, objective truth and universally beneficial progress through scientific discovery are very appealing, especially to those who have been defined as incapable or merely the objects of such feats. Furthermore, it is conforting to believe that Reason can and will triumph – that those who proclaim such ideals as objectivity and truth will respond to rational arguments. If there is no objective basis for distinguishing between truth and false beliefs, then it seems that power alone may determine the outcome of competing truth claims. This is a frightening prospect to those who lack, or are oppressed by, the power of others.[4]

Feminist political theories are also partially dependent upon liberal ideals in the ways claims to and visions of women's emancipation have been formulated. Concepts like natural rights, due process and equality are connected to ideas about essential (pre-political) human properties. These properties are supposed to compel the state to act, since it is required as part of its contractual obligation to protect the rights it did not create. Such pre-existing 'natural rights' are also meant to be barriers *against* state intervention – as, for example, in the use of the 'right to privacy' doctrine to legitimize abortion. While many reasonable arguments have been made about the limitations of liberal concepts and practices of citizenship, no persuasive alternatives exist. Given the enormous risks involved, it is reasonable for feminists to be sceptical about abandoning these practices before most women have fully enjoyed their admittedly limited and ambiguous benefits.[5]

Yet, feminist theories and post-modernist ones undermine the plausibility of many of the constituting assumptions of previous political theories. Both discourses are deconstructive; they distance us from and make us sceptical about ideas concerning truth, knowledge, power, history, freedom, law, the self and language which are often taken for granted within and serve as legitimations for liberal western theories and practices of politics. In these 'mainstream' political discourses claims to equality or justice seem inextricably linked to a disembodied, abstract, impersonal rationality. The capacity of 'reason' to transcend 'interests', including those of empirical experience and personal obligations, guarantees the legitimacy of its claims, procedures and laws.[6]

The problems of difference, dualism, hierarchy and a disembodied, ahistoric reason are central to both feminist and post-modernist discourses. Post-modernists do not seek 'equality', whether this is understood as 'equal treatment for equals' or due process for all. Feminists have begun to question whether 'equality' can mean anything other than assimilation to a pre-existing and problematic 'male' norm.[7] Neither the feminist nor the post-modernist seeker of justice can assume an ahistoric, transcendental posture or the possibility of a 'veil of ignorance' behind which all concrete, particular situatedness disappears. Nor can the post-modernist seek or ground claims to justice in 'natural law' or in abstract rules or decision procedures such as the categorical imperative said to be binding on and recognizable by all rational persons. Rather, post-modernist and, increasingly, feminist discourses call into question our belief that any such transcendental faculty or 'neutral' law is either possible or desirable.[8]

Like post-modernists, feminist theorists decentre Enlightenment concepts of a unitary or essentially rational self. Such a notion is the necessary grounding of either a Lockean 'rights' or a Kantian 'rational man' theory of justice. However, since feminists do not equate subjectivity with its stereotypically white western masculine expressions, they do not necessarily argue that all notions of a self must be abandoned. Indeed, theories and practices of justice and subjectivity seem inextricably linked. Since there are good reasons why such concepts cannot simply be abandoned, we have to offer more adequate ones.

Feminists displace unitary, essentialist and asocial or ahistoric ideas of the self by analysing the ways gender enters into and partially constitutes both the self and our ideas about it. They have shown that the stories philosophers or psychologists tell about the self tend primarily to reflect the experiences, problems and acts of repression of a stereotypically white western masculine self. Ideas about 'the' self are dependent upon and made plausible by the existence of specific sets of social relations, including gender. For example, Kant and other philosophers distinguish our phenomenal and embodied self from a (higher) noumenal, rational and transcendental one. The noumenal self can be free precisely because it is removed from empirical contingency. The possibility and plausibility of such distinctions rest in part upon the prior existence of a gender-based division of labour. In this division of labour, women take responsibility for and represent bodily processes, leaving the (male) philosophers 'free' to contemplate the noumenal world. In turn, the lack of conscious involvement with such processes and the existence of a whole class of persons who share similar social experiences render a split between the noumenal and phenomenal plausible.[9]

Only when persons with different sets of experience enter into or question philosophic discourse do these distinctions lose their 'intuitive' plausibility. Different questions then emerge; for example, not what is the relation between mind and body, but rather, why would anyone assume such a distinction is meaningful or central to philosophic discourse? Or: why is the contingent seen only as a source of unfreedom? This evaluation of the contingent and the predominance of certain questions within philosophy reflects in part the prevalence of relations of domination in which only the unfree care for our contingent existence.

Many feminist theorists also stress the central importance of sustained, intimate relations with other persons or the repression of such relations in the constitution, structure and ongoing experiences of a self. In this feminist account, the self loses its asocial, isolated qualities and is reconceptualized as a complex 'inner world' with its own systems of internal relations. Each self is partially constituted in and through networks of relations, fantasies and expectations among and about 'internal objects'. Feminists pay attention to the location of persons (and families) within wider contexts of social relations as well. Some of these relations are structured by and through domination, so that families, for example, are conceptualized as constituted by far more than the dyads (or triads) of many psychoanalytic accounts.[10]

In some ways post-modernism makes it more difficult to discuss questions of justice at all. These discourses disrupt master-narratives of the west and the language games in which terms like 'freedom', 'emancipation' or 'domination' take on meaning. Post-modernist deconstructions of representation and the 'innocence' of truth raise fundamental questions about the position and self-understanding of intellectuals, including feminist theorists, and about the relationships of theory and practice. Lacking 'privileged' insight into the 'laws' of history or reason's operations, no longer serving as the neutral instrument of truth or the articulator of 'humanity's' best hopes, what authorizes the theorist's speech or connects it with the experiences of others? We become hesitatnt to speak for or prescribe our good(s) for others. It is harder to separate normative discourse from potential exercises of power or to conceptualize power as other than domination.

Indeed, it is not clear that post-modernism has or could offer (a) positive vision(s) of justice. Post-modernists have had little to say so far about how or why totalizing discourses could or would cease their imperialist expansion. Consideration of gender as a relation of domination is noticeable by its absence in even the most radical of male post-modernists. Unlike many feminists, most post-modernists have remarkably little to say about the concrete practices and knowledges that could replace current ones. Writers such as Rorty and Lyotard argue that pragmatism is most congruent with post-modernist projects.[11] However, as anyone familiar with the history of western political thought is aware, pragmatism is far from unproblematic as either a theory or a practice. Post-modernists ignore or fail to acknowledge many of these important difficulties. The political problems intrinsic to pragmatism include: how to resolve conflict among competing voices; how to ensure that everyone has a chance to speak; how to ensure that each voice counts equally; how to assess whether equality or participation is necessary in all cases or in which cases; how to effect a transition from the present in which many voices cannot speak, or are necessarily excluded, or are not heard, to a more polyvocal one; how to instil and guarantee a preference for speaking over the use of force; and how to compensate for the political consequences of an unequal distribution and control of resources. Furthermore, the complex relations between speech and action are elided by privileging 'conversation' as the modal human activity. Aspects of human experience not easily grasped by or through the metaphor of 'conversation', such as child-rearing, fantasy and asymmetric relations of power, disappear behind a new kind of 'veil of ignorance'. The absence of discourse on such questions reinforces a suspicion that deconstruction may be most appealing to those who are accustomed to and confident of having authority, of comfortably occupying and controlling any space, and therefore need feel no particular worry about such details.

Despite these difficulties, neither feminist nor post-modernist theorists can abandon all consideration of a problem that modern liberal theory is meant to solve: that of domination (at least in the public sphere). A post-modernist–feminist approach to the problem of domination would entail a search for ways to free the play of differences.

The post-modernist engagement in and preference for play, fragmentation and differentiation have a quite serious, even normative, purpose. The sceptical and disrespectful rhetorical, anti-foundational and anti-essentialist moves of writers such as Lyotard, Foucault or Derrida are partially strategic devices. They are meant to disrupt and erode the power of the grand 'normalizing' discourses that put into action and legitimate patterns of dominance characteristic of post-Enlightenment states. This deconstructive project is to contribute to the clearing of spaces in which many disorderly or local forms of life could flourish.[12]

The more divergent forms of life become, the more salient justice is.

However, as it is presently articulated, post-modernism inhibits the development of alternative concepts and practice of justice. This is so partially because many theorists do not pay adequate attention to the concrete workings of contemporary forms of domination (especially gender and race). Equally important, since many post-modernists collapse all notions of subjectivity into one very flawed form of it, they are unable to articulate concepts of subjectivity adequate to and necessary for practices of justice. Justice above all is a problem stemming from and about relations among persons. Problems arise because people's deeply held or felt needs, wants, ideas and purposes differ and often conflict. At the same time justice is both possible and necessary because of the interdependent and social aspects of human subjectivity. Hence the need for justice arises out of the complexities of human subjectivity. Discourse about one cannot be abandoned without completely abandoning the other.

Feminists focus more directly on relations of domination. They do not recount history as the story of the tyranny of the 'metaphysics of presence', but rather as the persistence of asymmetries of power between men and women, the denial of being and justice to women by men in and through concrete social relations and the at best partially successful struggle by women against these relations of domination. Feminist theorists search for explanations of gender and women's experiences, reasons to and methods of struggle against domination, ways to understand our own complicity in them and evidence that struggle against domination by ourselves and others is worthwhile.

Feminist theorists also feel compelled to offer something new: concepts of politics which do not presuppose or require asymmetric gender relations for their realization. Feeling themselves oppressed now, feminists cannot be indifferent to questions of how transformations are to occur. Given the disappointing results of previous, allegedly radical practices, feminists also have no reason to trust that what will show up even in potential deconstructive spaces will be for our own good(s).

Thus, while Rorty may be correct that talking about 'justice' in the abstract may not help us to do right, there are also very good reasons why we cannot stop doing it. A purely pragmatic approach of examining our current practices is not satisfactory, because justice is often most noticeable by its absence. Our practices do not necessarily compel self- and social criticism or reflection. In fact, as critical theorists point out, they may operate to negate or disarm exactly these qualities. There is no reason to assume, as Rorty implicitly does, that our conversations are self-correcting, especially if these are made possible by the silencing of certain questions and voices.[13]

However, we can be more clear about what purposes are served by talk about justice. In a sense, justice is an anticipatory concept. Talk about justice provides a partial answer to the questions, why is domination wrong; why do you think any other forms of relations are possible; and what alternative forms might there be? While it reflects possible ways people can or do relate to each other, justice like any other concept or practice is context dependent. There is a pragmatics of justice which may have little relevance outside its appropriate environment. Outside its context, justice has little effect other than to remind us of possibilities not yet expressed. Furthermore, concepts or practices of justice cannot tell us how to move from an unjust context to a just one. Justice and domination are not binary opposites, so that the overcoming of relations of domination will not necessarily bring about justice. Contexts of injustice are ones in which relations of domination predominate, and the pragmatics of injustice have much more to do with power and force than with the playful recognition of differences. In the pragmatics of injustice strategic and tactical decisions must be made. Appeals to justice are simply one means of addressing domination or of inspiring the dominated to rebel. At times it may make sense to act as if one's opponent's sense of justice can be appealed to; at other times this would be suicidal.

Thus, it is no criticism of concepts of justice to say they are of no use in all contexts or for all purposes; there is no master virtue or practice within political life. Rather, the conditions and contexts in which justice can flourish must be delimited, and we must identify what existing human qualities or activities make us think such practices are possible. How to create such practices and to explain why they do not exist are different questions. The possible texture and consequences of proposed practices of justice can also be imagined. But new possibilities and problems will arise when relations of domination are relatively absent and we are able more fully to develop just ones. Justice is not a finite state or set of rules instituted once and for all. It is an ongoing process in which our very idea of what we are trying to achieve will change over time.

TOWARD FEMINIST–POST-MODERNIST THEORIES OF JUSTICE: A PROLOGUE

The liberal political theories we have inherited and depend upon in the contemporary west have produced impoverished and unsatisfactory concepts of reason, subjectivity and justice. Feminist, psychoanalytic and post-modernist theories force us to question the definition of reason in transcendental terms and the claim that liberation, stable meaning, insight, self-understanding and justice depend above all on the primacy of reason and intelligence. Indeed, they call into question whether there are *any* necessary or intrinsic relations between reason, however defined, and justice. There are many factors upon which the development of subjectivity, self-understanding and justice depend: political practices; the absence of economic, race or gender-based relations of domination; empathy; fantasy; feelings; imagination; and embodiment. On what grounds can we claim reason is privileged or primary for the self or justice? The claim that this privilege exists because only reason is independent of contingencies and is universal and available to everyone is untenable. Both psychoanalysis and feminism undermine the belief that reason is, can or should be independent of the contingencies of intersubjectivity, embodiment, language, social relations or the unconscious. The claim that reason is universal is equally problematic. Such a claim could only be justified by positing the very thing we are trying to prove – some transcendental standpoint from which what is universal and what is not can be distinguished. We would have to be persuaded that reason is historically and culturally invariant so that it could work in the same way in any person, thus providing a stable measure for what is just an unjust. But how could culturally situated persons claim to justify recognition of an invariant reason?[14]

More important, it seems unnecessary and even dangerous to assume that the existence and practice of justice require a, or any, transcendental grounding. Foucault's analysis of the relations within our episteme between truth and power is particularly germane in untangling such beliefs. We believe that there must be connections between truth and any form of power, including just ones, but this is not necessarily the case. Even if we abandon any notion of transcendental truth and a reason capable of grasping it, we can still formulate and articulate theories and practices of justice. Our choice is not necessarily between grounding justice in objective truth claims (judged by reason) or domination. Nor need we assume that only a transcendental reason can impel or recognize claims to justice. It is both possible and necessary to develop non-rationalist concepts of both 'the self' and justice.

Post-modernists are correct to argue that more adequate theories of justice cannot depend upon a transcendental or abstract reason that has a privileged relation to truth, knowledge or universally binding rules or principles or visions of the good. Feminist–post-modernist theories of justice would have to eliminate all recourse to foundational, essentialist, teleological and transcendental qualities, concepts or categories. However, while theories dependent upon such notions are untenable, it does not follow that all discourse about justice and subjectivity can or should be abandoned. Post-modernists are not justified in denying meaning to such discourses or in claiming that they necessarily entangle us once again in the dangerous myths of humanism. This is so for at least three reasons: (a) post-modernist discourses themselves are incoherent without some notion of self; (b) the post-modernist wish to do without such notions may be rooted in part in gender bias; (c) theories of justice depend upon and reflect certain dilemmas of human subjectivity, including those of interest to post-modernists, such as the question of difference.

Post-modernist discourses all contain and require some implicit notion of a self. For example, Foucault stresses the existence and importance of 'suppressed discourses' and local and particular forms of knowledge.[15] It is

202 Beyond Equality and Difference

incomprehensible that such discourses could persist despite the 'disciplinary and surveillance' aspects of power without the existence of some form of self. Something within and among persons must exist that is not merely an effect of the dominating discourse. Otherwise, how could conflict and struggle against domination continue even in the most totalistic discursive formation?

In both Lyotard and Derrida, a form of subjectivity is restored in and through its relation to the unrepresentable other. As in high modernism, the writer (writing/text) re-emerges as hero. Against the banalities of mass culture, he 'wage(s) a war on totality (and) activate(s) the differences'[16] which have their (non-originary) origin in the unrepresentable other. Writing transgresses the limits of language and at least evokes something beyond or outside of contemporary cultural practices. A coherent, subjective faculty must exist in order for the artist/writer to enter or be affected by the 'scene of writing' or for anyone to have an experience of the sublime as defined by Lyotard or Derrida. This faculty cannot be merely a knitting together of the 'same' conventional historical and social practices in and through which the 'beyond' is said to be produced or it could not go 'beyond' the given. Shifting the metaphor from the individual artist/author to 'writing' or the 'sublime' cannot successfully conceal the congruence of this view with the 'high culture' modernist view of the work of art and the artist. In this view 'true' art signifies and refers only to itself, yet, at the same time, it and the artist can represent a 'higher' dimension of reality and being 'outside the words of the tribe'.[17]

In Foucault's work the aesthetic is connected with subjectivity in his idea of replacing the technologies of self with the ideal of making one's own life a work of art.[18] Yet paradoxically, despite his criticism of Derrida's mystification of writing, Foucault does not ask himself the question, 'what forms of life make such a notion possible?' about his own aesthetic ideal. Such a constant remaking of the self presupposes a socially isolated and individualistic view of the self. It precludes the possibility that one might have enduring attachments or responsibilities to another in which the other can rely on one's stability and continuity of being. Indeed, despite Foucault's criticism of Sartre's 'humanism', this aesthetic self seems to have some of the empty, projective qualities of Sartre's monad. This monad is driven to throw off the 'slime of history' in its constant search for freedom. I do not see how this highly individualistic and atomistic quest for the beautiful life could be reconciled with, for example, the care of small children or with participation in a political community. Despite Foucault's critique of the notion of the 'universal intellectual', it betrays a romantic hope that the beautiful can rescue us from the totalizing discourses of modern western culture.

Another reason to be suspicious of post-modernist treatments of the self is that, while some post-modernists wish to maintain an aesthetic notion of subjectivity, they demonstrate an almost complete disregard for aspects of subjectivities rooted in intimate social relations. These post-modernist views are deeply antithetical to feminist concepts of self in relation to others. Such social relations are displaced by the post-modernist insistence on the self as a 'position in language' (Derrida) or an effect of discourse (Foucault or Rorty). From a feminist viewpoint, it is striking that a primary strategy adopted by these post-modernists to deconstruct essentialist concepts of self is to juxtapose and insist upon a notion of the self as 'fictive'. An alternative strategy would be to argue that 'the self' is (in some aspects) social and in important ways gendered. Hence any self or concept of it must be differentiated, local and historical. Gender can be used as a lever against essentialist or ahistoric notions of the self. A feminist deconstruction of the self, however, would point towards locating the self and its experiences in concrete social relations, not only in fictive or purely textual conventions.

A social self would come to be partially in and through powerful, affective relationships with other persons. These relations with others and our feelings and fantasies about them, along with experiences of embodiedness also mediated by such relations, can come to constitute an 'inner' self which is neither simply fictive nor 'natural'. Such a self is simultaneously embodied, gendered, social and unique. It is capable of telling stories and of conceiving and experiencing itself in all these ways.

In most cultures, the first person we are in an intimate, social relationship with is a woman, a mother or her substitutes or relations. Hence, many feminists are suspicious of theories that require a denial of the centrality of human relatedness or obviate the ways these relations become part of a complex inner world or distinctive subjectivity. Feminist theorists have argued that the repression, especially by men, of these primary relations and the relational aspects of our subjectivity is necessary for the replication of male dominant cultures.[19] A feminist theorist might well conclude that certain post-modernist deconstructors of the self are merely the latest in a long line of philosophic strategists motivated by a need to evade, deny or repress the importance of early childhood experiences, especially mother–child relationships, in the constitution of the self and the culture more generally. Perhaps it is less threatening to have no self than to have one pervaded by memories of, longing for, suppressed identification with or terror of the powerful mother of infancy.

Discourses about justice cannot do without concepts of subjectivity. The necessity for and problems about justice arise in part out of the complexity of human subjectivity and our relations with others. As Hanna Pitkin argues:

> In a way, political theory has always been concerned with this transition from private to public and the relationship between person and political ... the problem is always: How shall we understand ourselves as simultaneously private and public beings?[20]

She suggests that 'the road to a better' account of justice goes by way of conceptions of what a person is. The beginning of such conceptions is available in psychoanalytic-feminist 'object relations' theories of subjectivity. These theories offer the possibility of conceptualizing subjectivity and justice in ways that are congruent with both post-modernist and feminist projects. Such concepts eschew appeals to abstract rules, reason or a transcendental subject. Rather, both justice and the self can be conceptualized as complex processes that are necessarily imperfect, incomplete and without an end, justification or ground outside of themselves.

Justice can be understood as belonging to the 'transitional space' as D. W. Winnicott describes it – a 'third world' that is neither subjective nor objective, neither purely inner or outer. This world has its own processes, tasks and ways of making sense out of experience. This space is transitional only in the sense that it bridges the gaps between self and other and inner and outer reality. It is a permanent facet of our mental life; it is not part of a stage of development that is necessarily incorporated into some subsequent or higher state. It does, however, continually grow in complexity and richness.

Originally this is the space of play and of attachment to special 'not-me' possessions (a blanket, toy, etc.) that must always be accessible to the baby. The child's ability to choose and utilize a transitional object also signals that it has begun to engage in the process of symbolization. The capacity to play, and the process of symbolization associated with it, eventually 'expands into creative living and into the whole cultural life of man'.[21] Culture, like play, exists in this third area, the potential space between the inner life of the individual and objective reality. Without something to make use of (tradition out there), no creativity or culture is possible. The creative transformation by the individual of what exists independently in shared reality is what distinguishes art from dreams or individual delusion. On the other hand, the individual can creatively transform what is given in part by bringing something of inner reality into the process. The subject is not only a signified but can also disrupt or transform the pre-given chain.

Unlike Freud or Lacan, Winnicott does not conceptualize symbolization and culture itself as something alien to the individual, imposed over and against the inner self. Nor is culture built out of the repression and sublimation of instinctual impulses or from a logic purely external to those subjected to it. Culture arises out of that third space remaining within us, giving us pleasure and a sense of aliveness and continuity. However, in Winnicott's view each relatively healthy individual experiences conflicts that are endemic to human subjectivity. Each of us must engage in lifelong processes of reconciling self and other and inner and outer realities:

It is assumed here that the task of reality acceptance is never completed, that no human being is free from the strain of relating inner and outer reality, and that relief from this strain is provided by an intermediate area of experience . . . which is not challenged (arts, religion . . .). This intermediate area is in direct continuity with the play area of the small child who is 'lost' in play.[22]

Both our capacity to seek justice and our need for it arise in part out of the lifelong process Winnicott describes. Justice teaches us how to reconcile or tolerate differences between self and other without domination, how to differ with the other without feeling a need to annihilate her and to restrict the playing out of hurtful fantasies to the inner world.

Justice is best understood as an ongoing process rather than a fixed set of procedures or a pre-given standard to which we must conform. Like the transitional object, justice cannot relate inner and outer reality if it is conceptualized in purely objective (transcendental) or subjective (values or arbitrary wants or power) terms:

> The transitional object and the transitional phenomena start each human being off with what will always be important for them, i.e. a neutral area of experience which will not be challenged. Of the transitional object it can be said that it is a matter of agreement between us and the baby that we will never ask the question: 'Did you conceive of this or was it presented to you from without?' The important point is that no decision on this point is expected. The question is not to be formulated.[23]

Understood as a process, justice is one way the individual manages the strain of being simultaneously public and private, alone and in relation to others, desiring and interdependent. On a collective level, justice is one way groups manage the strain of mediating between the individual subjectivities of which they are composed and the objectivities such as limited resources, past traditions and the consequences of past decisions and practices which those individuals did not create but to which they must respond. The management of such tensions necessarily involves the exercise of various forms of power, as Foucault argues. However, depending upon *how* the tensions are managed, empowerment and relief may result; the political space may remain open or 'neutral' rather than objectified by the direct imposition of external standards upon individual subjects. Relations of domination are not the necessary result of the conflicts and strains endemic to individuals singly and collectively. Such outcomes depend upon the relative absence of justice as a process.

As a process, justice incorporates at least four aspects:

1 *Reconciliation* of diversities into a restored but new unity. Justice requires a unity of differences, mutuality, incorporation, not annihilation of opposites and distinctions. Claims to justice may be made on the basis of preserving the play of difference rather than mutual obligation to a uniform standard or sameness.

2 *Reciprocity*. Reconciliation is not passive – justice requires the active complementarity of reciprocity. Reciprocity connotes a continuous though imprecisely defined sharing of authority and mutuality of decision. It does

not require equality of power but does preclude domination. Domination may be present whenever the third space is transformed into a mirror of one set of 'objective' standards or 'normative' practices.

3 *Recognition* – in at least two senses: (a) acknowledging the legitimacy of the others; this involves the necessity of taking others into account or giving them due honour and consideration and of accepting their fundamental separateness and difference from oneself: (b) identifying with the other, seeing her in some way like oneself, or even part of oneself.

4 *Judgement*: a process of balancing and proportion, of evidence and reflection, of looking forwards and backwards. This involves the capacity to see things from the point of view of another and hence calls upon qualities like empathy and imagination as well as logic and objectivity. Judgement is also connected to action; we must evaluate the consequences of past decisions and place current, potential choices within the context of the needs of both individuals and collectivities. Thus justice calls upon a quality of care that arises out of a sense of connectedness and obligation to others. We must be able to imagine vividly the (potential) experiences of concrete others and yet sometimes distance ourselves from them, to think about the more abstract needs of the collectivity as a whole.

While the need for and the capacity to engage in justice depend in part on 'private' aspects of human experience, justice can only be exercised in public, intersubjective spaces. Justice is necessarily connected to an active notion of citizenship. Indeed, citizenship is another transitional practice that helps manage the strain between the 'subjective' and 'objective' worlds. Citizenship has at least two major aspects: the transformation of private need into public action, and the transformation of necessity into freedom. The transformation of private need into public action requires at least the following three processes: (a) To see a need as publicly actionable – that is, not just as one's private misery – is part of the feminist claim that the 'personal is political'; not that the two are identical or should be collapsed but rather that what was formerly borne as one's private misery is now understood, at least to some extent, as caused and transformable by a pattern of human decisions and practices. (b) In bringing a private need to the public, the spirit in which this is done must itself be transformed. The 'I want' must be transformed into the 'I and others in my situation are entitled to'. (c) This necessarily situates oneself as a member within a public which is shared by others. In some ways these others are like the self, and yet each person, even those we may share a claim with, is not exactly like us. For example, women may suffer from certain pervasive cultural practices (such as rape), but the ways we articulate claims on the basis of this experience may differ. Women of colour may be more mindful of the past racist uses of rape law than white women and hence may wish to frame remedies in different ways. In recognizing differences as well as mutuality, one is forced to negotiate with others and to see the boundedness of one's claims as well as one's mutual responsibility for and dependence upon the character of the 'we'.

In this process of recognizing and negotiating with the we, one begins to see the self as not completely driven by necessity but as part of a community which can collectively act to change its joint practices, to take responsibility for the social forces in which we are individually and collectively embedded. To take responsibility collectively requires at least these three conditions: (a) a community of discourse that cares for its transitional space; (b) individuals capable of desiring justice; (c) visible connections between speech, deliberation, empathy and outcomes. To have a community of discourse there must be rules, norms and practices which govern and nurture collective discourse and action. These themselves are open to renegotiation and must be understood as generated by the community itself, as dependent on nothing 'outside' it. To have individuals capable of desiring justice requires persons who need connections with others, who are able and willing to see how their own acts affect others and who are able to tolerate the prospect of engaging in an open process without a guaranteed end or result or privileged position within it. Such individuals will also seek out and be mindful of differences; they will worry when discourse becomes too mono-vocal, stable or unitary. Discourse is not meaningful outside contexts of action and power. To be aware of the consequences of acts, either individually or collectively, one must be able to take responsibility in a meaningful way. Responsibility is not meaningful without power to act and without having more than an illusion that one is the author of one's acts. To be able to see the consequences of one's acts also requires the elimination of relations of domination, for such relations are in part made possible by rendering some of the community's members and the consequences of individual or collective actions invisible.

In order to have and sustain these processes of justice, there must be a self which desires reciprocity, which can acknowledge without terror our interconnectedness and mutual dependence but can also honour and do justice to our separateness, to the distinctiveness and integrity of each other person. Such a self would also be able to recognize that there is nothing outside our tissue of practices, our mutually created transitional spaces, that can help us make decisions and relate to each other justly within them.

One of the negative consequences of transcendental notions of justice and reason is that they release us as concrete persons from full responsibility for our acts. Such notions are instances of what Nietzsche calls the 'longest lie', the 'notion that outside the haphazard and perilous experiments we perform there lies something (God, Science, Knowledge, Rationality, or Truth) which will, if only we perform the correct rituals, step in to save us'.[24] The belief that humans can construct an 'objective' set of rules or neutral laws that will protect us from each other is another facet of this lie. The power of law lies in the collective human agreement to be bound by it and to include one's fellow humans within its protective space. Lacking such agreement, and rejecting the practices such agreements codify, some of us will not be secure against the aggression of others. People are quite capable of defining some groups as less than fully human and hence as beyond the relations of justice or the protection of law such relations offer. Such has been the experience of women throughout much of history, of people of colour in colonial and post-colonial regimes and of Jews in Nazi Germany. What inhibits this aggression and keeps it at bay is a whole complex network of practices, beliefs and feelings. Our obedience to law and the meaningful inclusion of persons within its protection are *symptoms* that such a network is in place. Law alone – or the attribution of natural rights, or a theory of transcendental justice or natural law – can never create such a network nor compensate for its absence.

While feminists and post-modernists diagnose the sources of our attachment to the longest lie in rather different ways, both attempt to free us from it and its necessary consequences. Feminists point to the pervasive effets of gender relations, to the splits between nurturance or caretaking and autonomy or history making.[25] Such splits impede the development a subjectivity that can live comfortably within and make use of transitional spaces. Postmodernists point to the 'logocentrism' at the heart of western culture, to the equating of the rational and the human, and the collapsing of the rational and the real.[26] Both kinds of theorist seek to awaken us from the dreams of modern western liberal thought. They hope to persuade us that justice as well as truth is of this world and that its existence is dependent solely upon our fragile and unstable selves. As feminists, we have much to gain and little to lose in this ongoing process of dis-illusionment.

NOTES

1 On the gendered nature of concepts of equality see M. Thornton, 'Sex equality is not enough for feminism', in C. Pateman and E. Gross (eds), *Feminist Challenges: Social and Political Theory*, Boston, Mass., Northeastern University Press, 1987.

2 On the exclusionary and gendered characteristics of liberal political theory see J. B. Landes, *Women and the Public Sphere in the Age of the French Revolution*, Ithaca, NY, Cornell University Press, 1988, esp. part 2; C. Pateman, *The Sexual Contract*, Stanford, Calif., Stanford University Press, 1988, ch. 6; and L. J. Nicholson, *Gender and History*, New York: Columbia University Press, 1986, esp. ch. 5.

3 On the 'hom(m)o-sexual' tendencies of western thought see L. Irigaray, 'Women on the market', in L. Irigaray, *This Sex Which Is Not One*, Ithaca, NY, Cornell University Press, 1985; and H. Cixous and C. Clément, *The Newly Born Woman*, Minneapolis, Minn., University of Minnesota Press, 1986. The complex relations between post-modernism and feminism are discussed in my 'Postmodernism and gender relations in feminist theory', *Signs*, 12(4), Summer 1987, pp. 621–43; the special issue of *Feminist Studies*, 14(1), Spring 1988; and N. Fraser and L.

Nicholson, 'Social criticism without philosophy: an encounter between feminism and postmodernism', in Andrew Ross, *Universal Abandon?*

4 Cf. Sandra Harding's arguments in S. Harding, *The Science Question in Feminism*, Ithaca, NY, Cornell University Press, 1986, ch. 6.

5 See J. Mitchell, 'Women and equality', in A. Phillips (ed.), *Feminism and Equality*, New York, New York University Press, 1987.

6 The most recent and influential statement of such a position is J. Rawls, *A Theory of Justice*, Cambridge, Mass., Harvard University Press, 1971.

7 L. Irigaray, '"Frenchwomen," stop trying', in Irigaray, *This Sex*; Phillips, 'Introduction' to Phillips, *Feminism and Equality*: and J. B. Elshtain, 'Aristotle, the public–private split and the case of the suffragists', in J. B. Elshtain (ed.), *The Family in Political Thought*, Amherst, Mass., University of Massachusetts Press, 1982.

8 All the essays in Pateman and Gross, *Feminist Challenges*, call such ideas into question. See also I. M. Young, 'Impartiality and the civic public', and S. Benhabib, 'The generalized and concrete other', both in S. Benhabib and D. Cornell (eds), *Feminism as Critique*, Minneapolis, Minn., University of Minnesota Press, 1987; the essays in M. Griffiths and M. Whitford (eds), *Feminist Perspectives in Philosophy*, Bloomington, Ind., Indiana University Press, 1988; R. Rorty, *Consequences of Pragmatism*, Minneapolis, Minn., University of Minnesota Press, 1982; J. Derrida, *Writing and Difference*, Chicago, University of Chicago Press, 1978; and M. Foucault, 'Truth and power', in M. Foucault, *Power/Knowledge*, New York, Pantheon, 1980.

9 On philosophy, gender and the division of labour see the essays in E. Kennedy and S. Mendus (eds), *Women and Western Political Philosophy*, New York, St Martin's Press, 1987.

10 J. Flax, 'Contemporary American families: decline or transformation?', in I. Diamond (ed.), *Families, Politics and Public Policy*, New York, Longman, 1983.

11 R. Rorty, 'Postmodernist bourgeois liberalism', in R. Hollinger (ed.), *Hermeneutics and Practice*, Notre Dame, Ind., University of Notre Dame Press, 1985; and J. F. Lyotard and J. L. Thebaud, *Just Gaming*, Minneapolis, Minn., University of Minnesota Press, 1985.

12 J. F. Lyotard, 'Answering the question: what is postmodernism?', appendix to J. F. Lyotard, *The Postmodern Condition: A Report on Knowledge*, Minneapolis, Minn., University of Minnesota Press, 1984; M. Foucault, 'Powers and strategies', in Foucault, *Power/Knowledge*; and J. Derrida, *Positions*, Chicago, University of Chicago Press, 1981.

13 R. Rorty, *Philosophy and the Mirror of Nature*, Princeton, NJ, Princeton University Press, 1979, ch. 8. On the limitations of Rorty's view see C. West, 'The politics of American neo-pragmatism', in J. Rajchman and C. West (eds), *Post-Analytic Philosophy*, New York, Columbia University Press, 1985. On the politics of post-modernism more generally see the essays in Andrew Ross, *Universal Abandon?*; and H. S. Kariel, *The Desperate Politics of Postmodernism*, Amherst, Mass., University of Massachusetts Press, 1989.

14 N. Scheman, 'Individualism and the objects of psychology', and J. Flax, 'Political philosophy and the patriarchal unconscious', both in S. Harding and M. B. Hintikka (eds), *Discovering Reality: Feminist Perspectives on Epistemology, Metaphysics, Methodology and Philosophy of Science*, Dordrecht, Reidel, 1983.

15 M. Foucault, 'Two lectures', in Foucault, *Power/Knowledge*, and 'The subject and power', in H. L. Dreyfus and P. Rabinow (eds), *Michel Foucault: Beyond Structuralism and Hermeneutics*, Chicago, University of Chicago Press, 1983.

16 Lyotard, *Postmodern Condition*, p. 82. On 'writing' see Derrida, *Writing and Difference*, ch 4, 9.
17 R. Rorty, 'Habermas and Lyotard on postmodernity', in R. J. Bernstein (ed.), *Habermas and Modernity*, Cambridge, Mass., MIT Press, 1985; and also Michael Foucault's critique of writing in 'What is an author?', in M. Foucault, *Language, Counter-Memory, Practice*, Ithaca, NY, Cornell University Press, 1977.
18 M. Foucault, 'On the genealogy of ethics', in H. L. Dreyfus and P. Rabinow, *Michel Foucault: Beyond Structuralism and Hermeneutics*, Chicago, University of Chicago Press, 1982.
19 N. J. Chodorow, 'Gender, relation and difference in psychoanalytic perspective', in H. Eisenstein and A. Jardine (eds), *The Future of Difference*, New Brunswick, NJ, Rutgers University Press, 1985; Griffiths and Whitford, *Feminist Perspectives in Philosophy*, chs 5, 7, 8, 9, 11; and J. Benjamin, *The Bonds of Love*, New York, Pantheon, 1988.
20 H. F. Pitkin, 'Justice: on relating private and public', *Political Theory*, 9(3) August 1981, p. 348.
21 D. W. Winnicott, 'The location of cultural experience', in D. W. Winnicott, *Playing and Reality*, New York, Basic Books, 1971, p. 102.
22 D. W. Winnicott, 'Transitional objects and transitional phenomena', in Winnicott, *Playing and Reality*, p. 13.
23 ibid., p. 12.
24 R. Rorty, 'Method, social science, social hope', in Rorty, *Consequences of Pragmatism*, p. 208.
25 D. Dinnerstein, *The Mermaid and the Minotaur*, New York, Harper & Row, 1976, esp. part 3.
26 Derrida, *Writing and Difference*, chs 4, 9, and *Positions*; these approaches intersect in the work of writers such as Cixous and Clément. Also J. Kristeva, 'Women's time', *Signs*, 7(1), Autumn 1981, pp. 13–35.